The Subject of Murder

The Subject of Murder

Gender, Exceptionality,
and the Modern Killer

LISA DOWNING

THE UNIVERSITY OF CHICAGO PRESS   CHICAGO AND LONDON

LISA DOWNING is professor of French discourses of sexuality at the University of Birmingham, UK. She is the author of *Desiring the Dead: Necrophilia and Nineteenth-Century French Literature*, *The Cambridge Introduction to Michel Foucault*, and (with Libby Saxton) *Film and Ethics: Foreclosed Encounters*.

The University of Chicago Press, Chicago 60637
The University of Chicago Press, Ltd., London

ISBN-13: 978-0-226-00340-5 (cloth)
ISBN-13: 978-0-226-00354-2 (paper)
ISBN-13: 978-0-226-00368-9 (e-book)

Library of Congress Cataloging-in-Publication Data

Downing, Lisa.
   The subject of murder : gender, exceptionality, and the modern killer / Lisa Downing.
      pages. cm
   Includes bibliographical references and index.
   ISBN 978-0-226-00340-5 (hardcover : alkaline paper) — ISBN 978-0-226-00354-2 (pbk. : alkaline paper) — ISBN 978-0-226-00368-9 (e-book)   1. Murderers—Press coverage.   2. Women murderers—Press coverage.   3. Murder in literature.   4. Wuornos, Aileen.   5. Lacenaire, Pierre François, 1800–1836.   6. Hindley, Myra.   7. Lafarge, Marie, 1816–1852.   8. Nilsen, Dennis Andrew, 1945–.   9. Jack, the Ripper.   I. Title.
   HV6513.D685 2013
   364.152'3—dc23
                                                                    2012024191

Contents

Acknowledgments

For a number of reasons, some having to do with the subject matter and others with circumstance, this has been an especially challenging and difficult book to write. It has been reconceptualized numerous times, and several drafts have been produced and discarded along the way. The current version, however modest, is the most compelling narrative I can tell about the ways in which modern Western society, with its norms, iniquities, and structural neuroses, dreams the figure of the murderer as an exceptional outsider, rather than as a product of our own making.

Several organizations and individuals are owed thanks for the advice, help, and support they have provided over the six years in which this process has unfolded.

Firstly, the Arts and Humanities Research Council (AHRC) awarded me a Research Leave Scheme grant in 2006, which enabled me to draft several chapters of the book (in the form in which I originally imagined it: a study of the figure of the murderer in nineteenth-century France). Secondly, the award of a Philip Leverhulme Prize in 2009 enabled me to extend my institutional research leave from the University of Exeter in order to reformulate the book project as a more ambitious and historically wide-ranging study of the modern murdering subject. I am grateful to both of these funding bodies for the valuable research time they enabled, and to Queen Mary, University of London and the University of Exeter for granting periods of institutionally funded leave in, respectively, 2005 and 2009.

The following individuals provided—variously—ideas, references, source materials, discussion, opportunities to present work, and/or feedback on various aspects of the project and chapter drafts: Heike Bauer,

Chiara Beccalossi, Lara Cox, Peter Cryle, Richard Dyer, Alex Dymock, Michael Finn, Miranda Gill, Robert Gillett, Louise Hardwick, Peter Hegarty, Marian Hobson, Michael G. Kelly, Katherine Lunn-Rockliffe, Francesco Manzini, Rachel Mesch, Lorna Milne, Alison Moore, Douglas Morrey, Dany Nobus, Kyra Pearson, Dieter Rossi, Elizabeth Stephens, Ricarda Vidal, Caroline Warman, and Valerie Worth. I am indebted to them all for their kindness and valuable input.

An earlier version of part of chapter 2 was published as the article "Murder in the Feminine: Marie Lafarge and the Sexualization of the Nineteenth-Century Criminal Woman," by Lisa Downing, in *Journal of the History of Sexuality* 18(1): 121–37, copyright ©2009 by the University of Texas Press. All rights reserved. One section of chapter 3 first appeared as part of "The Birth of the Beast: Death-Driven Masculinity in Monneret, Zola, Freud," by Lisa Downing, in *Dix-Neuf*, the online journal of the Society of Dix-Neuviémistes, no. 5 (September 2005). I am grateful for the permissions received to reproduce this material.

Finally, I would like to thank Doug Mitchell, Tim McGovern, and the team at the University of Chicago Press for their kindness and efficiency, and the three expert readers, Keith Reader, Calvin Thomas, and David Schmid, for their invaluable feedback and advice on the manuscript.

Introduction

Serial killers are so glamorised . . . as to tempt others to . . . revere them as the prophets of risk and individual action, in a society overwhelmed and bogged down by the dull courtiers and ass-kissers of celebrity culture.
—(Ian Brady, *The Gates of Janus*, 2001)

[Murderers] share certain characteristics of the artist; they know they are unlike other men, they experience drives and tensions that alienate them from the rest of society, they possess the courage to satisfy these drives in defiance of society. But while the artist releases his tensions in an act of imaginative creation, the Outsider-criminal releases his in an act of violence.
—(Colin Wilson, *Order of Assassins*, 1976)

Jack the Ripper, along with many of his followers, has achieved legendary status. Such men have become world famous, awesomely regarded cultural figures. They are more than remembered; they are immortalized. Typically though, their victims, the uncounted women who have been terrorized, mutilated, and murdered are rendered profoundly nameless.
—(Jane Caputi, *The Age of Sex Crime*, 1987)

As reflected in the epigraphs above—the first written by an incarcerated serial killer; the second by a respected writer, thinker, and murder "expert"—a pervasive idea obtains in modern culture that there is something intrinsically different, unique, and exceptional about those subjects who kill. Like artists and geniuses, murderers are considered special individuals, an ascription that serves both to render them apart from the moral majority on the one hand and, on the other, to reify, lionize, and fetishize them as "individual agents." And, as the third epigraph by a feminist cultural critic announces, this idealization of the murdering subject needs to be understood in gendered terms. Such discourses, by highlighting the exceptionality of the "individual," effectively silence gender-aware, class-based analyses about murder. Analyses of this kind might notice which category of person (male) may "legitimately" occupy the role of killer, and which category of person (female) is more generally relegated the role of victim in our culture. Female murderers, by extension, become doubly aberrant exceptions in this culture, unable to access the role of transcendental agency since, as Simone de Beauvoir made clear in 1949, only men are allowed to be transcendent, while women are immanent.[1] From a feminist critical viewpoint, then, the figure of the killer described by Brady and Wilson is not out of the ordinary at all—he is merely an exaggeration, or the extreme logical endpoint, of masculine patriarchal domination, and his othering as "different" serves to exculpate less extravagant exhibitions of misogyny.[2] The ways in which—and purposes for which—murderers are seen as an exceptional type of subject by our culture is the central problem this book seeks to address.

In *Natural Born Celebrities* (2005), resonating with Brady's observation regarding a celebrity-obsessed society to which the figure of the murderer appeals, David Schmid has compellingly described the cult of sensationalist fame enjoyed by the "idols of destruction" that are serial killers in contemporary North America.[3] Where Schmid's aim is to explore and account for a "specific, individuated form of celebrity"[4] that accrues to the serial killer within that national context, my aim here will be to unpick, both historically and in contemporary culture, the terms "specificity" and "individuation," rather than the related concept of "celebrity," that work on and through, and that are exemplified particularly well by, the figure of the murderer. The contemporary, ambivalent idea of the murderer as a special and aberrant subject, and as an object of fascination that can lead to him (and to a lesser extent *her*) becoming a celebrity, has a history that predates twentieth-century North America, where it is perhaps most prevalently seen today, and that originates in paradigmatically European intellectual ideas.

The ubiquity of the idea of the murderer as a figure of fascination can be testified to by an example from the work of historian of systems of thought Michel Foucault, whose analyses of discourses of criminality and subjectivity will be central to the critical work undertaken in this book. In discussing the case of a rural parricide, Pierre Rivière, who, in 1835, murdered his mother, sister, and brother and produced a long, complex confessional account of his crimes, Foucault reports feeling "a sort of reverence and perhaps, too, terror for a text which was to carry off four corpses along with it."[5] Foucault's team of sociological researchers was drawn to the Rivière dossier as an object of study initially because it was the thickest of all the files they found, but Foucault admits that it held his attention ultimately because of "the beauty of Rivière's memoir."[6] He describes the fascination he and his team experienced reading the confessions in the following way: "We fell under the spell of the parricide with the reddish-brown eyes."[7] This admission of having been mesmerized by the murderer's confession—and, by extension, seduced by the figure of the murderer himself—is a surprising one for Foucault, an arch demystifier of discourses of individuality, to make. It is a perfect illustration of the widespread and pervasive nature of the problematic that this book seeks to expose and understand.

The Sadeian Subject

The discourse of the murderer as an exceptional individual has been a feature of our cultural imaginary at least since the Marquis de Sade's eighteenth-century writings, in which the person who kills a fellow human being is described as a sovereign self, obeying only the destructive force of nature. However, it was not until the nineteenth century that the figure of "the murderer" became a scientifically recognized subject, constructed and concretized in a series of interrelated and overlapping disciplines and discursive fields (both artistic and scientific). It is precisely through the lens of nineteenth-century taxonomies of the subject that Sade's idea of the murderer retroactively makes sense as a defining pre-echo of an eminently modern phenomenon. And it is unsurprising that a number of real-life murderers, including Ian Brady, as well as producers of fictional representations of murderers, draw on Sade as a source of "inspiration."

Donatien-Alphonse-François de Sade (1740–1814) authored a philosophy that took to the logical extreme a number of the fashionable ideas of his time. Sade transformed the Enlightenment's prioritizing of reason over superstition into a triumphant atheistic dogma, resulting in his being accused of the then-serious charge of blasphemy against the Catholic Church. In Sade's godless universe, nothing that nature[8] is capable of carrying out (killings, devastation) can be considered wrong or unnatural if practiced by human beings. He summarizes this principle thus in *Justine ou les malheurs de la virtu* (1791): "Can [nature], when she created us, have placed in us what would be capable of hurting her? Ah! Were murder not one of the human actions which best fulfilled her intentions, would she permit the doing of murder?"[9] Sade takes his logic

further in positing that adherence to the law of "nature" as he interprets
it, rather than obeisance to man-made regulations and legislation, brings
not only pleasure, but also truth: he effectively refutes the belief of contemporaneous *philosophes* that the human being is naturally "good" until corrupted by culture.

He expounds this theory via exaggeration and deformation of the
literary trope of libertinage, defined by Diderot and D'Alembert simply as "the habit of yielding to the instinct which delivers us to sensual
pleasure."[10] He argues in numerous texts that the most rarefied erotic
pleasure is found in murder, and that the true libertine should not spare
himself this experience of radical freedom, but should follow the principle by which he lives all the way to its logical limit.[11] The unfinished
work *The 120 Days of Sodom* (*Les Cent-vingt journées de Sodome*, written 1785, first published 1904) is an encyclopedic account of the vast array of possible sexual practices available to the connoisseur of pleasure
for pleasure's sake. (In this formal respect alone, it presciently foreshad-
ows nineteenth-century sexology's taste for the taxonomy and enumer-
ation of what will, by then, have become the "perversions.") The book
recounts the tale of four aristocratic male libertines who sequester themselves in a remote castle with a cast of prostitutes and intended victims
of all ages. Their sexual activity escalates from mild flagellation and
wounding, through blasphemous and coprophilic practices, to finally
culminate in mass torture and annihilation by various methods of killing, described as the 150 *passions meurtrières* (murderous passions).

While the act of murder is lauded throughout Sade's writing, then, as
at once natural, authentic, and sexually satisfying, the acts of "sadism"
he committed in his own lifetime were less extreme in degree than those
he imagined. He is known to have imprisoned a young woman, Rose
Keller, in his château in 1768, where he sexually and physically assaulted
her. He is also known to have poisoned (non-fatally) two prostitutes with
cantharide bonbons four years later. Crucially, then, it is Sade's textual practices, rather than his acts, that have ensured the legend he bequeathed to us. "Sade" becomes an "author function" in Foucault's sense
of the term,[12] that is, a proper name that immediately suggests an array
of cultural ideas and associations, rather than simply designating autho-
rial identity. Some of these ideas have to do intimately with our sense of
what "murder" and "the murderer" have come to mean.

Radical feminist texts that treat lust murder as an extreme symptom
of systemic cultural misogyny trace the mode of masculinity that privi-

leges murder as the *nec plus ultra* of sexuality directly to the influence of Sade. Andrea Dworkin dedicated her treatise *Pornography: Men Possessing Women* (1981), which includes a chapter on Sade's writing, to the memory of his victim, Rose Keller. And, according to Deborah Cameron and Elizabeth Frazer, "if [Sade] had not existed, the history of sex murder might well have been quite different,"[13] since "the extent to which he underwrites 'the murderer as hero' is almost impossible to overestimate."[14] Moreover, for Cameron and Frazer, Sade succeeded in making pleasure through cruelty into a principle of transgression, widely recognized and celebrated as a philosophical and aesthetic blow against the petty social status quo and its conventions. (According to feminist reasoning, of course, it merely ends up reinforcing the not-at-all transgressive, but rather habitual and reactionary, principle of the supremacy of the strong—especially men—and the victimhood of the disenfranchised—especially women and children.)

Conversely, Angela Carter has written a spirited and counterintuitive defense of Sade as protofeminist, arguing that in texts such as *Juliette* (1797), the story of that rare being, a female libertine, Sade allows more fully for the possibility of female agency than other writers of his time. Women are not reduced to their biological functions of gestation and lactation in Sade, but are permitted to be sovereign murdering subjects, on a par with men, even if this murderousness will necessitate a form of monstrosity. Carter writes:

> A free woman in an unfree society will be a monster. Her freedom will be a condition of personal privilege that deprives those on which she exercises it of her own freedom. The more extreme kind of this deprivation is murder. These women murder.[15]

Sade's model of freedom through domination is fashioned after the way in which he perceives Eros to work: via a "natural" instinct to dominate. But Sade does not insist that only the biological male should be the attacker. As Carter states, in *Juliette*, "Sade declares himself unequivocally for the right of women to fuck . . . aggressively, tyrannously and cruelly."[16] While Sade may allow for the possibility of the sexually aggressive and murderous woman, however, he cannot conceive of a paradigm of social interaction that is not based on the polarity of dominance and subordination. The "free" woman's immanence will be achieved by transcending the will of the other: the victim, the less "personally privileged" individual. The classist implications of Sade's philosophy are all too evident, then: social "superiors," whether male or female, may occupy the role of the radically free sovereign individual, in Carter's words "fucking," "fucking over," and, ultimately, killing those belonging to disadvantaged classes. It is one of the legacies of the Sadeian imaginary that the figure of the modern murderer will emerge as an individual imbued with the aristocratic privilege of a Gilles de Rais or a Catherine the Great, both historical figures lauded by Sade—a privilege of which Citizen Sade was summarily dispossessed after the Revolution.

Foucault contends that the particular fusion of sex and violence and the model of privileged individuality contained in Sade's texts became a template for the way in which desire, society, and self were to be understood in modernity:

> Sadism is not a practice finally given to a practice as old as Eros; it is a massive cultural fact which appeared precisely at the end of the eighteenth century, and which constitutes one of the greatest conversions of Western imagination: unreason transformed into delirium of the heart, madness of desire, the insane dialogue of love and death in the limitless presumption of appetite.[17]

The eighteenth and nineteenth centuries find their meeting point, then, in the figure of Sade, a figure via which the ideal of pure Enlightenment "reason" becomes corrupted by the extravagant taint of murderous lust. In Richard von Krafft-Ebing's coining of "sadism" as a type of sexual perversion in 1886, an aesthetic and philosophical influence is inscribed into the systematization of selfhood that would be a key strategy of the sexual and medical sciences in the nineteenth century.

The Disciplined Subject

In his early works, *The Birth of the Clinic* (1963) and *The Order of Things* (1966), Foucault isolates a specific shift in the disciplinary practices of, respectively, medicine and the human sciences. Namely, he shows that, in those disciplines, human beings began to take themselves as *both the subject and the object of scrutiny and knowledge* for the first time. (So, for example, medicine began to study the diseased individual not the disease process, resulting in the construction of the subject of "the patient.")[18] Foucault explains how modernity—the nineteenth-century imaginary—distinguishes itself from what went before by this precise technique of seeing the self through discourses of knowledge that result in the construction of a "subject." Foucault's aim is to show us that this subject is a *culturally and historically located subject of discourse.* In so doing, he refutes the supposition of humanistic philosophy that the subject is universal, transhistorical, and self-knowing. In an interview in 1982, Foucault stated:

> Through . . . different practices—psychological, medical, penitential, educational—a certain idea or model of humanity was developed, and now this idea of man has become normative, self-evident, and is supposed to be universal. Humanism may not be universal but may be quite relative. . . . For instance, if you asked eighty years ago if feminine virtue was part of universal humanism, everyone would have answered yes.[19]

The degree to which this perception of the universal human subject and the myths that inhere in it still need questioning and exposing for their woeful ahistoricism will be analyzed in this book. The murdering subject (who can become an exceptional celebrity) only makes sense if understood in a context of modern acculturation and as a result of specific historical systems of thought that establish human "norms" from which the exception can differ. The gendering of the subject of humanism is equally of relevance. Foucault's suggestion that "feminine virtue" (a patriarchal projection of essence onto women) is no longer assumed as a part of universal human nature will be shown, in the analyses of discourses surrounding female murderers that follow, to be somewhat optimistic. As well as figuring prominently in discourses of husband-poisoning nineteenth-century killer Marie Lafarge, as we might expect, the virtues of nurturing and gentleness are *still* expected facets of the subject born female, as made only too explicit by the especially vilifying discourses surrounding the cases of Sade-reading child-murderer Myra Hindley in 1966, and murdering prostitute Aileen Wuornos in 2002, both considered more "monstrous" than any man with a comparable body count.

As an attempt to redress the ahistorical humanism that he takes to task here, Foucault meticulously exposes the specific systems of thought that gave rise to the construction of "normal" and "abnormal" subjects. In the first volume of *The History of Sexuality* (1976), Foucault explains how the disciplines that developed during the nineteenth century—alienism (the precursor of psychiatry), criminology, and sexology—gave rise to a "specification of individuals," namely, a taxonomy of aberrant individuals.[20] Here he writes specifically of the personages of the homosexual or "invert" and of the "pervert" (including the "sadist") whose diagnoses crossed law and medicine. He tells how, prior to the rise of those medical technologies that take human beings as their subject matter, a person's acts would be judged in just those terms—as acts—without those acts taking on the status of ontological truths about that subject. The figures of the homosexual and the pervert came into discursive being, according to Foucault, at roughly the same time as the figure of the criminal—and all were constituted by similar means. The criminal was an amalgam of two "types": "the moral monster,"[21] a freak of nature that was an inheritance of earlier centuries, and the subject of "abnormality," constructed by means of modern technologies of normalization. The role of the expert or psychiatric witness served the very function in the case of the criminal subject that the sexologist (and later the psychoanalyst) would serve in the case of the sexual pervert and invert. By the extraction of confessions, designed to establish the person's "nature," the subject's criminal guilt could be proven and his or her nature confirmed.

Foucault shows how the defendant's behavior prior to his or her crimes was retroactively examined and *made* to be commensurate with his or her identity as a criminal: "The aim [of expert testimony] is to show how the individual already resembles his crime before he has committed it,"[22] providing "proof of a form of conduct, a character, and an attitude that are moral defects while being neither, pathologically, illnesses nor legally, offenses."[23] No longer simply neutral pieces of behavior, all the characteristics of the individual about to be written into discourse as a criminal subject are read as symptoms of an abnormal—or exceptional—essence. By means of these technologies of individualization and normalization, then, modern discourses that attempt to isolate the special "nature" of the murderer transubstantiate his or her crimes from acts committed into facets of ontological essences.

Throughout his work, Foucault gives us a model for understanding that subjects are not only constructed discursively by authority disciplines; rather, they also construct themselves in relation to these dominant discourses. That Ian Brady and Colin Wilson share a language for describing the "uniqueness" of the murderer is rendered explicable by this insight. Murderers draw on the resources of a common cultural memory bank about the meaning of the act and ontology of murder to understand—and to *produce*—themselves as murderers too. One of Fou-

cault's key questions in both his work on criminals and his work on in-
verts/perverts is precisely: "How had the subject been compelled to decipher himself?"[24] And his writing on the case of Pierre Rivière highlights
how the murderer's written narrative is poietic, not mimetic. The fact
that Rivière's confession was in part constructed *before* he committed
the crimes demonstrates that it does not make sense to say that a confession is merely a retroactive representation of what has taken place in the
world. Rather, discourse can bring the acts it describes into being; it can
be productive of them. And, by extension, the act of writing *as* a murderer
contributes to bringing the subject of murder constitutively into being.

What is of especial interest to me, and what is not fully explained in
this account of the disciplinary means by which murderers are discursively constructed as abnormal criminal subjects, is the fact that this specific form of "abnormality," has, since the moment it was constructed,
attracted as much fascination as it has received moral condemnation—
a phenomenon noted in my earlier anecdote about Foucault's own personal response to Rivière. In the same century that criminology and sexology were gaining authority, a series of parallel European discourses
about the nobility and beauty of the abnormal or exceptional subject
arose. It obtained in the aesthetic philosophy of Romanticism early in
the century and that of Decadence toward its end, and it continued to
color artistic and literary representation into the twentieth century. In
these aesthetic modes, the murderer paralleled the artist and genius as
exceptional and exempt from adherence to ordinary morality. In his *Discipline and Punish* (1975), Foucault makes mention of this celebration,
writing of a literary mode in which

> crime is glorified, because it is one of the fine arts, because it can be the
> work only of exceptional natures, because it reveals the monstrousness of the
> strong and powerful, because villainy is yet another mode of privilege.[25]

The mode of writing about murder that Foucault describes above is a
contemporaneous, but distinct, trend from the narrative of detection,
which seeks to identify the criminal's guilt and restore social order, often pitting an exceptional, but morally "good," detective figure against
an exceptional, and demonized, murderer. In the conceit of murderer-as-
artist, conversely, the murderer is neither detected nor dethroned, and
the triumph of transcendence promised by the violent act is celebrated
for writerly and readerly identification and vicarious thrills.

The Murderer-as-Artist

Central to the making of the subject that is the modern murderer is the fantasy, visible already in Sade's writing, that an act of destruction is, or has proximity to, an act of creativity. In nineteenth-century European culture, the aesthetic movement of Romanticism presented the murderer as a refined personage, above moral codes, whose acts bore a creative dimension. The most famous exponent of this idea was Thomas De Quincey, who, in a series of three tongue-in-cheek essays published between 1827 and 1854, argued that murder should be considered as one of the fine arts. The parallels drawn between the murderer and the artist include the following amusing analogy:

> Awkward disturbances will arise; people will not submit to have their throats cut quietly . . . and whilst the portrait painter often has to complain of too much torpor in his subject, the artist in our line is generally embarrassed by too much animation.[26]

The extended simile is ludic, but it is difficult to tell when De Quincey is simply joking and when a more serious agenda is being played out in his texts. Some of the assertions about domination and powerlessness in the scene of murder are particularly ethically problematic. For example, he locates the aesthetic response to murder precisely in the pathos of an unequal struggle between a superior agent and a weaker victim, casting the artist-murderer as a particularly powerful subject. The preferred mode of violence is the "clean" annihilation of the weak, especially the murder of a whole family, rather than a banal fight between equals that results in a death.[27] "When a brawl in an inn turns into murder," according to De Quincey: "farewell to all the genuine effects of the art."[28] The aesthetic quality of murder for De Quincey thus lies in its ability to "cleanse the heart by means of pity and terror," evoking a similar response in the beholder to the one that Aristotle suggests tragedy should elicit from its audience.[29]

It has been argued that De Quincey's murder essays are an attempt to explore the Kantian elision of the distinction between aesthetics and ethics. Within the philosophical concept of the transcendental, Kant claimed that destructive elements in nature could be "beautiful." With this in mind, as Joel Black points out in *The Aesthetics of Murder* (1991), "once natural violence was considered as a possible source of aesthetic experience, what was to prevent human violence . . . from making aesthetic claims as well?"[30] Kant argued, counter to this hypothesis, that human violence appeared instead as *monstrous*, and as distinct from the sublime power of destructive nature, contemplation of which could edify man's morality.[31] Yet an atheistic, Sadeian logic (one that Jacques Lacan would later place directly in dialogue with Kant in his essay of 1962)[32] would hold that, since human beings are creatures of nature, human acts of destruction are merely *extensions* of nature's violent power, and thus the two cannot be neatly disentangled. The murder-as-art trope essayed by De Quincey can thus appear as an exploration of the logical limit of Kant's thought, resulting in a "subversion of ethics by aesthetics."[33]

However, it is also undeniable that De Quincey's essays articulate recognizable Romantic ideas about ontology and subjectivity expressed through aesthetic extremes, such that it is not satisfactory either to dismiss them as "just" humorous texts or to elevate them to the status of a pure, philosophical redress. Instead, they must be understood as both productive and reflective of prized fantasies of the time about subjectivity, agency, and beauty. German Romantic writer Friedrich Schiller had written in 1802 of the lack of aesthetic potential of "the thief" as poetic subject matter, stating that if this man were also found to be a murderer he would be condemned more severely by moral law and yet "raised one degree higher" in terms of "aesthetic judgement," since a homicide elevates its perpetrator above the level of the person who commits a petty "*vile* action."[34] And, as we will see in chapter 1, during the trial of poet-murderer Pierre-François Lacenaire in Paris in the 1830s, the killer's poetry was discussed in relation to his crimes, and vice versa, as if they are two sides of the same coin of exceptionality. A later example of this phenomenon is Oscar Wilde's description of the real-life killer Thomas Griffiths Wainewright in "Pen, Pencil, and Poison" (1889) as "not merely a poet and painter [but also] a subtle and secret poisoner almost without rival in this or any age."[35] The aesthetic philosophy of Decadence, of which Wilde is an English exponent, celebrated the perceived social decay of the end of the century. Decadents took the murderer-artist as a key trope and often deformed Romantic sensibility into a lugubrious morbidity.[36]

This Romantic and Decadent discourse has not entirely disappeared in the pragmatic twentieth and twenty-first centuries, but has been absorbed into the fabric of the language and logic used to represent murderers. W. H. Auden claims in 1959 that murder is "negative creation" and that "every murderer is therefore the rebel who claims the right to be omnipotent."[37] The notion that both creating art and killing others are means of exercising power is central to this—very masculine—fantasy. Special attention continues to be paid in the twentieth century to those murderers who also create art works: Dennis Nilsen is discussed as an amateur artist, symphony composer, and memoir-writer, in addition to being a necrophilic murderer. And, as Ricarda Vidal and David Schmid have shown, a vibrant market exists for what Schmid calls "murderabilia": artworks and objects produced by incarcerated murderers, such as the paintings of the American serial killer of boys John Wayne Gacy, who dressed as a clown and visited children in the hospital as part of his civic duties.[38] Vidal has argued that those who purchase killers' artworks seek to possess—albeit by proxy—the lure of aesthetic transcendence that continues to accrue to the exceptional figure of the murderer and to all that he or she does.[39]

The phenomenon of murder-as-art is thoroughly explored in Black's *The Aesthetics of Murder.* Yet Black's work does not interrogate the ethical or cultural implications, or the gender politics, of the fantasy of murder-as-art and murderer-as-artist; rather it takes its subject matter as its critical position, considering a variety of texts and films—and indeed real-life cases of murder—"from an aesthetic rather than from a moral, psychological or philosophical perspective."[40] Where, in Foucault's *I, Pierre Rivière*, the instance of confession of the author's "seduction" by the murderer is an unusual moment of rupture in Foucault's habitual critical style, for Black, as for Laurence Senelick in *The Prestige of Evil* (1987),[41] fascination and admiration for the murdering creative subject are intrinsic to the tenor of the prose, suggesting again the force and prevalence of this trope for scholarly critics as well as for fiction writers and murderers.

The Murderer as Superman

A closely related fantasy to that of the murderer as creative artist is the idea that the murderer is a subject so special that everyday morality does not apply to him. The mark of the transcendental criminal subject is the capacity to commit the perfect crime, a crime not tempered by "base" motive or self-interest, but rather motiveless and pure: an acte gratuit.

This idea has its roots in the notion of a purely aesthetic crime, such as those presented by De Quincey, but progresses philosophically via the Nietzschean concept of the "Superman," which becomes a key figure in the murderer-as-exceptional-subject discourse that we are exploring here. Nietzsche sought to expose and relativize the "dominion of morality" that Plato, Kant, and Hegel had, according to him, bequeathed to Western thought as absolutes.[42] He wished to destabilize the metaphysical categories that govern ethics (good versus evil) and epistemology (truth versus lies). In place of such polarized values, he asserts the need for "disinterested malice"[43] and claims that the subject who can fully transcend the common understanding of good and evil need no longer be bound by moral limits which, in his understanding, are nothing but a matter of convention and conformity.

Murderers and those who write about murderers alike have been obsessed by the idea of a perfect, pure crime committed by a superior subject. In French literature especially, authors working in the philosophies of absurdism and existentialism (the latter of which influenced contemporary English writer Colin Wilson) have touched on the possibility of motiveless crime. This idea is embodied most famously, perhaps, in André Gide's Lafcadio, hero of *Les Caves du Vatican* (1914), a conscious parody of Fyodor Dostoyevsky's *Crime and Punishment* (1866). While traveling on a train, the character pushes an unknown man out of his carriage and onto the railway tracks for no apparent reason other than the necessity to cede to impulse. This allows Gide to stage a discussion of the idea that the existence of disinterested, gratuitous acts disproves the proposition that human beings are capable of acting only out of self-interest and self-preservation. Albert Camus's absurdist work *L'Étranger* (1942) similarly features a character, Meursault, whose shooting of an Arab stranger on the day he learns of his mother's death is voided by the author of both motive and of meaning. It becomes instead a triumph of pure free will and the senselessness of human life. And Jean Genet, a real-life incarcerated thief and gay writer, idealizes the figure of the murderer throughout his plays and novels, as seen in *Notre Dame des Fleurs* (1943), when he imagines the state of mind of his cell mate, Clément Village, following his killing of his girlfriend:

> By a powerful effort of will, he escaped banality—maintaining his mind in
> a superhuman region, where he was a god, creating at one stroke a private

> universe where his acts escaped moral control. . . . Men endowed with a wild
> imagination should have, in addition, the great poetic faculty of denying our
> universe and its values so that they may act upon it with sovereign ease.[44]

The interlacing of discourses of the poet-murderer, the Superman, and
the sovereign subject is in evidence here. Tellingly, a chapter of Sartre's
paean to the writer, *Saint Genet*, is called "On the Fine Arts Considered
as Murder," showing the influence of De Quincey—or more precisely,
the ideas associated with him—on subsequent considerations of murder
as both art and act of free will.

Yet these considerations do not remain wholly within the sphere of
philosophy and literature. Ideas from the intellectual realm are also
played out in real-life contexts, and then those ideas become further reified as the matter of criminal folklore. The case of Leopold and Loeb,
two Chicago University students who murdered a 14-year-old boy in 1924
allegedly in order to essay the "perfect murder" and to prove themselves
Nietzschean "Supermen," has itself spawned numerous fictional and
filmic representations, including Hitchcock's celebrated *Rope* (1948).
The case was also cited as criminal inspiration by Ian Brady, who intended the murders he committed with his partner Myra Hindley to be
examples of "perfect crimes." Thus, theory, fiction, and fact are revealed
as interpenetrating realms in which discourse is made, repeated, and
reinforced.

The gendered nature of these discourses of aesthetic murder and of
the acte gratuit cannot be ignored. The lionization of the powerful, dominant agent in De Quincey's discourse is a fantasy of macho masculinity, and it is impossible to see any place for women in such discourses,
except as the victims of the "beautiful" crimes. This is because the gendering of agency in the nineteenth century was such that only the super-
rational male subject would be presumed capable of essaying the acte
gratuit, since reason in the post-Enlightenment imaginary was ascribed
to masculinity, while femininity was associated with emotion, material-
ity, and unreason.[45] Ultimately, of course, the acte gratuit itself is a sophistry, since even "the desire to commit a perfect crime" and "the desire
to act irrationally, unmotivated by gain" are, in themselves, motives,
even if not pragmatic ones. The acte gratuit, then, is "just" an idea, but
an idea that is particularly exciting to the modern imagination, I suggest,
because it hints at a (masculine) subject acting out a form of radical free-

dom that is antibourgeois, antipositivistic, and that elevates the aesthetic above the ethical.

The Murderer as "Beast"

At the same time that Romantic writers were conceiving of the idea of the murderer as artist and agent, another set of discourses about the modern murderer was emerging from the scientific systematization of the nineteenth century that Foucault has described. Alienism, criminology, and sexology took the idea of the aberrant individual and turned it into a diagnostic *typology* of aberration.

The higher form of free will and the artistic capacity that exempted the criminal from considerations of ordinary moral responsibility in the aesthetic philosophies of the nineteenth century are transformed in the language of early psychiatry and social science into a disorder of reason. The figure of the "homicidal monomaniac," popularized in the second decade of the nineteenth century in France by the originator of the monomania diagnosis, alienist Jean-Étienne Esquirol, describes a person who loses reason and self-control in one area only: that of his overwhelming urge to kill.[46] The term "alienism," used to describe the profession in its early days, reveals much about its ideology: an "alienated" person was one who had "lost possession" of himself, who was dislocated from the codes of reason that shaped accepted subjectivity. In the attempt to wrest authority from superstitious discourses of religion, which had conceived madness as possession by a demon, alienism sought to return afflicted subjects from a state of delirium to full possession of their senses. The very instinct that Gide's Lafcadio would elevate as a philosophical principle a century later was cast as a symptom of insanity in early psychiatry. Monomanias were supposed to be strictly of two kinds, either "erotic" or "destructive" in aim. Sexual instinct was termed in French alienism the *instinct de conservation* or *instinct génésique*, both terms suggesting strongly the centrality of procreation rather than pleasure as the aim of sexuality. In erotic monomanias, the sexual impulse would go awry, being too intense, inappropriately directed, or perverse in the acts sought in its service. In destructive monomanias, the otherwise "normal" subject found himself in the grip of a single-minded and overwhelming urge to kill. In the case of murders accompanied by sexual acts or feelings, the diagnosis of monomania came under strain, since the "single-mindedness" on which the diagnosis rested and the necessity of fitting into one or other binary "type" of disorder (erotic or destructive) were troubled by the copresence of erotic and destructive elements.[47]

In the course of the century, the monomania diagnosis declined in popularity and by the time the heyday of European sexology and criminology dawned—the 1880s and 1890s—the criminal subject began to be understood instead according to the popular theory of degeneration associated with German physician Max Nordau. In this system, sexual and moral abnormality were expected to coexist in the degenerate subject, since "degeneration" described a jointly sexual, moral, physical, and psychological condition whereby the individual afflicted—and the society to which the individual belonged—were perceived to be in the grip of decay and destruction.[48]

The criminal subject and the sexual pervert were principal characters in the dramatis personae of degeneration, as they embodied the central tenet of this conservative post-Darwinian social theory: that modernity, with its fast-paced progress and change, was heading for self-destruction as technology advanced more rapidly than human adaptive evolution. As the population, caught in evolutionary impasse, became weaker and more degenerate, moral and criminal perversions would increasingly occur, along with physiological abnormalities, such as club footedness and scrofula. The spectacle of the murdering subject became an embodied literalization of the perceived threat of modernity in this discourse. The figure of the "inborn criminal" popularized by the founder of Italian criminal anthropology, Cesare Lombroso, gains prominence in this intellectual context.[49] The inborn criminal is a degenerate subject, a product of tainted heredity, compounded with personal moral weakness. His or her criminal essence can be literally read in his or her facial features, cranial bumps, and physiological idiosyncrasies, according to the pseudoscience of anthropometry practiced by Lombroso.

The reliance upon the body as a map to the individual's nature is equally visible in the contemporaneous German sexology of Austrian-born Krafft-Ebing, author of the bible of sexology *Psychopathia Sexualis* (1886), and his followers. As well as soliciting written and spoken confessions from his perverts, Krafft-Ebing would perform a detailed analysis of their physiological condition and medical history (and those of their family members), in the hope of isolating the degenerate conditions thought to be linked with perversion and criminality. (Epilepsy was especially commonly identified.) The particular subject of murder to which German sexology gave birth was the "lust murderer," supposedly exemplified by Jack the Ripper. The lust murderer was a figure of sexual instinct gone awry, in whom the "normal" desire for penetrative coitus was replaced by the sadistic desire to kill.[50] The lust murderer is a strikingly and singularly male/masculine subject. The sadism of his desire is describable, in the sexological system, as an exaggeration of the naturally occurring "aggressive character" that is held to account for male dominance and violence.[51] While extolling the superior capacity for reason on the part of men as compared to women, as was consistent with the beliefs of his day, Krafft-Ebing nevertheless clearly saw male sexuality as potentially violent and dangerous, and as needing to be tempered and kept within the bounds of decency by the civilizing influence of marriage. The lust murderers Krafft-Ebing deals with are described using a language of animality and teratology. The discourse of male sexuality as a dangerous, potentially uncontainable and savage force, leading men to behave in primitive ways, provides a pre-echo of the tabloid "sex-beast" rhetoric of the twentieth century.

Despite the apparently contradictory character of the nineteenth-century discourses of murderer-as-artist, on the one hand, and murderer as "beast," on the other, these ideas were, in fact, intimately linked and not mutually exclusive. They were harnessed together by the idea of exception and otherness that accrued to the murderer, whether as a noble mantle of superiority or as the beacon of sickness. Sometimes, indeed, these ideas overlapped, as when Max Nordau wrote in *Degeneration* (1892), a work he dedicated to Lombroso, of the narrow line between the creative degenerate and the destructive one. Nordau saw Symbolist poets Paul Verlaine and Stéphane Mallarmé as examples of a degenerate culture, just as an inborn criminal would be. He espied in Decadent, Naturalist, and modernist textuality a linguistic decay that revealed to him, trace-like, "all the physical and mental marks of degeneration."[52] Likewise, Lombroso himself frequently coupled genius with criminality or madness, especially in the case of "criminal man." (He is, as would be expected, more circumspect regarding the potential for the genius of "criminal woman," as we will see in chapter 2 via exploration of his discussion of Marie Lafarge.) Just as "genius" and "criminal" are two facets of the same discursive production, so aesthetic philosophy and criminal science share the same cultural ideas and ideals about exceptionality and individuality, even if they bring opposing political views to bear on the morality of the exceptional individual they describe.

This articulation within the subdisciplines of the psy sciences of a link between genius on the one hand and abnormality on the other is an eminently modern idea, and other "outsiders" were constructed in precisely this way. Along with the murderer, the homosexual was described in the late nineteenth and early twentieth centuries in terms that draw on ideas both of genius and degeneracy, and the damaging presupposition that homosexuals had criminal tendencies stemmed from this epistemological and ideological conflation.[53] However, the very term "genius," as we understand it today, is an adaptation of an ancient idea given a modern twist. Just as madness was once seen as possession by evil spirits, so in biblical terms, "inspiration" (that which, since the nineteenth century, we have associated with Romantic geniuses producing great art) was not exclusive to the exceptional creative individual. Rather "inspiration" was a spirit that entered each person along with the breath (as the etymology of the word suggests), such that everyone had a personal "genius" that moved him or her in different directions.[54] So, for the ancients, just as divine inspiration may lead to great art, so a "great" crime could be provoked by a malign spirit who entered the individual. In the modern age, the "specification of individuals" leading to the construction of the abnormal subject described by Foucault resulted in genius, madness, and criminality being understood instead as characteristics proper to abnormal individuals who were exceptional by dint of their heredity.

Beauty *and* the Beast: The Twentieth-Century Murderer

Efforts to render the exceptional murdering subject both pathological and breathtakingly different from the civilized norm during the nineteenth century have, if anything, intensified in the twentieth. Antipsychiatry exponent Thomas Szasz has pointed out that historical ideas about the proximity of "genius" to criminality and madness continue to inform the way in which we understand exceptionality in the contemporary Western world. Szasz critiques the fact that contemporary psychiatry has simply *displaced* the locus of such abnormality from the realm of spirituality in the ancient imaginary to that of brain chemistry in our current one, rather than questioning the values of the social system in which the terms of normality and abnormality are understood. Moreover, he critiques the way in which certain forms of mental illness have been idealized, owing to the nineteenth-century Romantic heritage I have outlined above, while others are read as innately negative and inevitably productive of criminality (a remnant of the contemporaneous nineteenth-century scientific discourses of innate criminality). He writes:

> Alongside the romantic image of manic-depression as a cause of creativity that does not detract from the subject's intentionality for his conduct and responsibility for his good deeds stands the bleak image of schizophrenia as a cause of criminality annulling the subject's intentionality for his conduct and responsibility for his bad deeds. This interpretation, too, lacks objective proof. Instead, its "truth" is enshrined in, and is taught by, the modern clerical and clinical practices of the insanity excuse/defense.[55]

Szasz's point is that the construction of insanity and the labeling of mental disorders compartmentalize subjects into their pathologies and allow these labels to stand in place of any other analyses of behavior: social, political, ideological. While Szasz's antipsychiatry stance is particularly radical, his point here is relevant to my contention that obfuscation of the meanings of individuals' criminal acts via discourses of both exceptionality and pathology neatly obviates more systemic critiques and contextual understandings.

A particularly good example of an unsatisfactory psychological/psychiatric diagnosis that is used to signal both condemnation of and fascination with the murdering subject is that of "psychopathy" (often used interchangeably with "sociopathy"). The term originated with physician J. C. Pritchard in the nineteenth century, and it described a person who was "morally insane" but otherwise appeared "normal" and was able to lead a functional life.[56] Two FBI agents expand the description thus: "The individual is not psychotic, is not neurotic, is not mentally retarded, and frequently appears not only normal but supernormal."[57] The mention of "supernormal" suggests to us, perhaps, the philosophical discourse associated with Nietzsche. A person with a deficiency of moral consciousness, but the ability to "pass" in everyday life as unremarkable and unworthy of suspicion, appears indeed to be a Superman. Lionization of the kind applied to the nineteenth-century transcendental killer is visible in descriptions of the "psychopath" produced by medical experts, true-crime buffs, and fiction writers. Jane Caputi points out that Norman Mailer described the emotionally numb psychopath as the "hero of our age" in "The White Negro."[58] Similarly, in his book on psychopaths, Alan Harrington writes that they are: "detached and unconcerned" but "at times almost *magical* . . . , not merely dominating, but *bewitching* others."[59] A reluctant admiration and no small measure of mystification are evident in the terms of Harrington's description. The label "psychopath" is, as we have seen, somewhat lacking in diagnostic rigor, and was replaced in the APA's *Diagnostic and Statistical Manual of Mental Disorders* during the 1980s with a range of other diagnoses.[60] Nevertheless, it continues to be used in criminology and media to the present day, and is often indiscriminately applied to those murderers whose personae resonate with the mythic figure described above, the ambivalently admirable subject who lives "beyond good and evil." Conversely, "psychopath" is also often used in a derogatory sense, especially in the popular press, where it is to be understood as morally interchangeable with "monster."

Contemporaneously with the making of the "psychopath," in the United States, the psychological discipline of offender profiling, pioneered by the FBI at the Behavioral Science Unit at Quantico, has introduced a technique of identifying killers, especially "serial killers," by analyzing the modus operandi of their crimes. The term "serial killer" was defined by the unit's cofounder Robert Ressler to describe someone who kills four or more victims over a period greater than 72 hours, with a recognizable signature and for no apparent motive.[61] Behavioral science moves beyond the analysis of degenerate characteristics, as in the late nineteenth century, and sidesteps the late twentieth-century psychiatric model of neurochemical analysis critiqued by Szasz, in favor of analyzing *behavior* that is then charged with carrying the essence of the criminal's identity. By observing the choices a criminal at large makes, the profiler can adduce the "personality makeup" of that individual: the kind of childhood he is likely to have had, his tastes, and his habits. The idea is to compile as full a database of information on past cases as possible, so that offenders may be more quickly apprehended. In his book on serial killers, Mark Seltzer humorously describes the offender profile as "a 'job description,' a sort of 'most wanted' ad."[62] Seltzer has pointed out how public interest in the FBI's work in this field, as popularized by Thomas Harris's best-selling Hannibal Lecter books,[63] has led to a general familiarity with the idea of the serial killer, a familiarity available to both public and killers:

The designation of the serial killer as a type of person has had, we have noted, a sort of switchback or looping effect: public knowledge about kinds of people has a way of interacting with the people who are known about and how these people conceive of themselves.[64]

The "offender" who emerges from Quantico's research laboratories is thus the latest "individual" to be "specified" in this discursive tradition, albeit by means of a rather unpoetic calculation of probability and observation of statistics.[65] And yet, one characteristic of the "serial killer" is that his crimes are apparently "motiveless" or "senseless."[66] Paradoxically, then, despite the prosaic means by which the "serial killer" is identified (or rather produced), the belief underlying the diagnosis has something of the Romantic idea that constructed the perpetrator of the "pure act," the agent of crime for crime's sake, in the nineteenth-century philosophical discourses discussed earlier. Indeed, I would contend that this inheritance of an earlier set of meanings superimposed onto present-day discourse is partly responsible for the glamour of the serial killer.

The very notion of offender profiling and behavioral science would be anathema to those murderers who see themselves as unique and not capable of reduction to a "type." "Individuality is the supreme value," writes Brady in *The Gates of Janus*.[67] And his fictional counterpart, psychiatrist and killer Hannibal Lecter, is described in *The Silence of the Lambs* as "impenetrable, much too sophisticated for the standard tests."[68] The discourse of the nineteenth-century exceptional criminal-genius that Lecter wholly embodies trumps any twentieth-century scientific method. That Brady's attitude, received in the context of the current scientific moment, would be interpreted as a symptom of psychopathy (grandiosity featuring prominently in Hare's famous Psychopathy Checklist)[69] illustrates the extent to which disciplinary discourses are not only historically dependent, but hierarchized. As Szasz points out,[70] we look to the psy sciences for reassurance of the presence of diagnosable abnormality—for a label—to stand in place of the unquantifiable and archaic quality of evil, or, indeed, in place of the existential quality of radical freedom, which Brady, like his nineteenth-century forebears, perceived as being accessible through crime.[71] Moreover, the existence of the insanity defense (McNaghten, 1843) and the plea of diminished responsibility[72] (the 1957 Homicide Act) provides another way of relegating the criminal to the margins of culture. Although it changes the likely outcome of sentencing in a criminal case, an insane murderer being more likely to be hospitalized than imprisoned, the legally insane killer, like the "serial killer" (the two are by no means identical and a Venn diagram would show only some overlap), is both placed outside of any expectation that the average individual should understand him and is thereby othered from the norm. As Cameron and Frazer have made clear, this means that murder remains a matter of the exceptional individual, rather than becoming properly political and open to analysis.[73] Wendy Hollway illustrates this, pointing out with reference to the case of the Yorkshire Ripper, Peter Sutcliffe, who claimed that a voice in his head told him to murder prostitutes, that

> the explanation that it was a delusion does not show *why* the voice told Sutcliffe to kill women. Whether it was God's voice, the devil's voice or the projected voice of Sutcliffe's own hatred made no difference: the content derives from a generalized, taken for granted misogyny.[74]

In cases of twentieth-century murderers, the "exceptionality" discourse and the "offending type" discourse are juxtaposed with—and paradoxically intensified by—an insistence upon the apparent "ordinariness" of the individual before he or she was revealed to be a killer. The "good next-door neighbor," whom one would never have expected to have bodies under the floorboards or the patio, has become a cliché, embodied in the persons of such killers as John Christie, softly spoken reserve policeman and necrophilic strangler of at least eight women during the 1950s in London;[75] mild-mannered civil servant and trade union activist Dennis Nilsen, sometimes dubbed "the Kindly Killer"; and "nice couple,"[76] Gloucester-based Fred and Rosemary West, who between them were responsible for the rape and murder of at least 11 women and girls between 1967 and 1987. Seltzer analyzes the way in which the serial killer—like the "psychopath" described above—is "seen as utterly typical: 'abnormally normal' or 'too normal' or 'alarmingly normal.'"[77] So powerful is the myth of the "exceptional" murderer that for an otherwise "ordinary," apparently sane person to *also* be capable of atrocities gives rise to cognitive dissonance, despite Hannah Arendt's brilliant 1963 essay exploring why "banality" and "evil" should no longer be such unthinkable bedfellows.[78] The real issue, of course, lies in the fact that we assume that the "ordinary"/"extraordinary" binary is ontologically meaningful whereas, as Foucault has shown us, its construction is a technique designed to establish a safely demarcated norm with which "we" can identify and a set of abnormal types which can be relegated to the outside of the commonality.

Once the "truth" about an apparently ordinary person's crimes is known, the individual is transformed in the eyes of those who knew him or her, and facts about the person's life prior to the crime can be retroactively adjusted, in precisely the manner described by Foucault when exploring the role of expert testimony in foundational medico-legal practice as a technique designed to make the murdering subject a *consistent* one. One feature of the myth of exceptionality we are exploring is the insistence upon the unchanging and singular nature, upon the monumentality and one-dimensionality, of the murderer. Thus, Myra Hindley's biographer, Carol Ann Lee, points out the cognitive dissonance and concomitant outrage on the part of those learning that the much-reviled child-killer was made a godmother while in prison and even wrote, almost 20 years after committing her crimes, about her desire to have children of her own.[79] Such multifacetedness (or even the simple capacity to change over time) is not admitted of within our cultural expectation of murderers.

A sort of alchemy therefore takes place around murderers. Since the idea of an ordinary, rather dull, individual who commits atrocities is commonly held to be an impossibility, the "ordinary person" who is revealed to have done just that must retroactively *become* the extraordinary monster described in the press during the course of a murder hunt. As Cameron and Frazer put it: "The beast is relentlessly personalized. . . . The press is on hand to present him with a name: the M4 Rapist, the Beast of Belgravia, the Fox, the Ripper" and "in most cases, the beast will eventually be revealed not as a monster but as the man next door."[80] There is no more apt illustration of the acuity of Foucault's contention that a person's acts are made to define their essence, to constitute their very identity, than this tendency. The stakes are so high in proving the killer absolutely, categorically, a "different" kind of subject—the mythical "beast"—that shades of ambiguity, contradiction, and nuance simply cannot be admitted. Commenting on the Yorkshire Ripper's original conviction as sane in 1981 (he was later diagnosed as schizophrenic and transferred to Broadmoor Hospital), feminist journalist Joan Smith wrote:

At long last it seemed to have been publicly acknowledged that we live in a society in which sane men periodically embark upon the wholesale slaughter of women. But no, the outpouring of words after the trial . . . did as much as possible to mould Peter Sutcliffe into the Yorkshire Ripper . . . to prove he was some sort of monster. The Yorkshire Ripper was filed away as an aberration. The case is closed. The myth has won.[81]

Carol Ann Lee sums up the tendency described here succinctly. She states: "Contrary to what some sections of the media would have us believe, people who commit monstrous acts look no different to the rest of humanity and have likes and dislikes, strengths and weaknesses, too."[82] They are, moreover, *products* of a society and their beliefs are of course likely to reflect those that surround them—even if they exaggerate or literalize ideas that are usually kept in the realms of fiction or fantasy. But this is a rare insight. All too often the apparently ordinary elements of the murderer are supposed, post factum, to have been simply a deceptive mask, a Dorian Gray–like countenance, worn to distract attention from the "truth" hiding in the attic. Even less commonly expressed is the spin Peter Sotos puts on the persona of the serial killer as exceptional outsider in his angry "Afterword" to Brady's paean to moral relativism, *The Gates of Janus*. Sotos casts the figure of criminal exceptionality as nothing more than a tired cliché, writing of "the dime a dozen serial killer front of puffed-up superiority."[83] Sotos refuses to allow the "grandiose" killer to be "unique" or transcendental. Instead his potency, much vaunted as a subjective attribute in nineteenth-century philosophy, as in many subsequent examples of popular fiction, is debunked here as a banal and easily adopted "front."

Methodological Tool Kit and Case Studies

This book will explore a series of discourses woven around real-life murderers in order to analyze in depth the workings of the mechanism identified by Foucault, by which *acts are made to become identities* in the case of the murderer. It does this by means of a series of illustrative case studies of murderers who have been excessively represented and, in some cases, who have sought to represent themselves excessively, as unique, different, and outside of cultural norms. This book is not concerned with trying to access the individual psychological "truth" of what motivates a given murderer to kill; nor is it directly interested in the processes of policing that developed contemporaneously with criminology and psychiatry in the nineteenth century, and which gave rise to the narrative of detection and the personage of the detective, as these concerns are much discussed elsewhere.[84] Rather, it takes as its focus the cultural, scientific, artistic, and popular means by which murderers are represented, made to signify, and attributed meaning as individual subjects—and focuses too on the ways in which murderers themselves echo, repeat, and perpetuate these discourses about themselves. The book's title thus pivots on the dual meaning of "subject" theorized by Foucault and explained above: murderers are both the prized *subject matter* of the disciplines and discourses—psychology and psychiatry, law, criminology, literature, film, and popular press—that construct them, and at the same time they are *subjects of discourse* in the Foucauldian sense of individuals whose experiences and sense of "self" do not develop ex nihilo, but are constituted at the meeting point of these discursive networks of knowledge. "Subjectification" is the Anglicized term for Foucault's description of how individuals internalize and identify the discourses designed to describe them and thereby self-represent and self-police in highly codified ways, while believing that they are merely externalizing the truth of their reality: their identity.

The book has a tripartite methodology: firstly, it will employ a type of Foucauldian analysis of discourses that permits an understanding of the extent to which assertions about given subjects are never a matter of neutral observation, but rather shot through with the biases and interests issuing from the historically located disciplines doing the asserting. Crucially too, the discourses in question will be read as productive rather than simply reflective of the cultural fantasies with which they deal. The method described in Foucault's sociological work on Rivière is of particular relevance. Foucault comments that his team decided not to use any interpretative framework to try to understand Rivière's acts or state of mind, but rather allowed the confessional text to serve as a focal point "to gauge the distance between the other discourses and the relations arising among them . . . without involving it in one of the discourses (medical, legal, psychological, criminological) which we wished to use as our starting point in talking about it."[85] This will serve as inspiration for my own method in this book. Like Foucault, I do not wish to psychologize the murderers discussed, but to plot the interactions and conflicts of competing attempts to produce truth about the figure of the murderer from within the different discursive fields that will concern us (literary, scientific, media, autobiographical, etc). I will also be influenced by

Foucault's demonstration, alluded to above, that Rivière's confessional writing *prompted* and created the conditions for his crime, rather than reflecting on them after the fact. I will interrogate the usefulness of this conception of confessional writing as a means of constructing and claiming identity and agency for and by murderers, and as an attempt to preempt interpretation by the authority disciplines.

Secondly, and relatedly, the book will undertake close readings of the different types of primary text discussed in order to pursue an analysis of their rhetoric and ideologies. By "close reading" I mean a form of analysis that pays attention not just to statements or ideas, but to textual matter itself. Key terms are identified, as in other kinds of inquiry, but attention is also paid to the specific articulations in which they appear, the logic being that the meaning of these terms will be locally inflected and thereby revelatory of ideology. This method or set of methods, commonly practiced in literary studies and philosophy, is predicated on the assumption that language and thought are mutually constraining.

Thirdly, a feminist perspective and an awareness of the gendered character of the discourses of nature, abnormality, monstrousness, exceptionality, criminal agency, and artistry that accrue to the figure of the murderer will be brought to bear on my readings. In this way, the book moves beyond Foucault's work on the construction of the modern criminal subject, since analysis of gender politics is an often-noted blind spot in Foucault's work.[86] Feminist works on murder, including Caputi's and Cameron and Frazer's books, are key reference points for my analysis of discourses of the murdering subject that serve, via an appeal to "individuality," to try to make the murderer an exception to patriarchal culture rather than a symptom of it. Unlike these two works, which focus on the predominance of the male as murderer, however, the subject of the female murderer will be key to my investigations. Feminist criminology points out that those ideological discourses that create the "inborn killer" using assumptions about "nature" drawn from biology work to demonize female killers in ways that exceed the disapprobation directed at their male counterparts. In *Imagining Crime*, Alison Young explains:

> First, there is a tradition within criminology which deploys the notion of biology as exercising a causative influence over individuals. Second, that tradition has deleterious consequences for criminology's representation of women, since women are understood as being determined by biology in ways that make them inferior to men (making them over-emotional, unreliable, child-

ish, devious). Its status *as* tradition means that such propositions have authority and meaning, forcing feminists to *rebut* an existing conceptualization.[87]

Indeed, a very conservative and uncritical tendency is visible in many popular books about killers—both case studies of individuals and works that treat murder more broadly as a cultural phenomenon. Mainstream true-crime titles and nonfeminist academic studies of killers tend to choose titles that do not mention gender at all, such as *Serial Killers* (making silent and invisible the fact that most of these are, of course, men). Titles that make mention of the sex of the killer as a crucial and relevant factor tend to be chosen only when the ones doing the murdering are inappropriately female, for example, "Women Who Kill."[88] In published works about male killers (unless the book is precisely a feminist study of masculine violence, such as Caputi's or Cameron and Frazer's), the killer's maleness is seldom seen to *require analysis*.[89] In strong contrast, there are very few discussions indeed of female murderers in which the killings are *not* understood in relation to failed femininity or monstrous femininity, or—conversely—in which the female killer is not seen as the passive, cowed dupe of a male partner. Similarly, there is a subgenre of true-crime writing that focuses on "children who kill,"[90] making clear that the default "abnormal" subject is assumed to be a (straight, white, adult) male—just as the default "normal" subject is. Further, insights about the tendency of the heteronormative imagination to construct normality and health in line with heterosexuality, and monstrosity or aberration in line with "queerness," and the ways in which this impacts upon representations of killers whose sexuality is perceived to be somehow deviant, will underpin my readings throughout.[91]

I have chosen in this book to focus on equal numbers of case studies of female and male murderers, and to include a chapter on "underage" killers. I do this in full awareness of the potential danger I run, namely that of being perceived to be implicitly supporting a pernicious antifeminist myth of "equivalence" in terms of the likelihood of male- and female-perpetrated homicide. I am aware that in statistical terms, male murderers far outnumber female murderers, and that both women and children are much more likely to be the victims than the perpetrators of violent crime. Moreover, I write with the awareness that these statistics need to be understood in a larger systemic context: that of a history of Western patriarchy. My decision to focus on equal numbers of male and female murderers was made in the service of illustrating that the constraining social constructs of "masculinity" and "femininity," as they are appealed to in discourses surrounding killers, deserve equal amounts of deconstruction. I thus deem this, perhaps controversial, selection of case material a risk worth running in order to carry out this dismantling of pernicious gender stereotypes via close reading and analysis.

Although murder is an enduringly popular subject for academic books, as for journalistic and other forms of nonfiction writing, no other published work has the same remit as the current study. Other titles cover only single aspects of the scope of my book, meaning that the broad historical span, discussion of a wide range of textual and visual materials from disparate discursive fields, and comparative cultural dimensions are absent in existing titles. Historical works on the figure of the murderer tend to consider either European discourses about the murderer-as-artist, such as Black's *The Aesthetics of Murder* and Senelick's *The Prestige of Evil*, or those discourses that are concerned with the murderer as the pathological subject of criminology and sexology, such as Masters and Lea's *Sex Crimes in History* and Robert Nye's study of crime and politics in modern France,[92] rather than taking these two sets of ideas together and reading them as the two faces of the same coin of modern specification of individuals, as I do.[93] Other historical works look at instances of murder in a specific period and/or national context,[94] or focus on a specific high-profile murder case.[95] My book, by contrast, offers a series of detailed case studies of individual murderers, both male and female, from the 1830s to the 2000s as a way of illustrating and expanding upon my broader theoretical and historical contentions.

There exist a few works with a cultural studies focus that share some of the aims of my book, most notably Schmid's *Natural Born Celebrities* and Seltzer's *Serial Killers*. Both of these works have been influential in helping me to formulate the methodology and focus of this book. However, both works concentrate specifically on representations of one kind of murderer-phenomenon: the serial killer. This can risk further fetishizing this already overdetermined cultural figure and giving the erroneous impression that this type of criminal is a subject that signifies radically differently from that of "the murderer" in general. I contend and demonstrate conversely that the "serial killer" is merely the most recent discursive construction of the murdering subject that the criminological and psy disciplines have offered us. Both of these works concentrate too on one geographical-cultural locus—contemporary North America—and focus on US-specific concerns: the rupture in the public-private division and the omnipresence of spectacle being central to Seltzer's analysis, while Schmid's final chapter treats post-9/11 culture. I believe that the US-centrism of Seltzer's and Schmid's works inevitably downplays the crucial factor of the European history of discourses that made the murderer intelligible. (Although Schmid includes an excellent chapter on Jack the Ripper, it concentrates only on the ways in which his case was received by an American public.) Richard Tithecott's intriguing *Of Men and Monsters: Jeffrey Dahmer and the Construction of the Serial Killer*[96] similarly restricts its subject matter to serial killers and to North America and, moreover, limits the discursive material it analyzes to the media coverage of murder cases rather than reading closely over a range of textual products from different discursive and artistic fields, as my book does. While pursuing rich arguments on which this book will draw where relevant, these three works present limited historical-geographical contextualization, or draw on a narrow corpus of textual material. My analysis of a variety of discourses from the 1830s to the present day, and my comparative focus on material from Europe and North America, allow a careful genealogy of this modern subject of exception to emerge.

The book takes the form of seven chapters, each of which examines a case study of a particular murderer or murderers. The case studies chosen for examination are intended to be paradigmatic, rather than comprehensive, and the book is not a survey volume. One criterion for choosing the murderers to be discussed is the sheer wealth of representation they have provoked and, in most of these cases, produced. In the first section, Pierre-François Lacenaire and Marie Lafarge, who came to trial in France in the 1830s and 1840s, respectively, are compared in terms of the treatment their crimes received in the press, by artistic figures of the day, and by doctors/criminologists. Both murderers wrote long confessional and creative texts that were published, such that the idea of murder as a creative act was complexified by the presence of actual creativity on the part of these murderers. The nineteenth-century attitude to female creativity as well as female destructivity is explored through the case of Lafarge. The third chapter considers the transnationally (in)famous case of British murderer Jack the Ripper in the 1880s and looks at the ways in which the murders and their anonymous perpetrator were received and represented throughout Europe by contemporary sexology (Richard von Krafft-Ebing in Germany), criminology (Cesare Lombroso in Italy), and literature (especially French novelist Emile Zola's portrayal of Jacques Lantier in *La Bête humaine*, 1890). Unlike many histories of the figure of the killer, my book argues that while Jack the Ripper may have inaugurated the figure of the "lust murderer" in the popular imagination and provided the prototype for the "serial killer," the anonymous figure was only one archetype of "the murderer," understood as an exceptional individual, to be produced in the nineteenth century, as evidenced by "aesthetic" French murderers half a century earlier.

The second section moves on to look at three twentieth-century murderers from England and North America who have been multiply represented in literature, art, and film, as well as in academic studies and the popular genre of true-crime writing: the Moors Murderer, Myra Hindley; homosexual necrophile killer Dennis Nilsen; and client-killing prostitute Aileen Wuornos. The gender, sexuality, and perceived class affiliations of these murderers are read as determining in interconnecting ways the kinds of representation that are made of their—paradoxical—singularity. The final chapter explores the cases of several child-murderers: Mary Bell; Robert Thompson and Jon Venables (killers of James Bulger); and Eric Harris and Dylan Klebold, the Columbine high school killers. The phenomenon of high-profile killings and mass murders perpetrated by children troubles conventional modern ideas about both childhood and the "nature" of the murderer, presenting a nightmare figure for a culture that constructs children as a class, rather than as "individuals"— and a class that signifies "innocence," as analyzed by historian of ideas Philippe Ariès.[97]

A second reason for selecting this case material is that the excessive representation of these particular crimes can be demonstrated to mark moments of historically and geographically specific cultural anxiety, namely, anxieties about threats to the dominant order by gendered/ sexual/class-bound "others." In each case discussed, the coincidence of a given cultural moment with its specific anxieties and a particular crime combine to produce a proliferation of discourse about the figure of exceptionality. So, Lacenaire embodies the perceived values and dangers of Romanticism, while his female near contemporary Lafarge raises anxieties about gender roles in the conservative French July Monarchy. Jack the Ripper is called to personify fin-de-siècle degeneration-theory-bound concerns about European societal decay. Hindley is a cipher for reactionary fears about the effects of the 1960s "permissive society" on morality in the UK. Nilsen's crimes became a metonymy for the AIDS panic and homophobia in Thatcher's Britain. The case of Wuornos speaks to a conservative North American backlash against the feminist gains made throughout the twentieth century. Lastly, the children who kill bespeak an Anglo-American turn-of-the-millennium anxiety about the weakened role of fathers and the family in a postmodern, post–nuclear family age. The strategy of those producing anxious discourse in each case is often to other the particular murderer as wholly exceptional, as an aberration rather than as a symptom or a reflection of a cultural moment, thus holding at bay the larger, cultural threat that that murderer may represent. Hence, the historical stereotypes of the Romantic figure of the outlier, the genius-criminal, the sex-beast, or the unnatural figure of the violent woman resurge in order to isolate those individuals from the rest of their culture and to maintain them as (sometimes glamorous) monsters, but never as *mirrors*.

PART I

Murder and Gender in the European Nineteenth Century

CHAPTER ONE

"Real Murderer and False Poet"

Pierre-François Lacenaire

Here's a gripping and terrible sensation; here's *Lacenaire*!
He carried a lyre and a dagger!
He was a poet and he killed!

—(Hippolyte Bonnelier, *Autopsie physiologique de Lacenaire*, 1836)[1]

At once soft and ferocious
Its form holds for the viewer
I know not what atrocious grace
The grace of the gladiator!

Criminal aristocracy,
Neither plane nor hammer
Has hardened its skin
For his instrument was a knife.

For sacred calluses of honest labor
One searches in vain the trace.
Real murderer and false poet
He was the Manfred of the gutter.

—(Théophile Gautier, "Etude de mains: Lacenaire," 1852)[2]

The lines of verse that form the epigraph of this chapter tellingly reveal a characteristic of the discourses that surrounded the case of Pierre-François Lacenaire (1803–1836), a murderer, forger, and thief, a dandy, and a poet, and the figure at the center of an aesthetic, media, and medical circus in the first years of the July Monarchy in France. Into his medical report on the phrenology and physiology of the killer,[3]

Hyppolite Bonnelier inserts lines of doggerel attesting sensationally to the qualities of Lacenaire—poet and murderer both. In his poem, which meditates on the severed hand of the infamous poet-murderer, Théophile Gautier meticulously dissects the appearance of the hand to read traces of the murderer's personality in a passable imitation of the methods of the science of the time.[4] Both writers, then, physician and poet alike, bend and blend their discursive resources in order to draw attention to the extraordinariness of Lacenaire and to celebrate the proximity of his artistry and criminality. These examples of testimonies to Lacenaire's singularity are only two of many, produced in the discourses of science, politics, the press, medicine, and art. The considerable proliferation of texts inspired by the case, and more specifically by the *figure* of Lacenaire, who was tried in 1835 and executed in 1836, bears witness to a very specific and long-lasting cultural fantasy of the links between destruction and creation, individuality and society, for which Lacenaire provided the locus in the French nineteenth century.

Lacenaire's actual crimes were neither particularly numerous nor particularly impressive. He was convicted of a double murder and a bungled attempted third killing. The murder victims were the Widow Chardon, whose body was found in a severely mutilated condition, and her son. The surviving victim was a bank employee, Genevay, whom Lacenaire attempted to kill with his sidekicks, the petty criminals known as "François et Avril" (Victor Avril and François Martin). Lacenaire had previously served prison terms for forgery and theft, and reputedly considered prison to be a "school of crime." As Edward Baron Turk has put it, Lacenaire "distinguished himself less for his crimes than for his aesthetic attitude toward them."[5]

If the case of Lacenaire excited a disproportionate wealth of reactions and opinions from a variety of ideological and political factions, this is perhaps due to his status as an educated, creative, and bourgeois killer—a "new" type of criminal subject. Foucault calls Lacenaire the "symbolic figure of an illegality kept within the bounds of delinquency and transformed into discourse—that is to say, made doubly inoffensive; the *bourgeoisie* had invented for itself a new pleasure, which it has still far from outgrown."[6] The idea that criminality might issue from, and appeal to, the bourgeoisie was seen as a different kind of danger than the one delinquency had previously been seen to pose. As Chevalier's influential book on crime in nineteenth-century France demonstrates,[7] criminality became a paranoid obsession of the nineteenth-century imaginary owing to the assumption that delinquency was a product of working-class insubordination, and that, like the "masses," its threat was plural and anonymous. Balzac summed up this idea that criminals constituted a subterranean group, operating secretly to destabilize society, when he described, in 1825, "a nation apart, in the middle of the nation."[8] In contrast to this perception, Lacenaire embodied dissidence from within the ranks of the artistic elite. The cult of personality that blossomed around Lacenaire announced the underside of the rise of the individual associated with post-Revolutionary society. For, in Lacenaire, crime had both a single name and a single face, and it articulated its reason in articles sent from prison to the newspapers and promptly published, and in rhyme.

Gautier famously termed Lacenaire "vrai meurtrier et faux poète" (real murderer and false poet), a formula about which I will have more to say later with regard to the discourses of subjective authenticity to which it appeals, while Lacenaire, in his own memoirs, had identified himself more simply (and flatteringly) as a "poète-né" ("born poet"), endowed with "a veritable natural gift."[9] The myth of Lacenaire as both murderer and poet is indeed extraordinary in its ability to extend beyond his own personal history and immediate cultural context. Not only did the case and trial of Lacenaire set the tongues of 1830s Paris wagging, but the figure of Lacenaire would go on to be associated with the creation of a particular kind of murderer in the European cultural imaginary—the artistic creator of the murderous act, who produced poems in addition to corpses, and both with the same attention to artistry and flair. While the figure of the criminal artist has a genealogy that extends back beyond the nineteenth century—Sade being its most obvious exemplar—I will be arguing that the specificity of this discourse in Romantic and post-Romantic French culture lies in giving rise to a recognizable (fantasy) identity for the murderer, an *ontology* that would cross seas and continents and endure for centuries, in order to give Western society an archetype of gentlemanly murderous subjectivity.

Lacenaire has been immortalized in works of literature and on celluloid by names as diverse as Victor Hugo, Théophile Gautier, Rachilde, Honoré de Balzac, Stendhal,[10] Fyodor Dostoyevsky,[11] Marcel Carné, and Francis Girod. Charles Baudelaire named him "one of the heroes of modern life" ("un des héros de la vie moderne").[12] It will be the task of this chapter to explore the precise filiations between commentaries on the murderer (both autobiographical texts and those authored by others) and the traces he left on the cultural imagination. By so doing, I hope to

articulate the ways in which the figure of the aesthete murderer became
a prized locus of debates about subjectivity, class, gender, sexuality, and
creativity in the 1830s in France and beyond.

Lacenaire in Context: The Most Frenetic of All the Romantics

The "popularity" of Lacenaire in the 1830s was not a phenomenon that
emerged ex nihilo, but rather the symptom of a cultural trend. The facts
of Lacenaire's case, as they were conveyed by a fascinated media, appeared to dramatize several of the philosophical, aesthetic, and political obsessions of the zeitgeist. For the group of young Romantic and republican writers of the 1830s, known as the *Bouzingos* or *Jeunes France*,
among them Pétrus Borel, Alexandre Dumas, Gérard de Nerval, and
Théophile Gautier, Lacenaire fulfilled the role of a talismanic hero, a
symbol of the transgression of artistic and lawful limits.[13] This group,
which pledged to fight against the philistinism associated with the new
order of Louis Philippe, was personally familiar with Lacenaire, who,
like them, frequented the workshop of the sculptor Duseigneur in the
early 1830s. During Lacenaire's incarceration, members of the group, including Dumas and Gautier, would visit him in prison, while their mentor, Victor Hugo, dedicated his first person narrative "Le Dernier jour
d'un condamné" ("The Final Day of a Condemned Man") to Pierre-
François. Following Lacenaire's execution, in a very literal and material,
if somewhat gruesome, gesture, Maxime du Camp allegedly acquired
the severed hand of the murderer, freshly cut from the gallows, inspiring
Gautier to pen "Étude de mains: Lacenaire."

The type of attention brought to bear on the case and figure of Lacenaire by his artistic contemporaries can be summarized under two head-
ings: political and aesthetic. In stark definition to the ordered, progressive new bourgeois class, the young Romantics (many of whom were, of
course, middle class or aristocratic by birth) cultivated an affectation of
bohemian eccentricity. The dandified figure of Lacenaire, producer of a
handful of political poems and famed for his insouciance in the face of
his own condemnation, was co-opted for their republican political project and made to signify against the society they hated. In "Quel malheur
ou Les regrets d'un doctrinaire" ("What misfortune or the regrets of a
doctrinarian"), Lacenaire concludes with the following two stanzas:

In this baneful age,
Repudiating even his name,
In this hated Paris
If he were to reign, despite being a Bourbon,
I am certain that our king
Would think today, like me,
What misfortune!
I say it with distaste
Our three glorious days were a waste!

To reassure the homeland
About a similar attack
Against the furious press
We need a coup d'état.
Fines and prohibitions
Have not put us back in surplus
What misfortune!
I say it with distaste
Our three glorious days were a waste![14]

The poem's stridently anti–July Monarchy sentiment, marked by its ironic appeal to the even more repressive fallen Bourbon monarch, belies the fact that elsewhere in his writings, Lacenaire declared that he was by no means a committed political activist and confessed himself indifferent to the details of political reality.[15] The availability of this stereotype of the committed rebel, corroborated by well-chosen sections of verse like the one cited above, was useful, however, for the aesthetic and political groups that adopted him as their byword for dissent.

For the press of the government, the politicization of Lacenaire was a dangerous gesture, according a revolutionary power to criminal force and providing a rhetorical weapon for oppositional factions. This explains, perhaps, the attempts to downplay the importance of Lacenaire as a man of his time in the conservative press. One commentator wrote in the *Journal de Paris* in November 1835:

The press has jumped on the trial of Lacenaire to incriminate either contemporary society or power. Some attack the corruption of the century, others what they call the immorality of the rulers. It would be more reasonable to re-

gard Lacenaire as a terrible exception, of the kind that have appeared under
all regimes and in all periods, but, happily for humanity, at rare intervals.[16]

Seeing the murderer as a "terrible exception" and as an ahistorical phenomenon—an aberration of the universal human genus that could occur in any epoch—rather than as the embodiment of the troubled and
divided zeitgeist was an attempt to diffuse the power that Lacenaire
wielded for his public and to make vanish the specters of the Revolution
that discourses surrounding him threatened to evoke. It was, perhaps,
precisely for this reason that the dissident writers of the day chose to
play up his doubtful political affiliation, making him appear as an aveng-
ing angel of the republican and revolutionary spirit rather than as (just)
an apolitical artist.

It has been argued that Romanticism presaged a democratization of literature. This obtained to some extent at the levels of both subject matter
and profession, and the two were inextricably linked. Romanticism's turn
away from the epic and collective concerns of neoclassicism toward individual and personal introspection was accompanied by the fact that the
profession of writer was increasingly potentially open to the bourgeois as
well as to the aristocrat. This elicited pessimistic commentaries from an-
tiliberal commentators. In a world in which anyone, regardless of class affiliation, could become a writer, according to Philarète Chasles, critic for
La Chronique de Paris: "the story of our literature and of our authors will
soon be told in the *Gazette des tribuneaux* [a popular, often sensationalist, publication giving details of crimes and trials]."[17] Lacenaire, under-
standably, was seen as the actualized embodiment of this premonition.

The figure of Lacenaire arrived on the Romantic scene as an amalgam of existing archetypes as well as an innovator of a new criminal
subject. The figure of the creative outlaw had already made his appearance in English Romantic literature during the 1820s with Byron's poetic heroes, and some newspaper articles went so far as to suggest that
Lacenaire was attempting deliberate imitation of these sublime role
models, citing "les ravages du romantisme" ("the ravages of Romanticism") which encouraged criminals to believe "that by dint of villainy
and cynical perversity, they can redeem themselves from the horror they
inspire and acquire admirers."[18] The problem, of course, was that this
was *exactly* the response Lacenaire received from his fellow Romantics
and a generation of ardent readers.

As well as the Byronic hero, acknowledged predecessors of Lacenaire include the figure of the dandified criminal Robert Macaire, eponymous hero of Antier, Lacoste, and Lemaître's play (1834). About the links between the hero of the melodrama and the figure at the center of the public trial of the decade, Jules Janin wrote:

> At least in the past, before Robert Macaire, vice was understood to be sullied and filthy; it inspired fear on sight; today Robert Macaire is dressed like the most elegant of men . . . what's more, crime on trial in the magistrate's court is quoting lines from Horace the epicurean poet. Robert Macaire, to be sure, is the father of Lacenaire.[19]

Lacenaire himself refuted this link, writing, "I've seen *Robert-Macaire* and *L'Auberge des Adrets*; these two ignoble works could have turned me off crime, given Robert's ostentation and the other one's stupidity."[20] Lacenaire's negative review of the production and its protagonist notwithstanding, significant parallels can be drawn between the theatre where the popular exploits of Robert Macaire were dramatized and the theatre of the courtroom, where Lacenaire kept the audience enrapt as they watched the drama of his trial unfold. His wider public consisted of the readers who followed its progress in the pages of the *Gazette des tribuneaux* which, as Foucault has pointed out, dedicated maximum column space to Lacenaire between 1835 and 1836, to the detriment of covering other murder cases such as that of his exact contemporary Pierre Rivière.[21] Moreover, the association of Lacenaire with theatrical melodrama was a strong one, and one which would resonate in the cinematic incarnation of Lacenaire in Carné's iconic film *Les Enfants du Paradis* (1945). Carné's Lacenaire, as well as being the archetype of the dandy-killer, is also a master of words: a public letter-writer and an author of melodrama, highlighting the performative and attention-seeking aspects of Lacenaire's persona, which the press of the time was also keen to point out.

Melodramatic rhetoric and exaggeration for poetic effect characterized the Frenetic Romantic style and are amply visible in Lacenaire's poetry. Frenetic Romanticism was famously described by Charles Nodier as the mode of writing that conforms "to the needs of a blasé generation demanding sensationalism at any cost."[22] Murder as both an attack on despised society and a stimulant for the nerves of a wearied population was prized subject matter for its literature. In his morbid and cynical "Champavert: le lycanthrope" ("Champavert: the werewolf") (1833), Pétrus Borel

employs the trope of violent death—enacted against self and other—
as a purer alternative to bourgeois society's hypocritical and pious self-
righteousness. The figure of the unmarried woman, Flava, who kills her
child rather than bear the stigma of its illegitimacy, is the symbolic victim of a destructive society, annihilating with conformity. The hero of
"Champavert," the eponymous "lycanthrope," murders the grief-stricken
infanticidal woman in turn in order to end her guilt and suffering, and
then turns a spirited attack on the society that forced this outcome:

> Infanticide. So many apparently shy virgins are already on their third, so
> many virtuous girls count their springs off by the murders they have commit-
> ted . . . Barbaric law! Ferocious prejudice! Infamous horror! Men! Society!
> Take her! Take your prey. I give her to you!!![23]

The writing is hyperbolic in the extreme, but the idea that the murderer
is the figure most fit to critique the complacency and moral turpitude
of society is a conceit which carried over to the treatment of Lacenaire.
The murderer himself wrote of moralistic (and therefore implicitly hypocritical) writers: "I prefer the blood that I have on my hands to the un-
clean mud that entirely covers theirs."[24] Here, having blood on ones
hands stands as a mark of authenticity, of getting ones hands dirty, in
contradistinction to theoretical pontificating. In both Lacenaire's statement and Borel's short story, an attack on hypocritical society goes hand
in hand with a glorification of extreme act and sensation.

However, despite the conscious and concerted attempts on the parts
of the *Jeunes France* and Lacenaire to emphasize the political (collective) implications of their movement, their frenetic aesthetic outpour-
ings bore witness primarily to a philosophical-ideological shift toward
the celebration of an eccentric sort of heroic individuality exemplified by
crime. Romanticism sought to portray the unique details of extreme, elevated, or uncommon sentiment and experience. Hugo's mourning lover
in his celebrated "Demain dès l'aube" ("Tomorrow at Dawn") speaks the
uniqueness of his sorrow, the *singularity* of his mourning. Lacenaire's
poetic writing similarly celebrates singularity, as in "Le dernier chant"
("The Last Song"), voiced by the unrepentant murdering hero awaiting
his date with the guillotine:

> Greetings to you, my beautiful fiancée
> Who soon, in your arms, will enfold me.

To you goes my last thought,

I was promised to you from the cradle.

Greetings, guillotine! Sublime expiation,

Final article of the law,

Which takes the man out of the man and cleanses him of crime

In the bosom of nothingness, my hope and my faith.[25]

Anticipating the "official" death of God with Nietzsche's pronounce-ment in 1882, Lacenaire writes of a world in which the only moral law is defined by the man-made juridical one which he held in contempt. He nevertheless welcomes its fatal punishment when he evokes "the bosom of nothingness" as sole source of "hope" and "faith." While this voice of singular revolt, not (only) against a political administration, but against an indifferent world, was an irresistibly seductive one for the poets of the 1830s, for the conservative and religious commentators of the day it signaled the worst outcome of the atheistic and materialist philoso-phies of the Enlightenment. For numerous commentators, Lacenaire's name was linked with those of Voltaire and Rousseau, especially when it was revealed that the murderer had allegedly been reading Rousseau's progressive, democratic work *Du Contrat social* (*Of the Social Contract*) shortly before committing one of his crimes.[26]

Lacenaire's biographer, Anne-Emmanuelle Demartini, has traced the history of the terms "égoïsme" (egoism) and "individualisme" (individu-alism), two words that entered frequent use in the 1830s and which recur in connection with the Lacenaire case. The former, dating from 1789, was defined by Moreau-Christophe in 1838 as "the cult of self-love" ("le culte de l'amour de soi"), while the latter, which increased in usage at least in its adjectival forms during the 1830s, "is a modern phenomenon with a democratic essence."[27] The rise of the individual and the rise of the creative criminal hero are, then, two indistinguishable faces of Ro-manticism. In their lauding of this real-life murderer as the embodiment of this principle, and in their creation of fictional versions of this deliv-ering angel of death, the Frenetic Romantics celebrated both democracy and the idealized cultivation of the self. These two ideas—if not directly in contradiction with each other—suggest at least a tension. The figure of Lacenaire came to stand in metonymically for this dual desire: the self-ishness of egoism and the aspirational collective of democracy.

The association of Lacenaire with his age (vehemently denied by those who sought to see him as a randomly occurring exception who

could plague any epoch) reached its apotheosis when Breton cited Lacenaire in the *Anthologie de l'humour noir* (Anthology of black humor) as
"an illustration of nineteenth-century thought,"[28] an opinion which has
apparently become part of mainstream literary-critical discourse today,
as evidenced by an entry in the *New Oxford Companion to Literature
in French* which lists Lacenaire's *Mémoires* alongside works by Gautier,
Nerval, and Borel as examples of *littérature frénétique*, canonizing the
writing murderer, even if within rather a marginal canon.[29] Ironically,
had Lacenaire never come to trial for murder, it is unlikely that the world
would have been made familiar with his writing, either in the form of the
journalism he had practiced throughout his life, or the poems which he
identified as his gift to the world, or yet in his memoir, written in prison.
It is in a very real sense, then, that murder was the final touch of artistry
that brought recognition to just another young man of his generation,
avid for the Romantic discourse of creative genius and longing for individual transcendence through words.

Head and Hands

To understand the rhetoric surrounding the figure of Lacenaire demands
a consideration of the peculiar networks of relations between art and
murder in the discourses of the early nineteenth century. I have shown
in the introduction how writings by Schiller and De Quincey in the first
decades of the century announced the attribution of aesthetic criteria to
morally problematic acts, in an attempt to work through the problem of
the relation between ethics and aesthetics, apparently elided in Kant's
model. Lacenaire's discourse at trial reveals a philosophy very similar to
De Quincey's in its concern for propriety and a "neat" execution of the
act: aesthetics trumping ethics.

Unconcerned with defending or exonerating himself, Lacenaire took
the opportunity instead to defame and decry his thuggish accomplices,
François and Avril, whose lack of "artistry" in crime had led to the bun-
gling of the murder of the banker, Genevay, and to the killer's capture.
The rhetorical qualities of Lacenaire's verbal performance in court,
meditating upon the philosophical and aesthetic imperatives governing
a killing, coupled with his cool refusal to offer any signs of remorse, led
to one journalist writing in the *Revue de Paris* that he was "the man
who invented the metaphysics of killing."[30] Though Sade, Schiller, or De

Quincey might more justifiably be said to have inaugurated this philosophical sophistry, Lacenaire had one advantage: as both a killer *and* a poet, a master of praxis rather than only of theory, the sheen of authenticity glimmered more convincingly about his name because he had *used his hands.*

The copresence of discourses of mental ingenuity and hands-on practice resonates throughout writing on Lacenaire. However, his competence as a criminal was by no means certain. Although Foucault reports that "François, Lacenaire's former accomplice, said that he had invented a method for killing a man without making him cry out and without spilling a drop of blood,"[31] accounts of Lacenaire's own criminal skills—even by his admirers—are less favorable. Maxime du Camp commented that Lacenaire "never succeeded in killing with a single blow."[32] Lacenaire's literary followers, then, seem to have known, at least on some level, that he was hardly a criminal mastermind. Thus, the myth of Lacenaire as artist seems to rely more heavily on his status as a poet and rhetorician—a creative artist—than on his skills as destructive agent.

It is, however, also far from certain that Lacenaire was an able poet. Gautier's poem summarizes the dual roles that Lacenaire embodies. The formulation "real murderer and false poet" reveals not—or not only—the complementarity between the terms "killer" and "artist," but equally a tension between murder, which undoes, and art which creates. The double logic of the poem is that if a murderer has the ambition of being a poet (but a flawed poet), then a poet is likewise touched by the ambition to be a murderer, but the ambition goes unrealized in any way other than symbolically. The formulation "faux poète" effectively dismisses Lacenaire's talent as a writer, but its counterpart "vrai meurtrier" suggests the mark of authenticity that shimmers around the experience of law breaking. In some ways, Gautier's poem represents the triumph of sublimation: writing is a substitute for action in the world. But it also suggests the relationship between the processes of aestheticization and the underlying fantasy of annihilation. In apparently oxymoronic formulations such as "la grâce du gladiateur" (the grace of the gladiator) and "criminelle aristocracie" (criminal aristocracy), Gautier's grudging admiration for action over sublimation becomes textually manifest, and the fascination which the murderer holds for the poet is evident. It seems, then, that what elevated Lacenaire, as a mediocre murderer and an indifferent poet, to the status he enjoyed was simply the fact that he combined the two.

In Lacenaire's own account of his life and crimes, the bloody or salacious details of the killing—the hands-on experience, as it were—are scrupulously avoided. His self-description relies on boastful accounts of his mental ingenuity and the clichés of the Byronic hero discussed above. Ironically, then, as Gautier reveals the poet's ambition to kill, Lacenaire's memoir concentrates rather on the killer's ambition to be a poet. These ambitions as a poet—generally rubbished by subsequent commentators—appear to be, for him, a more meaningful identity than that of murderer. Juxtaposing the poetic voices of Gautier and Lacenaire, a discourse emerges which holds that those who do not kill dream the transcendence of murder, while those who kill spin tissues of text around the real of annihilation, attempting to fix the noumenal in words.

Given the numerous examples of veneration for Lacenaire, despite the acknowledgment of his failings as both master criminal and creative artist, we cannot help but wonder whether failure itself is not an essential ingredient in his brand of heroism. Romanticism was particularly touched by an obsession with the hero who oscillates between greatness and failure. In her work on "the male malady," Margaret Waller has identified a strain of ambivalent masculine weakness in the protagonists of French novels from 1800 to 1840 (including Constant's *Adolphe*, Staël's *Corinne*, Stendhal's *Amance*, and Sand's *Lélia*). In these novels, "the fascination with the hero's self-punishment . . . is strongly mitigated . . . by an even greater instinct for self-preservation and aggrandizement."[33] Lacenaire offered an extreme real-life example of Waller's malady-ridden fictional male: a Romantic murderer with no wish to escape his own punishment, indeed who sought to glorify and further romanticize it, and who certainly engaged in flights of grandiosity.

In this discourse, the counterpart of the murderer is the suicide—most canonically Goethe's young Werther, the one dealing death sublimely, the other dying in the pangs of the mal du siècle and a general contempt for the positivism and materialism of the age. If killing (oneself or the other) takes on the status of a conscious rejection of the status quo, it seems that it was ripe for appropriation as both a heroic and an aesthetic act. Lacenaire compounded this by deliberately terming the execution to which he so willingly hastened a "suicide." Senelick has even gone so far as to opine that "in a sense, every romantic suicide from Werther onwards culminated in Lacenaire's ritual self-sacrifice."[34] Waller has commented on the strangeness of this recurrent discourse of "male disempowerment" and "alienation from the patriarchal status quo,"[35] in light of the hypermasculinist and misogynistic institutional and social climate after the setting up of the Napoleonic code in 1804, which relegated women to "moral rectitude, religious devotion" and "docile domesticity," a tendency "further intensified by the rise to power of the bourgeoisie in the July Monarchy of the 1830s."[36]

The ambivalent virility of Lacenaire—a violent yet dandified poet in a hypermasculine age—is a central feature of representations of him, both at the time of his crimes and subsequently. The aestheticization of Lacenaire happened at numerous levels, not only in the exultation of his acts to the status of works of art, or the lionization of his person as artist, but also in the literal aestheticization of his image and body parts, in a series of gestures that a Freudian critic would doubtless term fetishistic. Significantly, this creation of Lacenaire as fetish occurred in both artistic and scientific realms. In the artistic realm, the killer's head was immortalized on canvas and in clay. (Lacenaire sat for a portrait painter while in prison, and Jacques Arago had the sculptor Carl Elschoect mold his bust.)[37] His hands were memorialized in ink (in Gautier's poem) and, eventually, his image was reproduced on celluloid (in films by Carné and Girod). These transmutations from flesh to art have the effect of fixing Lacenaire's image such that it takes on the status of icon. In the medical sphere, Lacenaire's head was examined and molds made of it, both before his trial and posthumously, in order to establish the truth of his "nature" according to the popular contemporary pseudoscience of phrenology.

Gautier's "Etude de mains: Lacenaire" takes the form of a grotesque version of the *blason du corps féminin*, the sixteenth-century tradition that enumerates the parts of a desirable woman's body, before concluding that it is because of the sum of her parts, her totality, that she is beloved. Gautier's poetic evocation of Lacenaire never reaches this stage of summing up. He appears metonymically as a series of fragmented fetishes: hand and knife. Significantly, however, the erotic energy subtending the *blason* is visible also in this case. The hand is the part of the body that wields the knife and the pen with their obvious phallic attributes. It is also of significance that this poem, "Lacenaire," is one of a couple with "Impéria"—the study of an alabaster sculpture of a courtesan's hand. We are explicitly told in the first line of "Lacenaire" to contrast this male killer's hand with its "duvet roux" (reddish down) with the delicate woman's hand of the previous poem. Contrast soon shades into comparison, however, as Lacenaire's hand is similarly rendered passive, placed on a cushion like a benign decorative object. It is "en même temps molle et féroce" ("at the same time soft and ferocious"), a mixture of ideal attributes of the feminine and the masculine, an object wholly ripe for libidinal interpretation and appropriation. In the poem Lacenaire becomes reducible—literally—to the hand that did the killing.

In a discussion of Gautier's hand study poems, Joel Black has pointed out the implied link between the courtesan and the murderer in the masculine imagination: both use their hands skillfully on another person, but whereas the former uses them to give pleasure, in the case of the latter it is to destroy. Black writes, somewhat fancifully: "The two figures yoked together by Gautier in his poem, the courtesan Impéria and the assassin Lacenaire, are both artists who have the power to make their lovers or unmake their victims with their hands."[38] A set of complex and ambiguous associations linking murder, virility, effeminacy, and masculinity emerges here. The fact that Gautier has us compare the two hands to find not only differences but also similarities between them suggests proximity between the ideas of (aesthetic) violence and ambivalent sexuality.

This idea of Lacenaire as a sexual as well as a criminal subject calls to mind the popular discourse of the time regarding the women who clamored to write to Lacenaire and visit him in prison. According to an article in *La Chronique de Paris*, "women, overflowing with emotion, ensured Lacenaire's success."[39] And, in the words of another that appeared in *Le Vert-Vert*, it was the attention of these ladies that was responsible for turning "a simple writer of doggerel" ("un simple rimeur") into "un Pindare" (a Pindar—the celebrated Ancient Greek poet).[40] One significant strand of Lacenaire's myth, then, was that of "le Don Juan de l'assassinat" (the Don Juan of murder). It is significant that (male) commentators made much of Lacenaire's sexual appeal to women and prowess as a lover, since it shores up a Romantic myth of masculinity in which the combination of violent agency and art translates into sexual desirability. Demartini makes this point, when she points out that "the theme of the woman enamored by trials and criminals is a trope in the rhetorical sense of discourses about women in the nineteenth century."[41] Yet sexual ambiguity and homosociality are equally features of Lacenaire's life and myth. Like the character of Balzac's gentleman criminal, Vautrin, for whom Lacenaire allegedly provided inspiration, Pierre-François is known to have had partners of both sexes (though, in prison, same-sex sexual behavior was often an enforced reality).[42] Furthermore, the cinematic version of Lacenaire later put on-screen by Carné is unambiguously presented as homosexual.

The homosocial appeal of Lacenaire for the century relied on an admixture of violent, macho virility (the precursor, perhaps of Jean Genet's queer criminals) and of sentimentality. When at the end of the revised version of *L'Auberge des Adrets*, Robert Macaire declares: "Killing rascals and policemen doesn't stop a person having feelings,"[43] he announces a tenet of the cult of the Romantic murderer, embodied in flesh by Lacenaire, that is, the capacity of the murdering hero to transcend the moral turpitude into which his crimes might otherwise cast him because of his elevated status as a sensitive hero and artist, capable of a greater and more noble quality of feeling than would be revealed simply by sparing a victim. Lacenaire himself expressed it thus:

> A man alone against all others, but a man strong and powerful in his genius, rejected by society since the cradle, who has sensed his power and who has employed it for evil; a man who has studied everything, understood everything in depth; a man who would give his life twenty times over to repay a kindness; a man who feels wrong without being able to express it, but to whose soul is no stranger to anything beautiful or noble, a man, in sum, who, while despising his peers, has had to do more violence to himself in order to arrive at evil than many who have achieved virtue.[44]

The duality of which Lacenaire speaks—the simultaneous yearning for virtue competing with the instinct for evil—announces avant la lettre Charles Baudelaire's idea of the "two postulations" in man that pull him toward both good and evil at the same time. The idea that a morally or criminally punishable act is not only *not incompatible with* finer sentiment, but is in fact its counterpart, is a feature both of Lacenaire's psychology and of the nineteenth-century imagination.

In 1995, a tiny fragment of a lost work by the Decadent writer Rachilde was published.[45] This fragment, entitled *Cynismes: Lacenaire et Monsieur Papon* (Cynicisms: Lacenaire and Mr. Papon), takes the form of two prose poems, the first of which tells of a young man who is struck by the sight of a sleeping cat balancing on a narrow ledge. Shaken momentarily from his "dark thoughts" ("sombres idées"),[46] he approaches the cat and places it safely on the ground. The closing words of the little short story are, simply, "this young man was called Lacenaire" ("ce jeune homme s'appelait Lacenaire").[47] The second tale tells of an avaricious grocer who, too mean to feed his cat on milk, gives it water mixed with flour instead. Unsurprisingly, the cat dies. The message that Rachilde—arch elitist and lifelong member of the French Society for the Protection of Animals—wishes us to take away from these two fragments is that a killer who is also a poet is destined to be nobler in spirit by far than a petty merchant.[48] Killing transcends its problematical ethical status for the Decadent writer, Rachilde, as it did for the Frenetic Romantics 50 years earlier, so long as it is reinscribable in aesthetic terms.

It is notable that, just as writers wish to cast Lacenaire's persona and (criminal/creative) acts as purely artistic, rather than as having psychological or political meaning, so too the artist-murderer inscribes his crimes as aesthetic and metaphysical and shuns other interpretations. This is in part understandable as a desire to escape positivistic and pathologizing dissections of his motivations. It is also, significantly, the desire to have the last word about the meanings of one's own self and acts. Lacenaire wished his poetry, his crimes, and his own highly stylized self to be received by the world as the avid Romantic critic receives the artwork: appreciated or subject to disapproval only as beautiful objects, according to purely aesthetic criteria. In this, he opposed himself categorically to becoming a subject of the disciplines that will be under consideration in the next chapters: the burgeoning criminological and sexual sciences. In the preface to his *Mémoires*, Lacenaire writes with dread: "I can see from here a host of phrenologists, cranologists, physiologists, anatomists" wishing to inspect "the most minute and precise details of my tastes, my passions, and even of my life's adventures."[49] Lacenaire was right to suppose that he would be of interest to medical science. A report on his physiological and phrenological condition, undertaken by Dumoutier, appeared under the pen of Hyppolite Bonnelier on 15 January 1836. It tells, ironically enough, how the shape of the killer's head is found to denote, according to the accepted pseudoscientific indications, a benevolent and worshipful character. Yet the mismatch between the evidence provided by Lacenaire's crimes and atheistic attitudes, and that provided by the bumps on his head does not result in discrediting the controversial system of phrenology. Rather, the mismatch becomes a point of distinction, a sign of the extraordinary nature of Lacenaire and a way of enhancing his myth. As I pointed out above, when discussing the epigraph of this chapter, Bonnelier joins Gautier in celebrating Lacenaire's uniqueness as bearer of "lyre" and "dagger" and uses science to *authenticate* the myth.

This trope central to discourses about Lacenaire, marking the desire that the power of the artist-killer figure should thwart, exceed, and confound scientific principles, does not completely disappear as Romanticism gives way to positivism. Even in the late twentieth century, the power of this fantasy persists. Girod chooses as the opening sequence of his 1990 biopic, *Lacenaire*, scenes of the imprisoned murderer undergoing examination by the phrenologist, searching for the textbook morphological symptoms of the homicidal type. However, the doctor is frustrated in his attempts and is forced to reveal that the head displays instead signs of "intelligence" and "benevolence" ("bienveillance"), as reported by Bonnelier. The filmic image of a close-up on the cast of Lacenaire's head that the physiologist has taken is entirely in keeping with the legend of Lacenaire fostered in his own time. The bust provides a further simulacrum, another overdetermined object of awe that allows the shimmer of Lacenaire's persona to endure beyond his mere execution. This cast, like the object that is the hand in Gautier's poem, works like the poem and the film, to provide the material substance, a secular relic (fittingly, artificial and man-made rather than organic) on which the myth is constructed. The idea that this figure must be represented as having transcended not only moral condemnation, but also the system of scientific cataloguing, as remarked upon by Lacenaire's postmortem examiner Bonnelier, is a testimony to the continuing desire to believe in the power of the artistic murdering subject. The nineteenth-century mythic articulation of intellectual and criminal virility persists, disturbingly intact, in this late twentieth-century film.

Moreover, the figure of Lacenaire undergoes a significant and telling ideological shift in Girod's film from dissident rebel to mainstream figure of French history. Girod's *Lacenaire* falls into the category of the heritage film. The term "heritage film" describes a genre of history films with high production values made in the 1980s and 1990s, which were designed to celebrate French historical and cultural figures and institutions. Funded by subventions on the part of the French government, they are the prized national cultural product destined both for the home and export market. Lacenaire is played in the film by Daniel Auteuil, the face of other lavish French heritage pieces such as *Manon des Sources* and *Jean de Florette* (both Claude Berri, 1986).[50] Thus, the political and generic context of Girod's film works to transform Lacenaire from the antihero of society, beloved of the republican margins, to a mainstream icon of Frenchness. No longer a rebel, fêted for a (however imaginary) provocative stance by a few, the poet-killer is perversely inscribed into French history as the national hero.

Murder and Representation

Anne-Emmanuelle Demartini has written that

> Lacenaire establishes himself in this vast movement by which, in the nineteenth century, the criminal finds a place as never before in the discursive field, but he inverts its modes and meaning: whereas the criminal exists in discourse as an object, Lacenaire establishes himself as the subject of the discourse which concerns him.[51]

The question of the extent to which Lacenaire emerged as a subject rather than—or as well as—an object of discourses about criminality is central to my concerns here. That self-definition, rather than definition by others, is right at the heart of the project of the *Mémoires* is not in doubt. Demartini has written of Lacenaire's obsession in constructing the *Mémoires* with systematization ("système"),[52] that is with crafting a narrative of singularity, continuity, and consistency. Against the model of connections and groups—families and society—he crafted a myth of individual selfhood out of crime, which his commentators were only too willing to help shore up.

An extension of the cult of individuality is the fantasy of self-creation, of coming ex nihilo, rather than being shaped and formed by the family environment, by that rather general idea of "society" or "culture," by God, or alternatively, by the preordination of "nature." Lacenaire repudiates God, stating: "I act without fear and without hope, and by the sole force of my will."[53] He asserts self-construction over the determining influence of nature: "I have made myself what I am. Nature had nothing to do with me."[54] It is this same desire to appear as a self-created autodidact that led Lacenaire to respond forcefully to those who had attributed the cause of his criminality to his reading of rationalist eighteenth-century philosophers. He asserted that these readings had simply constituted the reinforcement of a system of thought that he had already adopted, that issued from his own intellect and temperament:

> Well, I read Diderot, d'Alembert, Jean-Jacques at an age at which I could hardly any longer be satisfied with Florian or Robinson Crusoe! Were I to permit myself some arrogance, I would tell you that in matters of morality and religion, my ideas were so similar to theirs that I sometimes thought I must have read them already and even have committed them to memory. I was often able to finish, without looking at the page, a thought or sentence that had been started.[55]

While Lacenaire's boast of having already formulated the same ideas as Rousseau at a tender age seems somewhat unlikely, it is doubtless the case that the very doggedness of Lacenaire's repeated assertions of grandiose self-creation account in large part for the fascination he provoked. A precursor of twentieth-century criminal celebrity, Lacenaire was a consummate PR professional of his age, adept at promoting his writing, his crimes, and himself as products.

The perceived impossibility of dissociating the murderer's acts from his textual production is visible in the many accounts of Lacenaire, issuing from differing ideological perspectives, that I have discussed above. Such a perception resonates with Foucault's claims about Rivière's confessions. Where Foucault points out that Rivière's murders may be seen as an *extension of* the text, rather than vice versa, in the case of Lacenaire both the texts and the crimes have been identified as lacking aesthetic perfection and artfulness. Yet somehow, when fused together, as Lacenaire and his followers ensured that they were, they became much greater than the sum of their parts and provided the material around which a myth of the perfect Romantic hero—the man who wielded both pen and dagger—could be crafted.

CHAPTER TWO

The "Angel of Arsenic"

Marie Lafarge

It is sad but true: among brutes, savages, and primitive people, the female is more cruel than compassionate, although she is not as cruel as the male.

With Christianity begins the heroic period of womanly pity. Christianity certainly did not create women's compassion, as some claim, since compassion was a slow, evolutionary formation; but Christianity unleashed it, put it in motion, brought it to life.

The female born criminal surpasses her male counterpart in the refined diabolical cruelty with which she commits her crimes.
—(Cesare Lombroso and Guglielmo Ferrero, *Criminal Woman*, 1895)

In 1839, a young orphaned Parisienne of noble descent, Marie Fortunée Cappelle (1816–1852), was married against her will to a bourgeois, Charles Lafarge. Six months later, he died in mysterious circumstances. In 1840, Marie Lafarge was found guilty of murder by poisoning (the poison having allegedly been slipped into a cake sent to her husband in Paris, and then fed to him incrementally in his sick bed). Marie served a term of life imprisonment, despite the widespread doubt regarding her guilt. During her imprisonment, Lafarge produced *Mémoires* in two volumes, a collection of correspondence comprising more than 6,000 letters, numerous articles, and a three-part, unfinished text, *Heures de prison* (Prison time), published shortly after her death.

In the previous chapter we saw how the case of Lacenaire, four years earlier, had provoked polarized commentaries. These were either reverential and admiring, lauding Lacenaire as an artist, or else damning, identifying the killer as a symbol of the perceived revolutionary spirit of the age and as proof of the dangers of Romantic philosophy. What both sets of discourses insisted upon, however, to a striking degree, was Lacenaire's uniqueness, his individuality (even as the ideal of individuality can be revealed as a generic—and therefore communal—prerequisite of Romantic subjectivity). This perception of a unique subjectivity hinged on the coexistence in the character of Lacenaire of murderousness and authorship. In examining the case of Marie Lafarge, we will see that the treatment she received in a series of cultural discourses (medical, literary, journalistic, criminological) differed considerably from that of Lacenaire, despite her own—even more prolific—output as a writer. Although a feature shared by conservative accounts of both murderers is the focus on the criminal dangers of reading and writing, the gendered specificity of the treatments afforded the reading and writing criminal subject will be given consideration here.

French society was divided by the case of Lafarge into two opposing factions: the Lafargistes and the anti-Lafargistes. The matter on which their difference came to rest—nominally at least—was the guilt or innocence of the woman in question of the charges of murder laid against her. The extensiveness of the medico-legal investigations concerning the physical evidence of the crime has led to the case being cited as the first instance of forensic toxicology.[1] Renowned toxicologist Mathieu Orfila responded to a letter from Marie's lawyer seeking his advice about the reliability of the forensic tests that had been carried out with the intention of establishing culpability. Orfila responded with a signed affidavit claiming that the results were meaningless. He was subsequently summoned to Tulle to carry out further tests himself and, to the surprise of the court, this witness for the defense found incriminating traces of arsenic in the body of the deceased. Marie was sentenced to life imprisonment without hard labor. In 1852 she was released from prison owing to the tuberculosis of which she would die later the same year. To the very end she and her supporters continued to proclaim her innocence.

In the newspapers and in literary society, discussion of the affairs of the day focused on little else but the Lafarge case. As the Goncourt brothers commented, a government could keep its population distracted from unrest if only it could provide "two things: a firework display every evening for the masses and a Lafarge trial every morning for the educated classes."[2] And in *L'Education sentimentale*, Flaubert evokes the zeitgeist of 1840 precisely by referencing the ubiquitous speculation in the salons of Paris surrounding the case: "Monsieur Gamblin immediately asked his opinion about Madame Lafarge. This trial, the obsession of the day, never failed to provoke a spirited discussion."[3]

Speculation on Lafarge's criminal intent and the justice of the verdict she received has continued to characterize writing on Lafarge, and much attention is paid to the incompatibility between Marie's feminine appearance, social respectability, and reportedly charming personality, on the one hand, and the fact of her crime on the other. Even as late as 1951, Edith Saunders's *The Mystery of Marie Lafarge* contains the following statement:

> A preoccupation with all that is good and beautiful seems to run through the best of her letters, and it is for that reason that so many people have believed that she was innocent. . . . I was, at first, very much predisposed to believe her innocent. The cold-blooded murder seemed so impossible an act for the charming, cultured girl to have performed that I wrote the first half of this book believing she was guilty of theft but not of murder. It was not until I had read the trial for murder for the third or fourth time very attentively that I realised that, had I sat with the jury, I too should have been obliged to say "yes the accused is guilty."[4]

I would argue that the real stakes of this debate were slightly different from the ones articulated by both Marie's contemporaries and later commentators. The concern with Marie's guilt or innocence with regard to the poisoning of her husband served to cover a different concern of modern society: an anxiety about gender roles and the incompatibility of narrow cultural perceptions of feminine nature with acts that are assertive, aggressive, or violent and, simultaneously, the equally persistent fear that women may embody exactly these qualities. Feminine pathologies, such as nymphomania, frigidity, lesbianism, and most especially hysteria, were coined or gained currency in the course of the nineteenth century, concretizing norms of gendered behavior by marking deviations from them. The criminal woman thus takes her place alongside the pervert in the nineteenth-century catalogue of deviance. The husband-poisoner in particular occupies a special place in such taxonomies of aberration. The woman who killed her husband from the very seat of the prescribed feminine domain—domesticity—threatened the social order from within. Moreover, masculinized by both her crime and by her writing, and yet insisting upon her own innocence and concerned in her writing with all that is, in Saunders's words, "good and beautiful," Lafarge offered a disturbing figure of gender and moral ambiguity for her age. Where Lacenaire's ambivalent murderous mixture of virility/melancholy and grandiosity/failure titillated the Romantic imaginary, Lafarge's surprising "virility" as a killer, juxtaposed with her feminine appearance and middle-class respectability, was readable primarily as threat. Debates about Lafarge's innocence or guilt may thus stand in place of unarticulated anxieties about the inappropriately active or masculine woman. At the level of cultural fantasy, if Lafarge could be proven innocent, the existence of the murderous feminine and its threat would be negated.

One term that recurs many times in the discussion of Lafarge, particularly toward the close of the century, is "hysteria" and its derivatives. If Lacenaire was the ambivalent masculine hero of the mal du siècle, Lafarge falls discursive victim to being labeled with the feminine maladie du siècle. As Janet Beizer,[5] Jann Matlock,[6] Martha Noel Evans,[7] and others have explored, hysteria was an extraordinarily plastic label, conveniently describing the exaggerated or excessive manifestation of any qualities deemed typically feminine. As Dr. Charles Richet put it in 1880, "Everything that we are accustomed to attributing to woman's nervous temperament can be found in the domain of hysteria."[8] Beizer has argued that the construction of hysteria as a medically codified phenomenon in the 1880s must be understood as a retroactive labeling of a long-term cultural unease (going back at least as far as Hippocrates in the fifth century BC) concerning the unpredictability and excess of the feminine. From the notion of the wandering womb to Charcot's extravagantly spasming female patients, the concept of hysteria is inseparable from a notion of femininity as out of control, teeming beyond the confines of its embodiment—tipping over, almost, into its opposite and becoming threatening, aggressive, *unfeminine*. The attribution of this label to Lafarge articulates a more widespread phenomenon of unease regarding the "excessive" outcomes of female passions and urges—and few behaviors are more excessive than murder. Hysteria is linked both analogously and causally to murderousness. Criminologist Cesare Lombroso points out that "hysterical women commit a variety of crimes. [They] stab, rob, poison, burn and testify falsely."[9] The inability of women to contain their passions spills into violent behavior, disrupting the masculine social ideal of reason.

Disturbingly and tellingly, this convenient, catch-all labeling of Lafarge as hysterical is found in recent critical work as well as in late nineteenth-century accounts. Senelick comments: "She repelled all of Lafarge's advances on the honeymoon, hysterically believing that to preserve her virginity intact was essential to her survival as heroine,"[10] and "these traits [a materialistic selfishness, a neurasthenic exoticism, and an autistic disconcern for others] are less obvious in her correspondence, but her style there is more hysterical."[11] Senelick's linking of Marie Lafarge's prolific correspondence with hysteria has particular resonance when one considers its proximity to female creativity in the history of medical discourse: hysteria was often diagnosed by Lombroso in patients or inmates displaying "a mania for letter writing."[12]

In Hilary Neroni's Lacanian study of violence and femininity in the specific context of contemporary North American culture, she proposes the fascinating reading that

> nothing can bring up the discussion of proper womanly traits like a violent woman. The character of the media response to a violent woman is, in almost every case, hysterical. Hysteria is a neurotic reaction in which the subject constantly questions the desire and position of the Other, especially as the Other relates to the subject. . . . When confronted with a woman's violent act, we immediately begin to question her desire, to wonder why she acted violently. In the manner of the hysteric, the media asks again and again what the violent woman wants, while it also speculates endlessly about the definition of femininity.[13]

The Lacanian (diagnostic) definition of hysteria, as explained here, is of a very specific kind, and differs from the nineteenth-century concept in various important ways. It offers a way of describing a type of relationality between the subject and the other, which is defined by a constant questioning as to the nature of the other's desire and the other's intentions toward the subject. Although it is devoid of historical specificity as a primarily structural analysis, Neroni's reading is a valuable and relevant one for me in that it turns the focus from the supposed "hysterical" nature of the woman killer herself onto the "hysteria" of the criminologist, doctor, journalist—or, indeed, twentieth-century male literary critic—who labels her thus. It helps us to ask what is at stake when the medics, press, judiciary, and public of the time debate in such detail and with such passion the guilt or innocence of Marie Lafarge of the crime of murder, and worry about her tendency to write.

Lafarge, Literary Persona, and Romanticism

Several existing works of feminist literary criticism have drawn attention to the importance of the figure of Lafarge for an understanding of gender roles and the treatment afforded women's literature in nineteenth-century Europe and France. Although the specific purpose of the current discussion of Lafarge is to see how the archetype of the Romantic murderer applies or fails to apply in her case, and to interrogate how her sex and gender trouble the established elements of this archetype, this endeavor is intimately tied up with questions of readership and authorship, such that existing work on Lafarge in this context must first be rehearsed here.

Jann Matlock discusses in detail the links between murderousness and hysteria in discourses about Lafarge and pays particular attention to what is written about her penchant for reading and writing.[14] Matlock makes the subtle and persuasive argument that the prospect of educated women reading and writing offered a specter of gender insubordination for the conservative nineteenth-century commentator that chimed with the anxiety occasioned by the prospect of the violent woman. Novels in particular were seen as a threat to young women's health and moral stability. In her study *Victorian Murderesses*, Mary S. Hartman describes Lafarge's much-discussed taste for Bernardin de Saint-Pierre's classic of sensibility *Paul et Virginie* and for the novels of Sir Walter Scott and George Sand, especially *Lélia* (1833).[15] And Matlock begins her discussion of Lafarge with a reference to the fact that at the time of her arrest, Marie was asleep with Fréderic Soulié's *Les Mémoires du diable* (*Memoirs of the Devil*) (1837) open by her bedside. Parallels were teased out between Soulié's Sadeian narrative of "sex, madness, prostitution, criminality"[16] and Lafarge's own story by public and press. The fact that a female murderer was physically apprehended while lying with a book by her head seemed to confirm nineteenth-century fears about the dangers for the female reader of the popular novel, that repository of erotic, violent, and criminal pleasures. Matlock argues that male commentators assumed an inability on the part of the reading woman to distinguish between fiction and reality, and self and (fictional) other, such that the desire unleashed by the text spills over into action in the world (much as the hysteric's desire—in the classic nineteenth-century clinical sense—spills beyond the bounds of her body and erupts into disturbing tics, spasms,

and symptoms). Lafarge seemed to offer the confirmation of this fear realized in flesh and act.

   The gendering of Lafarge as a writer, as well as a reader, has also been
the focus of critical feminist work. In a recent monograph on women's
prison writing, Anna Norris has argued that scant critical attention has
been paid to the writings of Lafarge in comparison with those of Pierre
Rivière and Lacenaire.[17] According to Norris, this reflects the broader
historical tendency to negate the significance of the female writing voice.
For Norris, the refusal of readers to accord Lafarge—and other incarcerated women writers—the status of "author" is an extension of the difficulty of professional women writers such as George Sand (herself a fa-
vorite author of the novel-loving Marie Lafarge) to be accepted, until
fairly recently, into the canon of French literature. Nineteenth-century
male criticisms of the female writing voice are perhaps typified by
Baudelaire's account: "Women write, write, write, with an overwhelming rapidity; they gossip their hearts out. They generally know nothing
of art, nor of measure, nor of logic; their style flows like their skirts."[18]
About George Sand in particular, or "La femme Sand" as he dismis-
sively terms her, Baudelaire writes acidly: "She has never been an artist.
She has the typical flowing style that the bourgeoisie loves. She is stupid.
She is heavy. She is gossipy."[19] The charges are familiar ones: women are
leaky (hysterical), gossipy, trivial, and nagging—and so is their writing.
Henri Didier, critiquing Lafarge's *Heures de prison*, writes in similar
terms to these that it contains "a breath of poetry, all the while overflowing with minute and frivolous details." [20] The prevalence and longevity
of such attributions are disconcerting. As late as 1987, Senelick repeats
wholesale the rhetoric of Lafarge's writing as sentimental, stylistically
uncontrolled, and prone to the logorrhea that we have seen in Baudelaire's critiques of Sand and Didier's critique of Lafarge, when he writes,
"Her autobiography lacks the elegance and terseness of Lacenaire's . . .
and often wallows in unbridled emotionalism after the fashion of her
great model Mme Sand."[21]

   Indeed, writings about Lafarge's crimes, in both the nineteenth and
twentieth centuries, have shown a tendency to silence her voice, while
romanticizing her story and her figure, casting her effectively as the
(anti-)heroine of a middlebrow, traditionally feminine genre such as the
roman feuilleton. In her own lifetime she was also the barely fictionalized heroine of the popular play *La Dame de St. Tropez* (The lady of
St. Tropez), which played throughout the 1840s. I would argue in con-

tradistinction to Norris that Lafarge has certainly *not* been ignored by commentators (there are more titles in the catalogue of the Bibliothèque nationale and the British Library containing the words "Marie Cappelle Pouch-Lafarge" than "Pierre-François Lacenaire"), but rather that there has been a greater tendency to objectify her in discourse, and to romanticize her as a feminine heroine *despite* her criminality, rather than to discuss her as the subject and producer of discourse and of crime. This silence on the matter of her active and discursive subjectivity may precisely signal the difficulty for the patriarchal imaginary of accounting for a criminal female presence in any way that is not either romanticized or pathologized. Shearing's *The Lady and the Arsenic* (1937) is a typical treatment of Lafarge in that it is "a biography in the form of a novelette,"[22] the diminutive "ette" conveying suitable femininity and frivolity. Even a work as recent as Laure Adler's *L'Amour à l'arsenic* (Love arsenic style) (1985), nominally a history of the Lafarge case written in a rather journalistic style, begins with the archly novelistic opening lines: "She is brunette, beautiful, adorable. A perfectly oval face, a complexion of an exquisite pallor, a sublime voice. She is intelligent, cultivated, possessed of a mad desire to live and to love."[23]

This discourse of the "Romantic woman" as a childlike figure with a naïve and irresponsible desire for pleasure is central to nineteenth-century culture, and is both treated by, and critiqued within, Flaubert's ambivalent characterization of Emma in *Madame Bovary* (1857). It is no surprise that Joseph Shearing uses a quotation from *Madame Bovary* about the disappointments of marriage as the epigraph of his "novelette."[24] The association between these two desperate housewives—one fictional, one real but excessively represented and thereby fictionalized, both driven to extremity by the constraints of their feminine social role—has been frequently drawn, both at the time of the publication and ever since. An obvious difference between them is that Emma Bovary, in taking her own life, violated one less gender and moral code than Marie: she did not do violence to another, but to herself. In *Female Perversions*, Louise Kaplan has argued that perversions have been theorized in the history of medicine and psychoanalysis as pathological exaggerations of culturally accepted masculine traits (so male perversions are excessive or deviant forms of male agency and aggressiveness, such as sadism and fetishism).[25] Kaplan claims that female perversions must likewise be understood as exaggerations of culturally ascribed female passivity, weakness, and masochism. She has theorized the characteristics of Madame Bovary's unhappiness and downfall—the self-destructive pursuit of romantic love and hedonistic pleasure through novels, imagination, and adultery—as a female perversion. In Kaplan's system, murder would be an exaggeration of masculine sadism, a male perversion. To apply this logic to Lafarge, we can understand how this female murderer, in embodying both a desire for ("feminine") sentimental escapism and the violent ("masculine") urge to kill, appears as a disturbingly ambiguous figure for a culture with strictly drawn codes of expected gender behavior—particularly for women.

The Lafarge case could potentially have offered a rallying point for the discussion of women's issues in nineteenth-century France, focusing on the desperate position of women married against their will. But instead of attracting political interrogation, the moral weighing of Marie in the most conservative terms—as an inadequately feminine woman because a criminal or, conversely, as surely innocent of criminality because a visibly "feminine" woman—was the resort of both female and male contemporaries. Sadly, even Lafarge's great literary heroine George Sand dismissed her case as irrelevant and uninteresting in a letter in which she wrote about the journalists' fascination with the *affaire Lafarge*: "I hadn't even given it a thought. I don't understand why such uninteresting and puerile stories are concocted for the public."[26] Given the absence of a sympathetic spokeswoman, one who would not draw on normative discourses about the "nature" of "femininity" to reduce Marie, it is perhaps not surprising that Lafarge was compelled to write so prolifically. Perversely, this attempt to voice an identity in writing simply contributed to the dismissive diagnosis of hysteric, or of unfeminine, woman, as I have already discussed.

Much discursive interest has focused on Lafarge's refusal to consummate her marriage on her wedding night, or indeed, according to the claims of her memoirs, at any other time (despite her suspicion of a pregnancy in December 1839, which she claims to have thought might be the result of a "miracle"). In a letter written on her wedding night, Marie begs her husband to take her fortune and let her go away, or even to let her kill herself, rather than to suffer the importunity of sex with him:

> I will leave you my fortune; may God permit that you prosper from it, you deserve to. Me, I will live off the profits of my work or my teaching. I beg you never to give another thought to my existence. If you want, I'll take arsenic. I have some. But let you receive my caresses . . . no never![27]

Rather than highlighting the social injustice of the patriarchal institution of marriage, in which a woman's bodily sovereignty was annihilated, Marie's refusal to lose her virginity and her wish to die rather than to consummate the marriage simply suggested colluding evidence of the "unnatural" nature of the female murderer for contemporary commentators.

However, it also formed a cornerstone of the discourse produced by her defenders. A medical expert of 1848, writing in the *Revue élémentaire de medicine et de pharmacie domestique*, explained the psychology of women such as Lafarge in the following terms, in order to attempt to construct grounds for an appeal:

> Delicate flowers, destined to remain barren, they close in on themselves at the least contact, at the slightest breath of love, because a single breath would seem enough to them to tarnish their virginal whiteness; beings, in a word, incapable of loving other than as angels love, a love of the heart and the mind, ethereal and having nothing to do with the vulgarity of corporeal organs.[28]

In this somewhat romantically, rather than pathologically, expressed medical defense, Marie's decision not to engage in penetrative sex is transformed into a strange sort of spirituality. The Romantic woman is desexualized and exalted as an ethereal being, without bodily or genital urges. Although Marie's sexuality is not presented as a specific pathological state by 1848 (frigidity as a taxonomical category not appearing until later in the century),[29] the copresence of abnormality revealed by Lafarge's murder and her refusal to engage in sexual intercourse (couched in similarly flowery language in the letter and the medical statement) are run together as twin symptoms of deviation, and suggest the precise terms in which the idea of the husband-poisoning woman is disturbing: she would be the literal as well as figurative destroyer of heteronormativity, an angel of death refusing fecundity as the outcome of wedded bliss. In this, she presented a particularly powerful threat to the conservative social climate of the July Monarchy.

Lafarge as Lombroso's "Delinquent Woman"

The heyday of criminal science—the 1880s in Italy—saw an intensification of systematic and scientific attempts to understand the problem of female abnormality. Marie Lafarge served as important raw material for Lombroso's theorizations, providing him with one of his famous head studies (as had Lacenaire before her) and contributing to his theory of inborn female criminality, as excerpts of her well-documented case are used to support several of his tenets regarding the nature of the woman with a predestined inclination to delinquency.

Lombroso's theory of the female criminal is riven with contradiction and paradox, a fact to which he readily admits, stating that "the most contradictory facts fit together like pebbles in a mosaic, making a full and living picture."[30] Feminist critiques of Lombroso (e.g., by Norris, and by Lombroso and Ferrero's translators, Rafter and Gibson) have pointed out reasons why Lombroso's idea of women should lead to such contradictions. In seeking to prove women's inherent inferiority, both physically and mentally, and therefore their predisposition to fall into the ways of prostitution and crime, Lombroso has to perform argumentational circumlocutions and contortions to explain away the lower rate of crime among women than among men. For if criminals are a less evolved, more degenerate, type and if statistics show that there are fewer criminal women than criminal men, then this would suggest that women are a "higher" and more "civilized" subset than males. Yet clearly, for Lombroso this conclusion would be unthinkable.

In order to perform the rhetorical feat needed, Lombroso first establishes the definition of "normal womanhood." Lombroso's idea of the normal woman is one who is physically feminine, maternal, passive, and virtually exempt from sexual desire. (The desire to procreate replaces the desire for erotic pleasure in the "normal" woman, maternity being seen as the highest and most natural achievement of womanhood.) However, Lombroso is also keen to state that as the normal woman is in many ways weaker than a man—intellectually, spiritually, and morally— she therefore has in embryonic form the characteristics of the delinquent woman: a tendency to calculate and manipulate, a limited intelligence, a similarity to children and animals in her simplicity and capriciousness:

> We have seen . . . that women have many traits in common with children; that they are deficient in the moral sense; and that they are vengeful, jealous and inclined to refined cruelty when they take revenge. Usually these defects are neutralized by their piety, maternity, sexual coldness, physical weakness, and undeveloped intelligence.[31]

Femininity is constructed here as a mixture of cruelty moderated by maternity and viciousness tempered by a "natural" physical and nervous inferiority to the male.

Lombroso's criminal woman is a strange hybrid; she embodies the "natural" cunning, deviousness, and duplicity of the "normal" woman to an excessive degree, but she is also disturbingly masculine. The criminologist writes: "The delinquent woman is closer to the man—criminal or not—than to the normal woman";[32] "virility . . . forms the nucleus of the criminal type. What we look for above all in the female is femininity and when we find the opposite . . . there must be some anomaly";[33] and "their eroticism differentiates them from normal women, in whom sexuality is weak and delayed, and makes them resemble males."[34] The excessively sexual woman is seen to constitute a particular threat in that she is too much like a man. The notion that too much female sexuality is masculinizing offers a clear view of the contradictory logic of the discourse as it reveals that for the nineteenth-century sexologist and criminologist, sexual desire per se is masculine, a theory that Freud would develop in his notion of libido as always active, whatever its aim. (Equally however, the lack of "proper" feminine receptivity, such as Marie's refusal to be penetrated on her wedding night, may be another sign of abnormality and delinquency.)

For Lombroso, the most abnormal woman is the most "masculine" (in one or all of the categories of appearance, sexual appetite, intelligence, and temperament). The masculine type of woman is found in three subsets: the lesbian, the inborn criminal, and the genius. However, on the subject of the genius woman, Lombroso gives with one hand and takes back with the other: Staël and Sand, he tells us, offer proof of the existence of exceptionally talented women, but on the other hand, these writers are hardly comparable with Balzac and Shakespeare in the "genius" stakes.[35] Elsewhere, in typically contradictory fashion, he plays down the possibility of female genius, as in the following strange passage regarding hysteria:

In some women generosity is a by-product of hysterical excitement. In these cases an excitement of the psychic centers of the cortex, provoked by hysteria, expresses itself in a spirit of abnegation and sacrifice. Epilepsy sometimes produces the same effect in men; but more often in them epileptic excitation of the cortex gives rise to genius or criminality. Hysteria, the twin of epilepsy, sometimes gives birth to crime in woman, but never to genius. One might say that altruism in women is the equivalent of genius in men.[36]

Unable to countenance female creativity, then, Lombroso falls back on the stereotype of the nurturing woman as the counterpart of the male deviant-genius.

The personage of Marie Lafarge is used to illustrate the very contradictory nature that universal woman—and, by extension and exaggeration within this logic, criminal woman—holds for Lombroso. It is when he illustrates the paradoxes and contradictions that his ideological position forces him to adopt that he uses the example of Marie. Thus, having explained the inferior intellectual and creative powers of both normal and criminal women, he is forced to consider the exception. Under the heading "Writing and Painting," he opines: "These two accomplishments are almost totally lacking in female born criminals. . . . We have found only three examples of memoirs by female born criminals: those of Madame Lafarge, of X and of Bell-star."[37]

Lafarge also appears when Lombroso has to account for the coexistence of apparent morality alongside criminal tendencies:

> The female criminal does not lack a paradoxical and intermittent goodness which contrasts strangely with her usual depravity. Madame Lafarge was extremely kind to her servants. In her own neighborhood she was called the godsend of the poor and she gave succor to the sick.[38]

This may remind us of the results of Lacenaire's posthumous phrenological examination, in which his head failed to conform to the criminal model of the vicious type, and revealed instead worshipful benevolence. Moreover, the Romantic rhetoric often used by the Lafargistes of Marie as a gentle, ethereal "angel," and her common sobriquet in the press, "l'ange de l'arsenic" (the angel of arsenic),[39] is evoked here by Lombroso. This is a case, perhaps, of Lombroso's self-prized "blind observation of facts" and "objectivity"[40] being subtly infected by the cult of Lafarge's persona, created by an amalgam of her life writing and her novelistic and journalistic following. Thus, the Romantic angel invades the scientific text, skewing the results prescribed by the guiding ideology, but in a fascinating example of self-undermining on the part of the scientist. Paradoxically, however, where the defenders of Lafarge sought to normalize her—to emphasize her characteristics of traditional, conformist femininity (sweetness, gentleness, etc.)—it is in the criminologist's account that she emerges as exception to the rule, as bearing the kind of individualism that we have seen attributed to Lacenaire by his literary fans and followers.

Subtle Women Poisoners

Martine Kaluszynski points out that the conclusions reached by Lombroso and his colleagues regarding the nature of the criminal woman correlate directly with contemporaneous European stereotypes and expectations of female sexuality and "femininity":

> It is thus for criminal woman, whose nature appears as an exacerbating factor in the crimes and to whom is attributed a typology of specific crimes: poisonings, theft (domestic or shoplifting), but also adultery, prostitution, abortion or infanticide—all crimes linked to sexuality, to the sex of their perpetrator, and which reveal through analysis the consensus on the danger of woman's sex.[41]

The association of women with poison is an old one, certainly one that predates the case of Marie Lafarge. Lombroso proposes evidence of the antiquity of this idea, and of its misogynistic consequences:

> Poisoning is one of woman's most frequent crimes. Caesar tells us that when a man died, the Gauls would burn all his wives along with him if there was even a suspicion that the death was not natural—an efficient procedure which must have originated in frequent poisonings.[42]

However, the simultaneity of the rise of criminology in nineteenth-century Europe and the fascination in which the Lafarge poisoning case was held throughout the whole century conspired to produce for the first time in history statistical accounts, as well as shared myths and stereotypes, of gendered poisonings. French criminologist Alexandre Lacassagne, detractor of Lombroso's theory of innate and predetermined criminality, but who did little to question his theories of femininity, reported in 1886 that between the mid-1830s and 1855—the heyday of the Lafarge scandal—poisonings in France were committed by an approximately equal mixture of the sexes; but that between 1875 and 1880, the number of poisonings overall declined, but there were 41 women accused as against only 19 men.[43] The accuracy of the statistics regarding female poisoners is of less interest and relevance to us than the fact that this question was being asked in the first place, and the answer drawn to academic and civic attention in publications.

In an article that appeared in *Le Figaro* in 1904, entitled "Femmes criminelles," Georges Claretie wrote:

> Monsieur Lombroso is right: a woman's crime, a feminine crime, has something particularly odious and more perverted about it. Women kill more readily for revenge, and therefore they bring to their killing a sort of refinement. And the female poisoner has a thirst like a drunkard—with this difference— she pours her drink down the throats of other people.[44]

Claretie says that women's crimes are more *refined*, because they are, by nature, premeditated and cold. Refined crime is a feature we have seen attributed to Lacenaire, but in the context of something to be admired, wondered at, approached with awe. However, the particular refinement of women criminals here is clearly intended to be understood differently. Lafarge and her murderous sisters are not accorded Lacenaire's status as artist-murderer (a Romantic amalgam of individualist and *homme du peuple*), but rather the status of duplicitous other. Moreover, where in discourses of the 1830s, *raffiné(e)*, meaning "refined," may bear positive connotations, by the end of the century it suggests rather the excessive and unnatural refinement of Decadence. Women are associated with poison because it is seen as unnatural and cold-blooded, rather than hot-blooded. Although by the end of the century humoral theories of the body (which hold that the woman is naturally cold, while the man is hot) have been surpassed by sexological models of perversion, a ghost of this discourse is clearly visible in Claretie's rhetoric.

Another version of this is seen as late as 1926 in Jules Marché's *Une vicieuse du grand monde: Madame Lafarge* (A vicious society woman: Madame Lafarge):

> She embodies the type of the criminal woman. There was something feline in her nature. . . . Women's crimes have, as their essential trait, a terrible duplicity. Lombroso called them diabolical. They are terribly premeditated. It's only in crimes committed by women that one encounters this genius for perversity; this prodigious ease in lying.[45]

Genius is finally attributed to the woman—but only a genius for deception. As Matlock has argued, duplicity and deception were to some extent necessary strategic tools if the female subject/agent were to think
or write herself into the active voice, in an epoch whose scripts wrote
agency (both creative and destructive) as always-already masculine, and
in a climate in which deviations from norms of masculinity and femininity were so little tolerated—especially in the case of the masculine woman.[46] An aesthetic of feminine murder—by poison rather than by means
of the dagger that we have seen fetishized in discourses of Lacenaire—is
thus visible here. This is an aesthetic that is projected onto criminal
women in which the characteristics of the mechanisms of the crime are
synonymous with the perceived nature of the perpetrator.[47]

Male criminologists concurred on the tendency of female offenders to
maintain their innocence after apprehension. Lombroso asserted that

> one peculiarity of female criminals, especially female born criminals, is the
> obstinacy with which they deny their crimes, no matter how strong the evi-
> dence against them. . . . Madame Lafarge maintained her innocence to the
> end, proclaiming it in her memoirs.[48]

Raymond de Ryckère added in 1899 that men tend to confess while
women dissimulate and resist.[49] These attributed characteristics construct the woman criminal as more wily and deceitful than the male.
Lombroso insists that women deny their crimes because of an innate
feminine deceptiveness, not because, in a cultural climate in which femininity bore the burden of signifying passive, gentle, maternal care, the
acceptance of one's own nonconformist violence would result in a monstrous self-identification that was ontologically impossible to assume.
If Lafarge's innocence was a matter of such high stakes to her culture,
we can only presume that she, as a product and member of that culture,
would have internalized and shared in the fantasy of the impossibility of
the murderous feminine.

Paradoxically, though, Lombroso's assertion also subtly complexifies
those familiar discourses that attribute physicality to the female and cerebrality to the male, positing a more calculating, and thereby more reasoned, criminal personality than that of the male killer who is aligned
with physical violence and passion—a sexual virility turned in the service of destruction. Indeed Lombroso, concerned throughout his opus
with insisting upon the intellectual inferiority of women in comparison

to men, makes the following point regarding female killers, particularly poisoners:

> Criminal women exhibit many levels of intelligence. Some are extremely intelligent, while others are ordinary in this respect. As a rule, however, their minds are alert; this is evidently why; relative to men; they commit few impulsive crimes. To kill in a bestial rage requires no more than the mind of a Hottentot; but to plot out a poisoning requires ability and sharpness.[50]

However any tacit admiration for this (fantasized) refined female murderer is not articulated within the discourse and remains foreclosed while the diagnosis operates at the level of moral indignation.

Beyond Gendered Logic

We have seen how the case of Marie Lafarge produced consternation and debate—could this pretty and apparently gentle woman really be culpable of murder?—in contradistinction to Lacenaire, who split public opinion along the lines of lionization of a virile criminal hero and demonization of a social deviant. Moreover, we have seen how Lafarge's creativity became a further factor in her construction as unnatural woman rather than the redeeming counterpart of her criminality, since authorship itself was seen as unwomanly in nineteenth-century Europe, despite the attempts of writers such as Madame de Staël in the early nineteenth century to celebrate female creativity. Where the male poet-murderer is a glorious Romantic monster, his female counterpart is merely monstrous. To quote Lombroso again:

> The female criminal is, so to speak, doubly exceptional, first as a woman and then as a criminal. This is because criminals are exceptional among civilized people, and women are exceptions among criminals. . . . As a double exception, then, the criminal woman is a true monster.[51]

What horrifies about the female murderer is not her excess, for excess is always-already constructed as on the side of the feminine, but her paradoxical cerebrality, her agency, her creativity. For these are the attributes of the Romantic hero in the nineteenth century, the ideal man. The figure of the murderess is thus an androgynous construction, presented as more aberrant than the murderer by dint of her violation of the norms of femininity, as well as her violation of the law, but resisting any principle of neat taxonomy. As a figure, she shows up the anxieties of a culture applying, despite its obvious lack of "fit," a strictly gendered logic to the attribution of reason/unreason, mind/body, and agency/passivity.

CHAPTER THREE

The Beast in Man

Jack and the Rippers Who Came After

Man is the hunter; woman is his game.
The sleek and shining creature of the chase,
We hunt them for the beauty of their skins;
They love us for it and we ride them down.

—(Alfred Lord Tennyson, "The Princess," 1847)

I'm not a butcher
I'm not a Yid,
Nor yet a foreign skipper,
But I'm your own light-hearted friend,
Yours truly, Jack the Ripper.

—(Included in one of many letters allegedly sent by the Whitechapel murderer, 1888)

Wild beasts remain wild beasts, and all attempts to invent better disguises will be in vain: there will still be wild beasts underneath.

—(Zola, *La Bête humaine*, 1890)[1]

The activities of Jack the Ripper, the still unidentified killer who terrorized London's impoverished Whitechapel in 1888, killing and dismembering at least five, and possibly several more, women in the most violent and bloodthirsty ways,[2] were disseminated and discussed avidly throughout both Europe and America. While "Jack" may not technically have been the first serial murderer,[3] he nevertheless stood at "the gateway of the modern age,"[4] inaugurating what Caputi calls the age of sex crime. The simultaneity of the Ripper killings and such modern cultural phenomena as a literary taste for the Gothic and detective fiction, the explosion of the pulp press, and the rise of sexual and criminological science suggests a complex network of discursive and social trends that interrelated to produce an event that would resonate beyond its immediate moment and shape the figure of the murderer in the cultural imaginary for centuries to come and across geographical boundaries. The anonymous Ripper became the archetype for that subject of modernity, the serial sex murderer. In Mark Seltzer's words: Jack the Ripper was "from the start a projective surface for all sorts of stories."[5]

The stories projected onto the figure of Jack include, of course, speculative stories about his identity, framed in discourses that are both of their time and recognizable. He was sometimes cast as the aesthete-killer, reminiscent of Lacenaire, as seen in the speculations of "Ripper-ologists," both at the time of the killings and in recent years, that the murderer may have been a poet, actor, or artist, "a gentleman of leisure . . . seeking after luxurious cruelties which could stimulate his jaded sensibilities."[6] Decadent poet Algernon Charles Swinburne and American actor Richard Mansfield, who portrayed Stevenson's Dr. Jekyll and Mr. Hyde with extraordinary skill at the Lyceum, were both contemporary suspects. And crime writer Patricia Cornwell has recently produced what she considers definitive proof that minor artist Walter Sickert was the killer.[7] Other theories have suggested that the killer was an aristocrat—even a minor royal (the Duke of Clarence). Given the extensive "gynecological"[8] mutilation of the victims' bodies, the theory that the Ripper was a doctor or butcher has also held sway.

The Ripper case also served as a hook on which to hang a story central to nineteenth-century criminological and sexological thinking: the narrative of civilization's decline, as dramatized by degeneration theory. The "degenerate criminal" suggested by the anonymous Ripper's crimes is an atavistic throwback, a "beast." The elitist aspect of degeneration theory is seen in the fact that this threat of destructive atavism was felt to issue primarily from the proletarian "masses," from socialists, and from nonwhite, non-Christian ethnicities and religions. The counterpoint to theories of the Ripper as artist or aristocratic gentleman was the idea that he was a member of the London East End's Eastern European Jewish community. While some theories cast him as an American, a more pervasive, if rather vague, description of the Ripper that circulated was of a man of "foreign appearance"[9] (implying, presumably, dark skin). This led to increased hostility toward Jewish immigrants, exacerbated by the allusion to an alleged Talmudic injunction that a Jewish man who had sex with a Christian woman should subsequently kill her.[10] The tendency of Western Christian culture to project misogyny onto non-Christian religions is a long-standing patriarchal strategy for distracting attention from more local examples thereof. The fact that the location of the Ripper murders was the cosmopolitan, largely Jewish, and extremely poor milieu of Whitechapel served to reinforce (despite the various contradictory conjectures that the criminal may have been an artist, doctor, or aristocrat) the belief that the socially deprived and the ethnic other posed an ineffable threat to the middle classes.

The East End of London was also, of course, the locus of prostitution, from which the Ripper profited in choosing his victims. It is of note that the prostitute was contemporaneously seen as a degenerate female and bearer of disease. One fanciful theory that circulated regarding the possibility of the killer being a doctor or medical student held that this man may have contracted a sexually transmitted disease, probably syphilis, from a prostitute and was "down on whores" and "ripping them"[11] as a form of revenge. Sander Gilman has argued brilliantly that the whore, the Jew, and the lust murderer are seen as the differently gendered embodiments of end-of-century diseased culture, such that, whereas police and physicians were powerless to remove prostitutes from the streets, "Jack could kill the 'source of infection' because he too was fatally diseased";[12] he became "the sign of deviant human sexuality destroying life, the parallel to the destructive prostitute."[13] The victim-blaming of murdered prostitutes implicit in this view of the Ripper murders is, as Cameron and Frazer have painstakingly shown, a phenomenon that the Jack the Ripper case bequeathed to subsequent sex murder cases, notably, but not solely, that of the English prostitute-killer, Peter Sutcliffe, in the 1970s and 1980s.

Jack thus became the archetype of a "new" murdering subject—the lust murderer—produced in the 1880s and 1890s in Europe. This figure of a sexually destructive male emerged as the seamy alter ego of the rational subject of progressive modernity. Bearing the mark of sexual excess, it provoked a fear of "uncivilized" animality. In the predominantly German science of sexology, the sexological type of the *Lustmörder*—proponent of what Foucault has rather fancifully called the "insane dialogue of love and death"[14]—found his place among the perverts carefully classified and catalogued by Richard von Krafft-Ebing and his sexological brethren. Although the Ripper crimes did not begin until two years after the first edition of *Psychopathia Sexualis*, in the numerous editions that followed, "Jack" provided Krafft-Ebing with exemplary illustrative material for his theory that in sadistic and murderous sexual perversion, the instinct to reproduce has been replaced with a desire to destroy. He writes of Jack: "He does not seem to have had sexual intercourse with his victims, but . . . the murderous act and subsequent mutilation of the corpse were equivalents for the sexual act."[15] This definition of the lust murderer, which persists beyond the epoch of German sexology, largely ensured that this figure would be male, as the idea that "sex" *is* penetration is a particularly masculine conception, a product of a patriarchal imaginary. While, as we will see, Krafft-Ebing's sexology reveals a definite suspicion of male sexuality as potentially dangerous (and therefore of men as a moral and social threat), it remains heavily conservative and misogynistic in gender political terms, since it assumes aggressivity as a "natural" quality of masculinity/ maleness (and passivity as a "natural" quality of femininity/femaleness).

This chapter analyzes some modern assumptions about sexuality, gender, class, race, and civilization that led to the production of the subject of the "lust murderer" or "sex killer," of which Jack is the exemplum, in a series of discursive fields. The ways in which nineteenth-century European medicine and sexual science figured male and female sexuality, and "specified as an individual" the murdering sexual pervert, will be analyzed in the first part. The second will consider in detail a near contemporary French response to the Ripper case and to Krafft-Ebing's *Psychopathia Sexualis*, Zola's novel *La Bête humaine* (1890), a work that functions as a fictional version of sexological and criminological discourse. In crafting the figure of Jacques Lantier, the innate criminal with an inherited compulsion to lust murder, it draws for inspiration on the aberrant pathological masculine typology described in sexology by Richard von Krafft-Ebing and in criminological accounts by Cesare Lombroso. It adheres rigidly to a model of predetermination and the belief in inherited moral, criminal, and sexual traits, while taking artistic license with some elements of the gendered portraits drawn. In a third section, I will examine how Jack the Ripper—in part owing to his continued anonymity, and therefore his qualities as a tabula rasa—provided the template for representing other sex-motivated multiple killers of both men and women that came after him, such as the "Düsseldorf Vampire" (Peter Kürten), the "Yorkshire Ripper" (Peter Sutcliffe), and "Son of Sam" (David Berkowitz). It explores how these later sex killers were culturally

represented—and how they actively self-represented—using the very discursive means made available by the nineteenth-century phenomenon of
Jack the Ripper and the language of the "beast" that issued from both
science and the popular press.

Medical Models

In the first chapter of his encyclopedic work of sexual classification, *Psychopathia Sexualis* (1886), Krafft-Ebing makes the following claim: "The
propagation of the human species is not committed to accident or to the
caprice of the individual, but made secure in a natural instinct, which,
with all-conquering force and might, demands fulfilment."[16] Krafft-Ebing
starts, then, from the assumption of a biological imperative: that the survival of the species guides the individual toward reproductive activity.
The strength of conviction here may strike us as a case of protesting too
much, given that Krafft-Ebing then goes on to devote some 500 pages
to cataloguing the many instances of sexuality's determined *resistance*
to acts that would lead to reproduction, in the form of the sexual perversions. Perhaps in recognition of this contradiction, Krafft-Ebing then appeals to the necessity for moral restraint on the part of men to prevent
the natural instinct from going awry. Men are instructed to apply reason
and moral sagacity in their sexual lives, as their natural predisposition
toward a higher sex drive than women makes them particularly vulnerable. Krafft-Ebing tells us—in terms that abundantly confuse nature and
class-bound culture—that "if [a woman] is normally developed mentally
and well bred, her sexual desire is small. If this were not so the whole
world would become a brothel and marriage and a family impossible."[17]
Whereas "from the fact that man by nature plays the aggressive *rôle* in
sexual life, he is in danger of overstepping the limits which morality and
law have set."[18] This normative description of the "natural" predisposi-
tions of men and women leaves in no doubt the danger that is perceived
to issue from the female prostitute and the male sexual sadist, the very
players in the Jack the Ripper drama.[19]

Two belief systems operate side by side and in tension with each other
in Krafft-Ebing's sexology. On the one hand, degeneration is innate and
inevitable: a degenerate pervert cannot be cured and, if he or she should
reproduce, the taint will be passed down the line. On the other hand,

corruption and contagion are consistently warned against and such pursuits as masturbation, that would be recognized today as harmless, could be sufficient to provide the foundation of ruin in a formerly "healthy" subject. The logic of sexual weakness in the *Psychopathia Sexualis*, then, is much the same as that of the alienists earlier in the century with their diagnosis of monomania, a single-minded compulsion that gripped the afflicted subject and robbed him of reason and free will. Sexual continence, like reason, is precarious. The biggest threat to the (male) individual and his society is loss of self-control, understood in sexology as giving in to sexual excess. But at the same time, men must retain just enough sexual aggressiveness to remain properly masculine. Krafft-Ebing states:

> The *rôle* which the retention of sexual functions plays in the case of a man, both in originating and retaining his feeling of self-respect, is remarkable. In the deterioration of manliness and self-confidence which the onanist, in his weakened nervous state, and the man that has become impotent, present, may be estimated the significance of this factor.[20]

Concerns over semen conservation and the potential of masturbation to lead to weakness, neurasthenia, and disease, as posited by Swiss physician Samuel-Auguste Tissot as early as 1760, raise their head here. Sexual excess risks not only undermining the masculine imperative to build society and propagate the next generation, but also weakening the nervous and moral system of the individual and laying him open to worse consequences. In a system haunted by the logic of corruption and contagion, masturbation could lead to depleted moral faculties, which could lead to more "serious" perversions such as sadism, necrophilia, and eventually, perhaps, to lust murder.

Lust murder is diagnosed by Krafft-Ebing, as we have seen, in cases where the act of killing can be said to have taken the place of the act of intercourse, as seen in Lombroso's patient Vincent Verzeni who, in 1783, made the following confession: "I had an unspeakable delight in strangling women, experiencing during that act erections and real sexual pleasure . . . much greater than that which I experienced while masturbating."[21] Krafft-Ebing further refines his definition, adding an element of mutilation to the consideration of the phenomenological killing/sex equivalence:

> The presumption of a murder out of lust is always given when injuries of the genitals are found, the character and extent of which are not such as could be explained by merely a brutal attempt at coitus; and still more when the body has been opened and parts (intestines, genitals) torn out and wanting.[22]

This conforms, of course, with the case of Jack the Ripper, who provides "an outline, a repository, a *type*"[23] for the diagnosis, even though he is far from being the earliest case of a lust murderer that Krafft-Ebing discusses:

> It is probable that he first cut the throats of his victims, then ripped open the abdomen and groped among the intestines. In some instances he cut off the genitals and carried them away; in others he only tore them to pieces and left them behind.[24]

It is in discussing lust murder that Krafft-Ebing deploys most freely a language of uncontrolled animal instinct. So, "a certain Grassi," who stabbed to death a female relative, is described as engaging in "acts of bestiality."[25] And the subjects in this category are referred to en masse as "psycho-sexual monsters."[26] It is perhaps not surprising that repulsion for such extreme violence should lead the doctor to use such emotive terms to describe the behavior in question. However, one cannot read this animal and teratological vocabulary as referring *only* to the specific and extreme acts and subjects it purports to be describing. The language of instinct leading to bestiality echoes Krafft-Ebing's words of warning regarding the citizen's socio-sexual duty to avoid "the lustful impulse to satisfy" the instinct of "sensuous love" (whether by adultery, masturbation, or other harmless acts, as well as by sadism and lust murder). For in doing any of this, he tells us, "man stands on a level with the animal."[27]

It was a Frenchman, Bénédict Augustin Morel (1809–1873), who in 1857 was the first to define degeneration as the source and cause of the rise of crime, in his *Traité de dégénérescences physiques, intellectuelles et morales de l'espèce humaine* (Treatise on the physical, intellectual and moral degeneration of the human species). This idea was expanded upon by Lombroso's criminal science in Italy and by Max Nordau in Germany. While, as Daniel Pick has pointed out in his study of this "European disorder," degeneration took varying forms in the distinct national cultures, it nonetheless shared common concerns, precepts, and obsessions.[28] Degeneration theorists pursued the logic that nonreproductive sexuality contributed to the moral, physiological, and mental deterioration they perceived to afflict the European population at the turn of the century. About sexual excess, that is, perversion, Nordau wrote that it renders the whole society, as well as the individuals in it, "too worn out and flaccid to perform great tasks."[29] This worn-out and flaccid population risked regressing from its position of evolved reason to an atavistic condition: "It is a descent from the height of human perfection to the low level of the mollusc."[30] Rather than being civilized men, the modern population risked becoming "anti-social vermin."[31] The regressive beast of degeneration, then, is described by Nordau in the same terms as the unreasoned sexual excess in Krafft-Ebing that devitalizes the population and turns its mind to destruction rather than procreation: from will and reason to animal instinct. Sexual perversions, writes Nordau, "run directly contrary to the purpose of the instinct, i.e., the preservation of the species."[32]

Sexual science, then, sets up the ideal of masculine agency, the "naturalness" of male aggression in sex, and the force of male sex drive. It warns, on the one hand, against weakening good virile male aggression by means of masturbation or effeminacy and, on the other, against the excessive pursuit of satisfaction of the sexual appetite, for this leads to an animalistic exacerbation of the instinct that could result in sadism and lust murder. It demonstrates a belief both in heredity (in the inherited predisposition toward mental and physiological dysfunctions) and in the corrupting or contagious power of exposure to sex. This is demonstrated by the fact that Krafft-Ebing rendered the most obscene details of his case studies in Latin, so that the uninitiated could not be corrupted into imitative behavior if their eyes should fall upon an open copy of his book. Effectively, then, the ideal of masculine behavior presented leaves little room for maneuver for those aspiring to it; the nineteenth-century male is trapped in a series of tautologies and logical double binds. The discourse of sexual science has high expectations of masculinity as the fantasized embodiment of reason, but also a fatal suspicion of male weakness. It only barely manages to disguise this latter by means of its misogynistic projection of passivity and low sex drive onto women, seen in Krafft-Ebing's comment on the high number of male sadists and lust killers as compared to female ones. Since sadism is, for Krafft-Ebing, "a pathological intensification of the masculine sexual character," it is inevitable in his system that "the obstacles which oppose the expression of this monstrous impulse are . . . much greater for a woman than for a man."[33] The perverse intensification of the natural "feminine" sexual character would be sexual masochism.[34] Indeed, Krafft-Ebing points out that so natural is the instinct of submission to the heterosexual female that feminine masochism is more or less the norm rather than a perversion: "ideas of subjection" are the "tone-quality of feminine feeling"[35] and "the male 'sadistic force' is developed . . . by the natural shyness and modesty of women."[36] Krafft-Ebing comes perilously close to suggesting that women's "natural" sexual passivity *causes* male sexuality to take an aggressive, violent form—effectively blaming the victim for the crime. Furthermore, dressing the absence of female sex murderers as a matter of natural submissiveness neatly obviates the need to consider the factor of male social domination of women, via such institutions as church and medicine, which inculcated in women a very *cultural* passivity from their youngest age. Neither does this explanation address the idea that the lust murderer is constructed a priori as a masculine subject by dint of the shared investment of this individual *and his culture* in a myth of male agency, potency, and aggression, in which penetrating and killing can be intelligibly interchangeable.

The figure of the lust murderer described by nineteenth-century scientists actualizes in the public sphere the destructive and disruptive potential of male sexuality gone awry that the onanist risks only in the confines of his bedchamber. This figure haunted the scientific and literary discourses of degeneration in the form of Robert Louis Stevenson's Mr. Hyde, the underside of "rational" man embodied by Dr. Jekyll; in the form of Bram Stoker's Dracula, a predator from an Eastern European land preying on Western women and infecting them with a voracious sexuality; and, of course, in the figure of the anonymous Whitechapel murderer striking after dark in the East End of London. The lust killer, to some extent, became the poster child of conservative medical and social discourses, then, for it would have been hard to convince the reader that foot fetishism or erotomania so directly threatened the survival of civilization. But there is no question that for Krafft-Ebing, these nonprocreative sexual activities lie on a continuum of masculinity. The hybrid figure of the lust murderer, uniting hypermasculinity and evirated masculinity, became an appropriate specter of beastly horror—and of fascination—for the culture that gave birth to him.

Strikingly and counterintuitively, then, the radical feminist analysis of the meaning of lust murder expounded by Caputi and by Cameron and Frazer, which holds that it is "a distinctly male crime"[37] and "male violence taken to its logical extreme,"[38] is already the unspoken subtext of the very authority discourse that produces the lust murderer as a subject (even if this is not the political *intention* of this discourse). To clarify: both nineteenth-century sexologists and twentieth-century feminist scholars perceive male murderous sexuality as a real threat, but, crucially, where Krafft-Ebing sees it as a symbolic threat to civilized (patriarchal) social order, feminist writers see it as a very real threat to female lives, safety, and subjectivity; where Krafft-Ebing sees male destructivity as rooted in biology, in essence, feminists see this rhetoric as the strategy of a culture invested in justifying and maintaining its constructed system of domination, in which men are dominant and women submissive.

Zola's Beast

Naturalism was the literary school that, in the words of Daniel Pick, dreamed both of "mastering disorder" and of providing a "master narrative of disorder,"[39] by trying to make literary craft approximate scientific method. It is widely acknowledged that *La Bête humaine* constitutes an attempt to construct, in literary form, a case history of the sexual criminal subject in conformity with the scientific theorization of the day. Work by Geoff Woollen,[40] Daniel Pick,[41] and Pauline McLynn[42] has demonstrated various filiations between Zola's text and the ideas of Krafft-Ebing, Lombroso, Morel, and Nordau. The response of the scientists in question to Zola's project differed considerably. Delighted to have a novelist popularizing his theories, Lombroso wrote approvingly of the physiognomical characterization of Zola's dramatis personae. Noting that Zola's lust murderer is described as a "handsome fellow with a round face and regular features, but spoiled by a too prominent jawline,"[43] he remarked that "this Jacques Lantier definitely has some characteristics of the inborn criminal."[44] However, he also argued that Zola's portrayal was not consistently psychologically accurate as the "real" murderer with a hereditary predisposition toward lust killing would never be able to enjoy sexual intercourse with a woman without feeling the need to kill her, as Jacques is shown doing in his early encounters with Séverine. For Nordau, on the other hand, Naturalist literature was a symptom and cause of degeneration, not a means of enlightening the population about it, and Zola's novels were among those that he condemned most forcefully. Nordau strongly believed that degenerate art, such as he termed

Naturalism, was rooted in the "sexual psychopathology" of its creator. In the context of a system in which artists and writers were seen to bear strong resemblances to the mentally ill, Nordau was able to write of novelists that "all persons of unbalanced minds . . . have the keenest scent for perversions of a sexual kind."[45] However, the ambivalence of degeneration theory comes in its concession that the genius as well as the mad man or the criminal is a "degenerate." In its adherence to the very idea of genius, and in approximating genius to criminality, degeneration theory bears no doubt unintended comparisons and parallels with the discourse of Romanticism. The focus on the unique, singular, better-than-normal individual persists, albeit with a different ideological bias.

As well as borrowing theories from scientific contemporaries, Zola drew, like them, on the popular press for case material. Sketches for a novel about a man with an overwhelming desire to kill women—"un homme qui a besoin de tuer"[46]—first occur in Zola's notebooks as early as 1874. However, Jacques Lantier owes both his name and certain characteristics to the sensationalist press coverage of the murders of Jack the Ripper (whom the French called *Jacques l'éventreur*—the verb *éventrer* meaning "to eviscerate"). And true to form, the narrative of Zola's text parallels Krafft-Ebing's statement that murder replaces penetrative sex for the inborn lust murderer (despite the episode criticized by Lombroso, in which Jacques is able to perform "normally"). When the reader is first made aware of Jacques's unorthodox desire, it is in the following terms: "Kill a woman, kill a woman! This rang in his ears, from the days of his youth, with the growing, maddening, fever of desire. As others, at the dawn of puberty, dream of possessing a woman, he was obsessed with the idea of killing one."[47] Jacques's murderous desire first occurs at puberty, suggesting an unhealthy parallel to "normal" development, the supplanting of sex with death-lust. Yet the choice of verb to describe "healthy" sex with a woman is telling: it is *posséder*, "to possess." Zola draws attention to the aggressive masculinity that is the "natural" sexual response to "the weaker sex" (and suggests, to a reader aware of gender politics, the domination paradigm on which heterosexuality is discursively founded). This passage about Jacques's youth is designed to read like the confessions included in the studies of individual patients in contemporaneous sexological manuals. And it succeeds in so doing; the following, taken from the confessions of the "Vampire of Montparnasse," the necrophile soldier Sergent Bertrand, tried in 1849, bears resemblances to the description of Jacques's adolescent desires:

At thirteen or fourteen I knew no limits. I masturbated up to seven or eight times a day; the mere sight of women's clothing excited me. While masturbating, I was transported in my fantasy to a room where women were at my disposal. There, after having sated my passion on them, and having amused myself by torturing them in every manner, I imagined them dead and exerted upon their cadavers all sorts of profanations.[48]

Both fictional and medical accounts of the pervert's and the lust murderer's experience are collated in the course of the nineteenth century, such that they eventually constitute a cultural repository of ideas about the phenomenon.

Geoff Woollen[49] and Philippe Hamon[50] have pointed out the probable influence on Zola of a short story by the little known Belgian Naturalist Camille Lemonnier, "L'Homme qui tuait les femmes" ("The man who killed women"), which appeared in *Gil Blas* on 2 November 1888, and which was also inspired by the Whitechapel killings. Lemonnier's treatment of the subject matter is, however, rather different from Zola's. The narrative is voiced in the first person by the murderer, who speaks of himself in the third person at one point, stating: "I bequeath to science . . . the perverse and complex being who, to me, will always remain an unfathomable problem."[51] In the change of person from first to third, Lemonnier's hero expresses a dissociation from the unknowable part of himself that feels the need to kill, whereas Jacques Lantier asks endless questions about the cause of his condition expressed via free indirect style, a narrative technique beloved of French Realist and Naturalist novelists of the nineteenth century. Musing on the origins of his sexual inclination, Jacques wonders: "Did it come from a distant time, from the evil that woman had done to his race, from the accumulated spite felt by male after male since the first deception?"[52] What is very visible in Jacques's speculation is the victim-blaming tendency that runs through discourses of sex killing—scientific, journalistic, and those produced by (fictional and real) lust murderers themselves. Here, the familiar projection of male aggression onto women is accorded ancient origins. The "first deception" reminds us of an atavistic, primal, perceived wrong wrought by a female: we may think of Pandora, of Lilith, of Eve. Too, Jacques's self-interrogation is consistent with the ideology of heredity and degeneration, since the more local explanation of the "first deception" is understandable in terms of the fact that Jacques comes of a degenerate line, that of the Rougon-Macquarts, whose taint of sickness originated with

the mentally deficient middle-class Adelaide Fouque, Jacques's grandmother, who had three illegitimate children with a low-class smuggler,
Macquart. The descendants of this coupling all bear degenerate traits:
alcoholism for Jacques's mother, Gervaise, of *L'Assomoir*; prostitution
for his sister, the eponymous Nana; and lust murder for Jacques, showing
again how the nineteenth century imagined gendered complementarity
between the "perversions" of whoredom and lust murder.

Vernon Rosario has argued that it is, in fact, the trace of the feminine that is feared and despised in the figure of the beast in man in a
culture in which weakness and lack of reason are associated with the
feminine: "La bête humaine crouching in the dark recesses of the individual and collective psyche was the primitive, pathological, deadly
erotic imagination, and its sex was female."[53] As we have seen, weakness
and a proximity to nature and the instinctual were codified as feminine
in nineteenth-century philosophy and sexual science, while the mastery
of reason connoted masculinity. However, as the following extract from
Psychopathia Sexualis reveals, the supposed greater capacity of the male
for sexual lust rendered him in danger of "feminine" weakness precisely
at the moment that he was apparently most masculine: "Undoubtedly
man has a much more intense sexual appetite than woman. . . . In ac-
cordance with the nature of this powerful impulse, he is aggressive and
violent in his wooing."[54] Yet "the weakness of men in comparison with
women lies in the great intensity of their sexual desires." The more de-
sirous he is, "the weaker and more sensual he becomes."[55] Here Krafft-
Ebing is describing the condition of the so-called normal, healthy male.
Jacques's fantasy of destructive revenge on the female ancestor who provoked his weakness is thus understandable as an exaggeration of a "normal" masculine attitude. We see, then, that Zola's lust murderer, Jacques
Lantier, and the sexologist Krafft-Ebing employ the same logic in relation to the female: the "weakness" that desire suggests for the male is
projected onto the object of his lust, from whom the weakness is errone-
ously perceived to emit. The fantasy of sexual and moral weakness with
which femininity was associated and the fantasy of a monstrous, exaggerated destructive masculinity both come to rest in the same site: the
figure of the "lust murderer."

A fascinating feature of *La Bête humaine* is that it seems to suggest at
moments that the representation of Jacques's desire to kill women may
not (only) be the result of the perversion of the instinct of conservation
peculiar to the exceptional perverted male, or the fatal trait inherited

from a degenerate family line, but rather a logical consequence of the ways in which heteronormative culture dreams the asymmetrical distinction between the sexes—a collective fantasy. Yet this is never *explicitly* given, and Jacques's status in the text is ambiguous, swinging between the two perspectives. If sometimes it is made abundantly clear that Lantier is intended to do no more than fulfill the criteria for a case study of the lust murderer, at other points in the novel, Jacques's proclivities suggest a paradigm of a more general model of (nonexceptional) masculinity in which sex and killing lie on an imaginary continuum, exactly as argued by Caputi and by Cameron and Frazer, and as fearfully posited by nineteenth-century sexology. It is by drawing the reader close to the perspective of Jacques that he is permitted to shift, sometimes, from the aberrant subject matter of a case study, to an agentic subject. Rhetorical questions such as the following draw the reader in, creating collusion with the character, and forcing us to question too: "possessing, killing; were the two equivalent?"[56] It is because of Zola's manipulation of the narrative point of view in *La Bête humaine* that our understanding of Jacques's perspective is allowed to slip from one of exceptional aberration to one of universality. Caputi has described the way in which the reader/viewer is commonly aligned with the point of view of the killer, rather than the victim, in most spectacles and narratives of lust murder, and this is certainly the case here.

The terms in which the murder of Séverine is framed are particularly revealing in this respect: "She inclined her submissive face and, with a supplicating tenderness, revealed her bare neck. . . . And he, seeing this white flesh, as in a burst of flames, lifted his fist which held the knife."[57] The strategy is one of dramatic irony. The reader, possessed of the knowledge of the secret of Jacques's desire, can anticipate the radical misreading of Séverine's signals that will occur. Intending to tempt her lover to have sex with her, Séverine fatally mismanages the other's desire and hastens her own murder—in another example of implied victim-blaming. It is, then, because the reader's attention is aligned throughout much of the narrative with Jacques's point of view—and crucially never with Séverine's—that the dramatic irony of this episode can function. We know that Jacques's desire is to "throw her onto her back, dead, like some prey that one has grabbed from the others."[58] The passage cited above, describing the moment, before Séverine's murder, shows how the woman's motivation is construed from the masculine viewpoint. The figure of Jacques fluctuates in the course of the novel between personifying the pathologized figure of the sexological object of inquiry and the universal masculine subject of the culture. At the moment when he should so clearly be the former, distanced from the reader as horrifically "other," the narrative point of view, which suggests irresistible collusion with him, forces the reader to relate to him as the latter.

The gender bias of the viewpoint of *La Bête humaine* is brought into even sharper relief if we compare the passage I have just quoted with an extract from a minor female-authored Naturalist text, treating similar subject matter, which places the female perspective into the foreground. Rachel Mesch has brought recent critical attention to Lucie Delarue-Mardrus's *Marie, fille-mère* ("Marie, child-mother") (1908), contending that this novel constitutes a spirited feminist response to Zola's famous novelistic account of masculine beastliness.[59] In one passage of *Marie, fille-mère*, we are given the following account of heterosexuality:

> She didn't know that desire is a hunter without pity. She had never asked herself why all female animals, more intelligent than girls, start to flee from males after having called them, because a sort of fear grips them in the face of the deathliness of sex. . . . She didn't know that there is struggle within love and murder in possession, that there is from one side attack and from the other defense, and that man, more cruel than any other beast, is stirred during his youth by the deaf desire to lay a woman out as he would a weaker adversary.[60]

Here, the language of murderous attack is used to describe romantic love. Drawing on the lexicon of the animal world: man as beast, and woman as prey, Delarue-Mardrus both cites and inverts Zola's formula. Using the figure of the lust murderer, Zola literalizes and puts at the surface the destructive misogyny and the paranoia regarding male sexual incontinence that run through nineteenth-century scientific accounts of heterosexual desire. The female novelist, on the other hand, dresses the socially prescribed act of sexual intercourse as a *metaphorical* murder. The difference is that our close collusion with Jacques's point of view at its most extreme naturalizes misogyny and makes lust murder appear inevitable, while our proximity to Marie's perspective here, invites us to question, in the terms of the scientific discourse itself, the inevitability of masculine destructivity and, crucially, the obligation of female collusion with it. This restores female subjectivity to what, in Zola's account, is only a victim-position.

Yet the figure of desire-as-destructivity that is at the center of Zola's conception paradoxically allows him, via the characterization of female protagonist Flore, to separate masculinity (which is aligned with destructivity) from biological maleness. As Hannah Thompson rightly points out, Philippe Hamon's division of Zola's dramatis personae into "personnages féminins" or "personnages masculins"[61] is too simplistic.[62] It conforms with the elision of the distinction between sexed bodies and cultural codes of gender that the French language presupposes. That is, it collapses masculinity unproblematically onto maleness and femininity onto femaleness, as if they are naturally linked rather than forced together by cultural constraints. This supposition is certainly the common belief of the time. However, the treatment of desire and identity in *La Bête humaine* is not quite consistent with this supposition. The character of Flore is presented to us in terms that are strikingly similar to the presentation of Jacques. Like him, she is troubled by a blood lust: "She had a fascination with accidents."[63] Unlike Séverine, defined as rape victim, abused wife, and finally murder victim—that is, archly feminine and heterosexual—Flore is described as impenetrable: "virgin and warrior; disdainful of men."[64] While Séverine is an unwilling and traumatized accomplice in the murder of her former guardian and abuser, Grandmorin, Flore's single-minded jealous passion gives birth to devastation, when her attempt to kill Jacques and Séverine leads to the derailment of a train and the death of many of its passengers. And, significantly, Zola has her die of her own volition after the mass murder, walking into the path of the oncoming train, like a warrior walking into battle: "She needed to walk right to the end, to die upright, guided by the instinct of a virgin warrior."[65]

The supposition of binary sex and gender difference determines the position one occupies in regard to desire in the master-slave paradigm of heterosexuality. In *La Bête humaine*, however, the binary difference in question is no longer simply the division and assumed complementarity between (aggressive) male and (passive) female, but that between destructive agency and passive victimhood. The fact that these are, in social reality, most often—and programmatically—mapped directly onto masculinity and femininity, and thence onto maleness and femaleness, is undeniable, but the text allows for a moment of doubt about the inevitability of this. The logic of desire in *La Bête humaine*, in which active sexual desire equates with the desire for death, results in an elaborate analogy of same- and hetero-desire, where the desired quality in the other is

not sex or gender but a position around destruction or victimhood: being "doer" or "done-to." Flore's desire for Jacques, who like herself is
an agent of death, suggests a model of desire analogous to homosexuality, but—crucially—from which the privileged term of sex/gender is removed. (She does not desire another woman, but another murderer like
herself.) Jacques, in preferring, ultimately, the tempting victimhood of
Séverine as complement to his murderous assertiveness, metaphorizes
the heterosexual choice.

This game with agency and passivity is not quite proto-queer, as it
still retains a binary logic and a domination-subordination paradigm
that run parallel to heterosexuality. Writing of homosexuality in a letter
to Dr. Laupts, Zola recapitulates the notion of homosexuality as the soul
of one sex in the body of another that was popularized by Karl Ulrichs
(1825–1895). By formulating homosexuality as understood according to
heterosexual principles, Zola gives in to regressive stereotypes: "the ef-
feminate, delicate, cowardly man; the masculine, violent, hard-hearted
woman."[66] Using the masculine-encoded desire for destruction, rather
than biological sex, as the crucial identity category in the case of Flore
and Jacques frees up gender attributes from biological sex (whether "appropriately" or "inappropriately" assigned), making a more complex
picture of Zolian desire than Hamon allows for, and making the human
beast a matter of *masculine identification* rather than *male biology*. The
effect of this is that it emphasizes its cultural constructedness, rather
than its naturally occurring status, and therefore suggests that male murderousness is culturally produced (and avoidable?) rather than eternally
and essentially inevitable.

What Zola's novel does, by dint of its novelistic, and more specifically
its Naturalist qualities (since Naturalist novels sought to depict objec-
tively the whole of human life in its minutiae), is to make the perspective of pathological marginalized masculinity into a universal of masculinity. The value of the literary narrative is that it allows us to see where
the subject and object of theorization touch. Zola's theory of homicidal
masculinity echoes the alienists' language of the "perversion of the instinct" and delineates the degenerate, pathological individual described
by Krafft-Ebing for whom murder replaces penetration. Yet it also
echoes the anxious voice of the scientists musing on the potential weakness and destructivity of *all* male sexuality if moral restraint cannot hold
men in check. That is, it crisscrosses continuously between the individual and the social, the apparently aberrant exception and the apparently

universal, demonstrating how the one segues irresistibly into the other, and thereby allowing for a reading against the grain that shows up the fictitiousness of the division.

The Invention of the Twentieth-Century Serial Sex Killer: The Rippers Who Came After

If the high-profile case of Jack the Ripper consolidated Krafft-Ebing's construction of the lust murderer and inspired Zola to create his "human beast" in the nineteenth century, the specter of the Ripper did not disappear as one century turned into another. Rather, he has remained a cultural figure of folklore through which the contemporary serial sex killer can be read and understood. As Caputi puts it: "Succeeding sex killers are not only incessantly compared and even identified with Jack the Ripper, but now as then, fictional constructs are superimposed upon the events of modern serial murder."[67]

The "fictionalization" of real killers is of key relevance to the concerns of this book, as it is by identifying with archetypes and antecedents that subjectification occurs in the case of murderers (both for the public and for the murderer). One way in which this happens is through the process of naming. Serial killers are often attributed a colorful moniker while at large, in the tradition of "Jack the Ripper" (who is again paradigmatic here as he remained perpetually at large, such that his nickname and all it conveyed trumped any revelation of identity). While some of these names are creations of the press, such as the derivative "Yorkshire Ripper" or "Boston Strangler," others are produced by the killer himself and included in letters written to the news or the police — as was the case with the founding father, "Jack." It has even been argued that, were it not for the catchy name and the wide press he received, the Whitechapel murderer might have been forgotten after his crime spree came to an end.[68]

The trope of the killer who writes witty or taunting letters to the press is often assumed to originate with the Ripper, even though a precedent is found in the case of Lacenaire, whose open letters were printed in the Paris press (though these came after, not prior to, arrest). The common critical tendency to assume Jack was the first murderer to write to the press is, perhaps, a symptom of the Anglophone-centrism of much writing on murder. That said, the Ripper correspondence is intriguing in that, although its authenticity remains in question (an issue hotly debated among "Ripperologists"), this does not in any way diminish the effect or influence it has undoubtedly had. Moreover, the whole question of authenticity of authorship is relatively unimportant here, since our focus is on the way in which myths of subjectivity are built. What is of especial interest, however, is that, given that some 128 pieces of Ripper correspondence were received by press and police, it is reasonable to assume that at least some of them were written by "ordinary" people who identified, aspirationally, with Jack the Ripper. The line between the killer and the "ordinary" citizen is again blurred here, since the desire to occupy the subject position of killer suggests the very potency and availability of that role in the cultural imaginary. The following, most commonly quoted letter, sent to the Central News Agency, on 18 September 1888, was the first to use the name "Jack the Ripper":

Dear Boss,

I keep on hearing the police have caught me but they wont fix me just yet. I have laughed when they look so clever and talk about being on the right track. The joke about Leather Apron gave me real fits.

I am down on whores and I shan't quit ripping them until I do get buckled. Grand work, the last job was. I gave the lady no time to squeal. How can they catch me now? I love my work and want to start again. You will soon hear of me and my funny little games.

I saved some of the proper red stuff in a ginger beer bottle over the last job, to write with, but it went thick like glue and I can't use it. Red ink is fit enough I hope. Ha! Ha!

The next job I do I shall clip the lady's ears off and send to the police, just for jolly, wouldn't you? Keep this letter back till I do a bit more work, then give it out straight. My knife's so nice and sharp, I want to get to work right away if I get a chance. Good Luck.

Yours truly

Jack the Ripper

> Don't mind me giving the trade name. Wasn't good enough to post this be-
> fore I got all the red ink off my hands; curse it. No luck yet. They say I'm a
> doctor now. Ha! Ha![69]

The letter gives a sense of the "personality" that the public would go on
to associate with the killer: brash, dry, teasing; in short, "a stylish, like-
able rogue,"[70] obscuring the horror and misogyny of his crimes. Moreover, the direct appeal to the readership to identify with the intention
to clip off the ears of the next victim— "wouldn't you?"—implicates
the (implicitly male) reader in the "funny little games," suggesting that
"Jack" is the active representative in the field of murder on behalf of all
those armchair enthusiasts who support, desire, and approve of his actions, but don't dare do likewise.

That the phenomenon of the Ripper letters inaugurated a tradition
among murderers and their public is beyond question. In 1977, in New
York City, David Berkowitz shot a number of young women walking in
the street or seated in parked cars. Berkowitz styled himself the "Son of
Sam" ("Sam" being a paranoid projection of the devil who was allegedly
ordering him to kill) in letters to both police and newspapers. Like the
Ripper in the letter cited above, Berkowitz uses his correspondence to
announce more crimes to come: "Don't think that because you haven't
heard from me for a while that I went to sleep. No, rather, I am still here,
like a spirit roaming the night. Thirsty, hungry, seldom stopping to rest.
Anxious to please Sam."[71] Extracts of Berkowitz's letters were published
in the *Daily News*, resulting in record sales. Then mayor of New York,
Abraham Beame, commented:

> Son of Sam. I even liked the name and that in itself was terrifying. I knew it
> would stick . . . would become his trademark. There had been six attacks, all
> laid at the feet of a single individual, and you could see it all building.[72]

The power of a name—of the assertion of identity—is certainly conveyed
by these examples.

In the case of the Yorkshire Ripper, active in the 1970s and '80s in
England, a cassette tape sent to the police, allegedly from the killer, was
found to be a hoax, produced not by Peter Sutcliffe, but by a wishful pre-
tender who called himself "Jack" after the press's naming of Sutcliffe as
a "Ripper." The tape announced, much in the style of the original Jack

and of Berkowitz: "I'm Jack. I see you are still having no chance catching me. . . . I'm not sure when I will strike again, but it will definitely be some time this year, maybe September or October—even sooner if I get the chance."[73] Three letters claiming to be from the Yorkshire Ripper were also received. The police took the decision to have the tape played on air in regular news broadcasts, and made a recording of it permanently available by calling a telephone number. It is estimated that 40,000 people per day called the number to listen to the "Ripper's" voice.[74] Samples of the letter-writer's handwriting were also published in the newspapers, with requests that readers should inform the authorities if they recognized the voice or hand. The confusion to which this led considerably delayed the progress of the police investigation, but it also had the effect, as Caputi has described it, of insinuating the Ripper "into every atmosphere,"[75] facilitating "fantasy identification with a Ripper."[76]

Perhaps most disturbingly, and offering the most persuasive corroboration of those theories that hold that a murderer-worshipping culture is a misogynistic one, is the following anecdote told by Cameron and Frazer: "In Leeds, football crowds adopted 'Jack' [the still-at-large Yorkshire Ripper] as a folk hero and chanted at one stage 'Ripper eleven, police nil.'"[77] This demonstrates persuasively that those dis-identifying with—seeing as worthless—the (female, mainly prostitute) victims of crime, and identifying instead with the masculine killer, cannot simply be dismissed as a rare few who could be properly termed "outsiders," eccentrics, the exception to, rather than the rule of, the cultural norm. Rather, such phenomena lend weight to Caputi's argument that "the myth of the Ripper—from its very beginnings—was a *collective* male invention,"[78] a myth of exceptional individuality with which all could identify. Furthermore, with regard to the Ripper case, it is striking that the lionization of the killer and disregard felt for the victims expressed by the Leeds football crowd finds an echo in a statement made by West Yorkshire's acting chief constable, Jim Hobson, writing of the fact that Sutcliffe's latest victim, 16-year-old Jayne McDonald, was not, like his earlier targets, a prostitute:

> He has made it clear that he continues to hate prostitutes. Many people do. We, as a police force will continue to arrest prostitutes. But the Ripper is now killing innocent girls. That indicates your mental state and that you are in urgent need of medical attention. You have made your point. Give yourself up before another innocent woman dies.[79]

In stating that it is normal and acceptable to "hate prostitutes," in implying that the public and police themselves share the killer's view in this regard, we see another disturbing, misogynistic echo of the case that gave Sutcliffe his pseudonym. Just as Jack the Ripper (and his culture) were "down on whores," so, for Peter Sutcliffe, the self-styled "Street-cleaner" (and his culture): "the women I killed were filth, bastard prostitutes who were just standing round littering the streets. I was just cleaning the place up a bit."[80]

The flip side of the lionization of the sex killer as a folk hero is, of course, the hypocritically moralistic tendency in the media to dub him a "monster" or "beast," discourses that persist since the nineteenth-century application of them to Jack, likening him to the vampires and other Gothic horrors that titillated the Victorian imagination, and which also appear, as we have seen, in the scientific writings of Nordau and Krafft-Ebing. This delineation of the killer as beast is not dissimilar in function to the naming of him as a hero. It serves, again, to mark him as different from other men, as an exception not a symptom, and to deliver the mawkish disapproval that is the flip side of titillation. "Sex-beast" is a staple of the Anglophone tabloid lexicon and the public readily adopts such othering, mythologizing discourses. Jayne McDonald's mother announced to Sutcliffe on television: "I think you are the devil himself. You are a coward. You are not a man. You are a beast."[81] And, in turn, Sutcliffe himself, assuming subjectification as a killer in the terms of available discourse, said of the voices in his head: "They are all in my brain, reminding me of the beast I am. Just thinking of them all reminds me of what a monster I am."[82] The language for making the killer other than human—a beast, a monster—belongs to, saturates, shapes, and has meaning for the culture as a whole, including murderers themselves.

Another way in which the influence of the Jack the Ripper case contributes to the discursive construction of later murderers is in their explicit familiarity—and identification—with the archetypal figure and the minutiae of his crimes. Peter Kürten, the "Düsseldorf Vampire," who killed at least 9 and possibly as many as 60 people of all ages and sexes, between 1913 and 1929, was one of a disproportionately large number of sex murderers active in Weimar Germany.[83] He produced extensive confessions which were written up by Dr. Karl Berg in 1931. Kürten was a sadist who, like Vincent Verzeni cited earlier, found strangling a victim to be a great source of sexual pleasure in itself (and sometimes stopped short of outright killing if he achieved sexual satisfaction before the vic-

tim was fatally asphyxiated). He also, like Zola's fictional "Flore," enjoyed witnessing train crashes and derailments, and bloody accidents
of all kinds. Kürten has made the following statement: "I did myself a
great deal of damage through reading blood-and-thunder stories. For
example, I read the tale of Jack the Ripper several times."[84] While we
might be cautious about assuming the straightforwardly imitative nature
of Kürten's crimes (the theory of moral contagion), what is suggestively
hinted at here is that his identification with the Ripper gave Kürten a
way of understanding his subjectivity as a lust murderer. This identification then led to active self-stylization: Kürten, like "Jack," wrote letters
to the press, acting knowingly in the style of his hero and, in his confessions to his therapist, was able to acknowledge consciously the influence
"Jack" had had on him.

Ordinary, Decent Men?

My gender-aware readings of discourses of the figure of the lust murderer
exemplified by Jack the Ripper in this chapter are influenced largely by
Cameron and Frazer's conclusion that misogyny alone does not account
for sexual murder, rather than by Caputi's more radical view that all sex
murder is "gynocide." As Cameron and Frazer point out, men kill boys
and men for sexual kicks too. Rather than focusing on women as the
sole victims of sex killers, it is helpful to focus on the gender of the murderer and recognize that "the common denominator [in lust murders]
is a shared construction of masculine sexuality, or even more broadly,
masculinity,"[85] which accounts, perhaps, for the fact that it is overwhelmingly men who kill in this particular way. For it is men, not women, who
are commonly culturally encouraged to identify as transcendental, agentic subjects, and to find heroism in an idea of freedom enacted at the expense of an "other" (often a female other). In the rare cases in which
a sadistic sex killer has been revealed to be female, English murderers Myra Hindley and Rosemary West (both of whom acted in tandem
with a male partner) being the two obvious examples, public condemnation wholly replaces the jokey, hero-worshipping discourses provoked by
cases of male Rippers who kill women. And, even more than the unadulterated hostility that accrued to Hindley and West as women involved in
the killing of children and young women, American serial killer Aileen

Wuornos, whose victims were solely men, was so vilified as to have rendered her execution an imperative, as will be discussed in chapter 6.

In the first section of this chapter, it was noted that foundational sexological discourse tends to exaggerate the stereotypical characteristics of "ordinary" masculinity and femininity, and to insist that these are "naturally" present in biological males and females. Also noted was the tendency to make women both the gatekeepers of male sexuality within marriage (as their supposed weaker sexual desire fits them to such a role) and the agents of their own destruction, in Krafft-Ebing's extraordinary statement that women are too naturally shy to lust murder and that their passivity therefore spurs men on to do it to them instead. (This is an idea encapsulated in the memorable episode in *La Bête humaine* in which Séverine submissively bares her throat to her lover—who just happens to be an inborn lust murderer.) It becomes clear that the creation of the categories of, for example, nymphomania or masochism in the female and sadism and lust murder in the male reveal more about the gender ideologies of the culture that produces the subjects diagnosed with them than about the so-called conditions themselves. Equally, however, it is less often noted that analyzing the ideology behind taxonomies of perversion, which locate antisocial acts and desires in an exceptional aberration, can contribute in turn to our understanding of the cultural ideologies governing expectations of "ordinary" masculinity and femininity.

We have seen how destructivity is related to sexual instinct and to maleness in the scientific discourses of the mid- to late nineteenth century. Sexual murder is understood as the reproductive instinct gone awry, the desire for intercourse replaced by the desire to kill, and is attributed to the pathological figure of the lust murderer, a subject who, in the personage of Jack the Ripper, came to center stage at the moment of burgeoning modernity. The popularity of Jack the Ripper—his capacity to give rise to fictional "sons," such as Jacques Lantier, and to influence the understanding of murderers who came after him, such as Kürten, Berkowitz, and Sutcliffe—can be understood as having had a paradoxical, at once sensationalizing and normalizing, effect on the understanding of lust murder. As Caputi has relentlessly catalogued, sex crime is everywhere. It is the titillating subject matter of crime fiction, television, film, men's magazines; naturalized and banalized in our culture as "entertainment." Yet owing to the persistence of traces of Jack's extravagant, Gothic persona that continues to accrue to representations of actual sex killers with their fanciful nomenclatures and media celebrity personae, these subjects are rendered exotic, exceptional, and different from "ordinary" men. Such mechanisms serve to obscure a clear assessment of the contemporary condition of masculinity and to prevent the understanding that casual cultural misogyny and sadistic male violence are not radically separate, but lie on a continuum: that, to recycle Cameron and Frazer's pun, the assumption of an absolute qualitative difference between "Jack the Ripper" and "Jack the Lad" is an ideological sleight of hand.[86]

PART TWO

The Twentieth-Century
Anglo-American Killer

CHAPTER FOUR

"Infanticidal" Femininity

Myra Hindley

Sooner murder an infant in its cradle than nurse unacted desires.
—(William Blake, "Proverbs of Hell," *The Marriage of Heaven and Hell*, 1790–1793)

I couldn't believe how exciting it would feel to do something really bad, how free you can feel when all is lost.
—(Myra Hindley, conversation with prison therapist, cited in Carol Ann Lee, *One of Your Own*)

Poor Myra. Life means life for Myra. For others it means just a few years. When they call her a beast or a devil, they don't know what they're talking about. They don't know her. She's still my daughter.
—(Nellie Hindley, Myra's mother, "My Myra Should Die in Prison," *The Sun*, 20 June 1985)

As early as 1748, materialist philosopher Julien Offray de La Met-trie wrote in his treatise *Man a Machine* (*Homme-machine*) that women who kill children should not be executed like other criminals, but rather should be examined by judges, who should ideally be "excellent physicians besides," so utterly incomprehensible and aberrant are this particular crime and the woman who commits it.[1] Despite the radicality of his thesis for its time (the blasphemous proposition that human beings are not possessed of an immortal soul, but instead are complex machines), the view of maternal instinct as natural, and the idea that women are subject to different emotions and ethics than the default human beings (men), are all too familiar tropes, recognizable from a long history of textbooks of patriarchy that both pre- and postdate La Mettrie.

When, in 1966, the so-called Moors Murderers, Myra Hindley (1942–2002) and her partner Ian Brady (1938–), were tried for the killing of three children, 12-year-old John Kilbride, 10-year-old Lesley Ann Downey, and 17-year-old Edward Evans,[2] in a working-class area of the North of England, the discourse that surrounded Hindley echoed La Mettrie's intimations of extraordinary aberration, even though Hindley was not a technical infanticide (a woman who kills her own child). But far from echoing his call for treatment rather than punishment, the press dubbed Hindley "The Most Evil Woman in Britain,"[3] and reserved for her a retributive hatred that far outstripped, and has long outlasted, that directed against Brady (or other male child-killers), even though Brady was almost certainly the brutal assailant in each case.[4] Many commentators were chagrined that Hindley came to trial just months after the implementation of an act suspending capital punishment in the UK.[5] Myra's aiding and abetting of the murders and lack of pity for the child victims were considered worst crimes—or, more accurately, more unnatural things—than the male-perpetrated violence. For, as we have seen in the commentary upon the case of Lafarge, gender role transgression constitutes an extra cause for condemnation in the case of the murderous woman. I have called this chapter "'Infanticidal' Femininity" in recognition of the fact that all women, whether technically mothers or not, are symbolically charged in this culture with maternity, with the burden of *caring for children*, and that dereliction of this duty carries a heavy penalty.

In their modus operandi, Hindley and Brady differ somewhat from the murderers discussed thus far in this book, insofar as they killed together, as a pair, rather than alone, problematizing the popular stereotype and "official" view of the serial killer as an exceptional, lone individual. (Fred and Rosemary West would, in 1995, provide another example of a much-hated heterosexual killing couple in Britain.) Too, they are far from being the first couple to have planned and executed killings together. Brady, in particular, was fascinated by the 1924 Leopold and Loeb murder case, and his ambition of committing a perfect crime, a "pure act," issues from his study of that widely represented case, which itself draws on the nineteenth-century fantasy of the acte gratuit, explored in the introduction.[6] The dream of exceptionality—here a *shared* exceptionality—is central to the self-representation of Brady and Hindley, who viewed themselves as social outsiders and outlaws at the time of their crimes. It is thought they considered themselves fortunate that, like Leopold and Loeb, each had found a partner who fitted the other's criminal and emotional needs "like pieces of a jigsaw puzzle."[7] This said, there has also been some contrary evidence and speculation that Hindley may have been psychologically controlled by, and emotionally in thrall to, the dominant partner, Brady.

My interest is not, however, in attempting to mitigate Hindley's guilt because of her own potential victimhood at Brady's hands (an agenda that has been pursued elsewhere by those who tirelessly and fruitlessly campaigned for her release from prison in the 1980s and '90s).[8] As in all the case studies in this book, my interest in Myra Hindley lies in examining how what is said and written about murderers as aberrant subjects is an index of socially constructed perceptions of (gendered) normality and abnormality, how subtle normative prescriptions and proscriptions about acceptable subjectivity and agency are embedded in this discourse that purports to be *only* about the immoral minority, the exception par excellence (attempting to negate the truism that exceptions can only exist in relation to the rule in the first place). What is inescapable is that the reaction to Myra Hindley bespeaks society's attitude to women in general; hence the first part of this chapter will be devoted to a discussion of the specifically gendered rhetoric about this murderer at the time of her arrest and trial.

Also of particular import in the case of Hindley (and Brady) is the role played by social class in defining subjectivity, social agency, and criminal transgression. The case provided a catalyst for conservative warnings regarding the repercussions of the "permissive" or "swinging" society,[9] and the dangers of allowing members of the uneducated but upwardly mobile classes access to literary material such as that found at Hindley and Brady's home (including Sade's *Justine* and Hitler's *Mein Kampf*). The second half of the chapter will examine in detail these debates about social class and access to morally corrupting materials (that echo, strikingly, nineteenth-century public hygiene discourses about contagion and debates about the dangers of "immoral literature" that have been discussed in previous chapters). Finally, in a third part, the chapter will explore the afterlife of the case and Myra Hindley's enduring role throughout her long prison sentence as a peerless public hate figure, which will give insights into the cultural perception of evil and the ways in which this abstract idea from moral philosophy maps onto sexed and sexual transgression in the modern age.

Femininity, Nature, and Normality

I am by no means the first writer to draw attention to the unusual degree
of negative emotion that Myra Hindley attracted at the time of her trial
and that her name is still capable—almost a decade after her death—of
conjuring among the British public, nor the first to suggest that the reason for this is rooted in her sex. In a chapter of her book, *Moving Targets*, Helen Birch poses the rhetorical question: "Why, more than any
other British criminal [of the twentieth] century, has Myra Hindley been
singled out for vilification?" She then, immediately, supplies the answer:
"her gender."[10] "There is," Birch goes on, "an implicit assumption that
for a woman to be involved in killing children is somehow worse . . .
than it is for a man."[11] The ideological ground on which such a belief
can be built is the societal assertion of the intrinsic moral and emotional
differences between men and women, differences that have, over time,
mapped on to and determined cultural roles, professions, duties, and re-
sponsibilities. For it to be particularly shocking for a woman to be revealed as callous in this way, the belief in, and expectation of, women's
"sweetness," altruism, and mothering instincts as ontological truths must
be deeply ingrained.

Indeed, it is telling of the attitudes of the times in which Myra Hindley was tried that the jury at her trial consisted entirely of men, the four
women who had been called to serve having been challenged and dismissed by Hooson (Brady's defending counsel) and Heilpern (Hindley's
defending counsel).[12] The law presupposes a rational subject that it requires its jurors to embody. Feminist lawyers and criminologists have
suggested that the very assumption of the existence of a universal subject of reason reveals a masculinist bias in law, given that women have
historically been excluded from male philosophy's definition (or wishful
imaginative construction) of perfect rationality.[13] In her highly problematical book about the Moors Murderers' court case, *On Iniquity* (1967),
which I shall discuss at length in what follows, playwright and essayist
Pamela Hansford Johnson writes:

> All the jurors were male, four women having been rejected. My husband said
> to me: "perhaps a poor comment on the views held by the defense about the
> sensibilities of men." Yet I myself think, somewhat against my own principles,

that three weeks of the horror ahead might have been a greater strain than many women could have contemplated.[14]

The value promoted here is that of a paternalistic protectiveness—a key feature of Hanson Johnson's book. Women, like the children that Myra Hindley helped to kill, are a class of person whom (male) society must keep safe, just as the working classes must be kept safe from inflammatory material. That the generation-on-generation insulation of adult women from social realities helps to keep women infantilized, and that the resulting forced innocence is then interpreted as female "nature," is not admitted of in these kinds of discourses. Instead, women are suspected to be less capable of coping rationally with the details of a brutal murder trial (especially one involving cruelty to children) by dint of their constitution, rather than by dint of lifelong training and cultural expectation. This is a self-fulfilling prophecy not recognized as such. The discourse that led to the prejudicial removal of the female jurors here is simply a different facet of the discourse that is widely applied to Hindley, explaining the shock and awe that she provokes: a woman who does not signify within the terms in which "woman" is constructed. Her transgression of the cultural imperative of female nurturing is accorded sufficient import that she becomes uniquely *exceptional among women* in the discourses that proliferate about her.

Of the many published accounts of the case, one of the most imaginative (and most vilified by Hindley and Brady)[15] is Emlyn Williams's *Beyond Belief* (1967). This semifictional/semibiographical work, an exemplum of a literary genre of New Journalism–inspired true-crime writing inaugurated by Truman Capote with *In Cold Blood* (1966), seeks to explore the societal pressures and conditions that led Brady and Hindley to commit their crimes. Williams crafts, via internal monologues, the inner worlds of Hindley and Brady as a way of trying to understand their motivations. He describes the conditions in which Myra grew up: a child who lived primarily at the house of her doting grandmother, with her mother, father, and sister Maureen living just a short walk away in a neighboring street. Williams refutes the assertions by other commentators that Myra's parents' decision to let her live with her grandmother, as the old lady desired, signified a childhood instance of rejection and instability. Instead, he makes much of the comforts of Myra's upbringing and the absence of "normal" expectations placed upon the growing girl:

While Nellie [Myra's mother] would have seen to it that her daughter learned to sew and cook like any other girl, little Myra sat back waited on by a doting old woman whom she took for granted and later despised.[16]

The assumption implicit in this passage is a strikingly gender-biased one. In not requiring Myra to carry out tasks that would never have been expected of the growing Brady, the doting grandmother is implicitly given responsibility here for having primed little Myra for her future role as an aberrant woman. Helen Birch has described the social climate in which Hindley grew up, the late 1940s and '50s in Northern Britain, as a particularly oppressive and conformity-demanding environment for women. Borrowing from Elizabeth Wilson's *Only Halfway to Paradise*, she suggests that the socially conservative values embedded in the new postwar welfare state led to an increasingly zealous policing of appropriate female behavior, strict delineation of what constituted "normal" and "correct" female sexuality, and an intensified burden placed on women to maintain, via their maternal and caregiving roles, marriage and the nuclear family as the primary units and cornerstones of society.[17]

This expectation is described also by Emlyn Williams, who reflects upon the options available to a young Myra, 18 years old and about to begin her job as a junior typist at Millwards, the chemical merchants where she would meet stock-clerk Ian Brady. Williams comments:

She was, at that moment, in a state of abeyance. As unconscious as an empty goblet waiting to be filled to the brim, whether the poison is to be harmless wine or arsenic. If . . . she had grown to take pride in her position as the wife of a successful man, and had become determined to share in that success, she would have exercised every ounce of her will-power to bring her character into line with his. She might not have been the most popular wife in their set, other women might have found her disconcerting, but her children would have helped.[18]

A young woman—any young woman—is a tabula rasa in this discourse, waiting to be written on by the man who will shape her destiny. The metaphor Williams chooses of a vessel "waiting to be filled" is surely pointedly sexual, suggesting the means by which the man will do the shaping: sexual penetration leading to impregnation. This half-life of achievement-by-proxy, then, is the woman's lot, her permitted options woefully limited in ambition and range. Williams permits himself no comment on the iniquity (to use Hansford Johnson's preferred term in its other meaning of "gross injustice") entailed in the narrowness of socially available trajectories he imagines for Myra Hindley, compared to what he hypothesizes Ian Brady might have achieved if he had not followed his criminal course. (Football star is one missed opportunity he imagines for young Ian, a fate relegated forevermore to a parallel universe when he flinched away from an oncoming ball in a key game.)[19]

Perhaps inevitably, Myra, *even as the most aberrant of women*, has been seen by many commentators to have reproduced in her unorthodox relationship with Brady the accepted gender roles within the heteronormative couple described by Williams above. Myra became Ian's driver, gunwoman, messenger, and procurer in the course of their criminal alliance. He was the ingenious plotter, the one with a personal vision: a philosophy of crime (heavily borrowed from the Marquis de Sade). Her role in the relationship, then, is characterized, at least by Williams, by the same function of proxy that the "average" wife plays, living every achievement (however bizarre those "achievements" may be in the case of this couple) through her association with a fully realized social subject: a man.

And indeed, Brady's and Hindley's testimonies in court conspire to suggest that he was the dominant partner in all respects in the relationship.[20] Hindley's defense counsel put the following to Brady:

> In general, Mr Brady, supposing that you and she were having a discussion about going anywhere or doing anything, and you had different views about it, whose view would prevail? —Mine.
> Why? —Because she was my typist in the office. I dictated to her in the office and this tended to wrap over.[21]

And in Hooson's questions to Hindley:

> Did Ian ever persuade you in any way to do things that you did not want to do? —He asked me to do some things, and if I objected, we argued, and I would do them eventually and go along with them.
> Miss Hindley, why? —Because I just did.
> Can you help us with the reason? —I cannot. (JG, p. 221).

The careful construction of the Brady-Hindley couple here apes the unchallenged gender politics of the hetero-norm, even as both partners

claimed to despise the form conventional heterosexuality took, reject-
ing the institutions of marriage, parenthood, and the family sold to them
as ideals by their society. Maureen, Myra's sister, testified in court how
Myra had "changed." Having once been a reliable and eager babysitter,
as well as a Catholic churchgoer, Myra, following the start of her relationship with Ian, claimed that "she didn't believe in marriage. She said
she hated babies and children and hated people" (JG, p. 69). Indeed, an
entry in Myra's diary from January 1962 corroborates Maureen's story
of a change of heart. Prior to the consummation of her relationship with
Brady, Myra writes, conventionally enough: "I have been at Millwards
for twelve months and only just gone with him. I hope Ian and I love each
other all our lives and get married and are happy ever after."[22] Neither
marriage nor motherhood issued from the coupling, however, and Hindley's willful barrenness as well as her murder of children constitutes an
affront to the expected role—the *very point*—of women in society.

At trial Mr. Hooson was keen to emphasize to the jury that they must
set aside their instinctive emotional responses to the crimes to be described: "It is terribly important that you dispose from your minds all
the natural revulsion one has in reading or hearing evidence connected
with the death of children" (JG, p. 162). However, the way in which
Brady and Hindley were questioned by the police and cross-examined
in court about their crimes makes it clear that they were expected, as
a man and a woman, to have different reactions to, and levels of toler-
ance for, violence and cruelty toward the young. The most emotive piece
of evidence to appear in the trial was a recording made by Ian Brady,
while preparing to take pornographic photographs of 10-year-old Lesley
Ann Downey. Hindley is heard to tell Lesley, in an attempt to stop her
screaming, to "shut up or I'll forget myself and hit you one" (JG, p. 114).
The pathetic and harrowing nature of the exchange is intensified by Lesley's repeated appeals to "Mum." It is unclear whether she is addressing
her absent mother or appealing to Myra for mercy as a surrogate "mum."
When questioned in police custody about this, Hindley revealed apparent remorse and shame for her involvement in the incident, but stuck to
the story that she and Ian did not kill Lesley; they merely photographed
her and then let her leave unharmed with two men in a van:

> Mr Benfield then played the tape recording of the voices of the two accused
> and Lesley Ann Downey. Hindley was sitting with her head bowed, and she
> started sobbing and a pulse at the left side of her throat was pulsating rapidly.

When the recording was finished, Mr Benfield said: "Did you hear that recording?" She nodded her head and in a very quiet voice said: "I'm ashamed." She then commenced to cry. This lasted a very short time and then she said: "I'm saying nothing." (JG, p. 138)

When Brady is being examined in court, his attitude toward children is not particularly thoroughly interrogated. "Mr Tyrrell said: 'Are you fond of children?' Brady said: 'I like children. I never thought of it'" (JG, p.159). Myra, on the other hand, is forced by the attorney general to account at length for her failure to conform specifically to the expectations of "maternal instinct" that govern what a woman should feel and do:

> The screams of a little girl of ten—*of your sex, madam*. Did you put your hands over your ears when you heard the screams of Lesley Ann Downey? —No.
> Why not? —I wanted her to be quiet.
> Or get the child out of the room and see that she was treated *as a woman should treat a female child, or any other child?* —I should have done, but I didn't. I have no defense for that.
> No defense? —It was indefensible. I was cruel. (JG, pp. 223–224, italics mine)

And, knowing Myra's passionate fondness for dogs, the attorney general accuses her pointedly, in connection with the words heard on the tape, "I'll forget myself and hit you one": "You would have hit her more readily than hitting a dog?" (JG, p. 234), a point that Hindley can hardly do otherwise but deny in the circumstances. It should be clear that my point here is, of course, not to suggest that Myra Hindley's crime—that of terrorizing a small child, assisting in the making of pornographic pictures of her, and then murdering her—is anything other than terrible. However, I wish to highlight the ideology underlying the fact that the crime is made to assume proportions of even greater magnitude because, in the course of it, Hindley transgressed not only morality, compassion, and the law but also the unwritten but powerful and binding social rule of what it is *supposed to mean* to be *a woman*. That this is not identical with what it is supposed to mean to be an adult *person* is the problem here. The ascription of the female sex role brings with it both limitations on freedom, opportunity, and autonomy, as we have seen, and extra expectations of specifically "feminine virtues": caregiving, compassion, and selflessness. The case of Myra Hindley posed a devastating challenge to the dearly held cultural myth that all women instinctively love and seek to protect children. Yet, since that myth is not allowed to be shattered, Myra's monstrousness must instead be asserted.

Further corroborating my point regarding the gender-specific treatment of Hindley and Brady at the trial, it is striking that Myra's appearance was as much the subject of intense media scrutiny as her behavior. As I have explored in the first half of this book, the physical appearance of the murderer of both sexes has long been assumed to be capable of reflecting his or her "nature," and we have seen that surprise and consternation ensued in the cases of both Lacenaire and Lafarge when their appearance was revealed to be at odds with their acts. However, in a society in which (to use an expression from feminist film theory) women connote "to-be-looked-at-ness,"[23] and in which women's appearance is always closely policed, the assumption of the appearance-nature symbiosis is markedly intensified in the case of female criminals and its stakes are higher.

It is by no means the exclusive province of men to measure women's appearance and behavior against gender norms. Carol Ann Lee notes, for example, that women far outstripped men as members of the public gallery at the trial, and that all of the women wanted "to get their hands on" Hindley, rather than on Brady.[24] Pamela Hansford Johnson makes much of the effect Myra had on those present in court: Ian Brady "looks ordinary," she writes. "Myra Hindley does not." In an attempt to describe this extraordinariness to her readers, Hansford Johnson goes on:

> Sturdy in build and broad buttocked, though her face, hands and feet appear to be narrow and delicate, she could have served a nineteenth-century painter as a model for Clytemnestra; but sometimes she looks more terrible, like one of Fuseli's nightmare women drawn giant-size, elaborately coiffed, with curled and plaited maid servants reaching no higher than her knees.[25]

And, later, she describes "the Medusa face of Hindley, under the melon puff-ball of hair."[26] The writer draws here on the imagery of myth and of teratology. She effectively dehumanizes, by further mythologizing, Myra Hindley, suturing together what she perceives her appearance to suggest with what we know of her crimes and the cultural/moral meanings they bear. Birch points out that blondeness, at the time, would have most readily connoted the femme fatale of film noir whose dual appeal and threat lie in her being unknowable, inscrutable—which chimes perfectly with the perceived nature of a female child-killer.[27]

Every detail of the murderess's appearance is fair game for Hansford Johnson: her hairstyle, "a huge puff-ball" is "far too massive for the wedge-shaped face; in itself it bears an uneasy suggestion of fetichism [*sic*]."[28] And "in the dock she has a great strangeness, and the kind of authority one might expect to find in a woman guard of a concentration camp."[29] However, what is—strikingly—missing here is any acknowledgment of the fact that Myra Hindley styled herself in such a way as to satisfy a range of cultural expectations of femininity and, no doubt, fantasies shaped by her intrasubjective imaginary world with Ian Brady. In fact, Hansford Johnson's analogy with the concentration camp guard is accurate: Brady nicknamed Hindley "Hess" or "Hessie," playing on the names of the celebrated pianist who shared Hindley's first name, Myra Hess, and Hitler's lieutenant, Rudolph Hess. The moniker also recalled infamous Nazi concentration camp guard Irma Grese, a photograph of whom Myra kept in her purse. Thus, Myra's appearance reflected her carefully constructed "self," a masquerade of the debased cultural ideals to which she and Ian aspired, but it did *not* emanate eerily and in socially unmediated fashion from a dark essence of evil within her, as Hansford Johnson would fancifully have it.

And, in describing the strange effect that the couple had on the press and public in court, the playwright is keen to assert that the otherworldliness they possessed was particularly strong in the case of the woman: Ian looked somehow "real"; Myra did not: "They looked real enough, *or Brady did*: but because we knew what they had done, somehow they were not."[30] Corroborating the idea of Myra as a personification of monstrous evil, Robert Spiers, the policeman who found Lesley Ann Downey's body in its shallow grave on Saddleworth Moor, comments on his day in court: "It was the first time I saw Brady and Hindley and they were truly faces of evil. All the goody-two-shoes who complained later that the mugshot of Myra was the only photo ever shown, it was nonsense. That was how she looked."[31] The infamous mug shot of Myra Hindley (fig. 1) to which Spiers alludes has been the source of much discussion of Myra's visible evil.

Here, for contrast, is Myra Hindley's version of the moment her mug shot was made, taken from the notes for her unpublished autobiography, written in prison, and commented on by her biographer, Carol Ann Lee:

FIGURE I. Myra Hindley's infamous mug shot. Photographer: Keystone; Hulton Archive/ Getty Images.

I was tired and frightened. When we left the [interview] room, they led me down what seemed like endless flights of stone stairs, dimly lit with 60W bulbs. I thought I was being taken to a dungeon somewhere. Then we came to some doors and a policeman kicked one of them open. I immediately thought they were going to interrogate me so I clenched my teeth, hard.[32]

Lee goes on, "the photographer told her where to stand, then draped a black cloth over his head and adjusted the focus of the lens. The lights flashed and an image of unparalleled British female notoriety was made."[33] Similarly, this is how Myra describes her famously "hard" appearance during police interviews and in court: "[I] took refuge behind the mists that swirled in my mind . . . my instinctive reaction to escape the unbearable reality was construed as arrogance and hard defiance."[34] Justifiably outraged by the murders that had been committed, those present found it easier in dealing with the traumatic details of the case to assume that the criminal was pure evil and never to admit of the potentially traumatized state of the accused herself—much less to consider that her appearance should be an irrelevance in adjudicating as to her guilt or innocence. For, as we have noted, and as Lee remarks, in the case of female criminals, "their appearance is regarded as uniquely relevant to their deeds."[35] What also went unspoken was the class prejudice that jostled for space with culturally acceptable misogyny at the "trial of the century."

Class and Control

As Josephine McDonagh has written in her history of child murder in Britain: "Discussions of child murder frequently seeped into debates on other issues, often providing a test case through which society examined its own values."[36] This is particularly true of the Moors Murders case, which came to stand in for conservative fears about the permissive society and the threat to traditional values in the 1960s. During the trial, the fact that 50 books on Nazism, torture, and pornography, including writings by the Marquis de Sade, had been found in the killers' house, was used not only to corroborate Hindley and Brady's guilt, but to fuel wider fears about the effects of looser morals on aspirant, socially mobile, young working-class people in the "swinging" 1960s.

The mistress of this discourse, Hansford Johnson, writes: "It seemed to some of us that April that we were seeing the results of total permis-

siveness in a rather comely young man and woman, ill-educated but neither of them stupid, on trial at Chester Assizes for multiple murder."[37]
The way in which commentators of the case discuss the murderers' backgrounds and educational achievements is extremely revealing—predominantly of the contemporaneous social biases and attitudes held by those
writers and by their culture. Emlyn Williams describes Myra Hindley's
roots in a way that says much about the accepted view of the relationship
between class, "ordinariness," and "exceptionality":

> She came of Lancashire working folk . . . —a class respected for its practi-
> cal humour and adjustment to hardship. If you went canvassing from door
> to door you would meet them in their hundreds: poor, respectable or trying
> to look respectable, nobody clever, nobody original, nobody sinister; a mul-
> titude of warily conventional human beings with a vocabulary just capable of
> communicating the small-talk of the day.[38]

For a serial sex murderer to emerge from this background of conventional banality seems hard to countenance for Williams, I would argue, because the idea of the murderer is still bound up with those exotic
discourses of either genius and exceptionality that issue from the nineteenth-century followers of Brady and Hindley's own master, Sade, or
with the idea of a degenerate beast. And while Brady's homeland—the
Gorbals in Glasgow—produces a regular population of *ordinary* petty
and not-so-petty criminals, these are far from the gentleman criminal
figure to which Brady aspired, a murderer who consciously envisaged
his crimes as "products of an existentialist philosophy."[39] And a murderess with a working-class Manchester accent is, somehow, assumed to
be more unreal, more of a mythical monster, than one with icy cut-glass
tones, which accounts, perhaps, for Williams's attempt to render local accent and dialect when writing dialogue between Myra and Ian, or evoking their inner thoughts. In a transcription of an imagined conversation
between Ian and Myra while driving through Gorton, we have "Myra"
responding in the following way to some unstated outré suggestion made
by Ian: "Well Massa Brady 'ow kinky can ye get? Ooh they're playing In
The Mood an' you've lit a cigar, you devil, you know what *that* does to
me, stop actin' about now, back into traffic before I lose me 'ead."[40] Since
we are supposed to understand the *Coronation Street* accent as associated with the prosaic, the homely—almost the comedic—and not with

transports of evil, passages like this can only be designed to create a grotesque and jarring effect.

On ordinariness and exceptionality in the realm of murder, MP and Baronet Francis Wyndham's account of the Moors case is striking:

> Both [Ian Brady & Myra Hindley] showed remarkable control which, in the circumstances, could only be constructed as callousness. But there was nothing heroic about their defiance: it was rooted in a lack of imagination, the ultimate mediocrity. In years to come, some myth may form around the memory of this couple who explored the sensation of evil to its furthest limits—a cult like the recent attempt to vindicate the "theories" of de Sade. It would be based on a dangerous error. These acts of destruction were neither superhuman nor sub-human; for all their hideous extravagance they were mean. In spite of its outrageous material coupled with scrupulous formality, this "sensational" trial seemed to have a hollow centre where the accused should have been. It was almost as though they were being tried by proxy, ghostly presences in an empty dock, as dead as their victims on the moors.[41]

On first reading, I was surprised, as I had the impression that Wyndham was essaying something that is rarely expressed: the debunking of the mythical status of the figure of the "exceptional subject" that is the murderer, an acknowledgement that a murderer could be *anyone*. However, if it sounds initially as though he is getting to the heart of the problem—the cultural construction that transforms the ordinary individual into extraordinary subject because we believe in the transcendental power of extreme acts—then, as the quotation goes on, it segues instead into what appears to be disappointment that, for Wyndham, Brady and Hindley don't rise above "mediocrity" *in order to be equal to* that mythic construction of the murderous subject. It is, in sum, an odd, ambivalent, and confused statement—and, I would contend, class-bound, like Williams's suggestion that no one extraordinary (such as a genius or a serial killer) should be expected to issue from such prosaic working-class origins as Brady's or Hindley's. And it was against this very assumption—that they *should* be ordinary because of the accident of the circumstances of their birth—that both Ian and Myra *consciously* struggled. Myra admitted, years later: "One thing which we shared was a dissatisfaction with belonging to the working class and being trapped in it."[42] And writing of the experience of committing the crimes, Hindley recalls that for her: "the prime motivation for the murders . . . was compensation in the sense of being different from other people and being set apart from the world."[43]

Brady and Hindley were marked by their class throughout their trial. And, at numerous moments within her account, Hansford Johnson uses a colorful lexicon of filth to describe the case, the crimes, and the criminals, a choice that I cannot help but feel is imbued with class meaning. She describes Brady as having used "dirty language that spouted from him like oil from a well,"[44] and, "over the whole of the trial," she avers, "there was a psychic stench."[45] Her language reflects the particular disgust that she admits she felt because the victims were children, and one cannot help but sense that the backgrounds of the people in the dock and the witness stand unconsciously call up this choice of words to her particularly middle-class sensibility. However, the use of the language of dirt is not original to Hansford Johnson's reporting of the case and was a feature of the trial itself. Witness the exchange between the attorney general and Brady about the latter's library collection:

> This was the diet you were consuming? Pornographic books, books on violence and murder? —Not pornographic books. You can buy them at any book stall. [The books in question at this point in the trial are sexology tomes about perversion.]
> They are dirty books, Brady? —It depends on the dirty mind. It depends on your mind. . . .
> Was your interest in them on a high medical plane? —No, for erotic reasons.
> Of course. This is the atmosphere of your mind. A sink of pornography, was it not? —No. There are better collections than that in lords' manors all over the country. (JG, p. 191)

Brady's response is intelligent. He points up the class-bound hypocrisy underpinning the line of questioning. Doctors and aristocrats are assumed to be immune from moral corruption (despite the glaring fact of Sade's own aristocracy); the "common man" is not.

This line of questioning paves the way for Hansford Johnson's central thesis in *On Iniquity*: the idea that society needed, in the mid-1960s, to start asking questions about the effects on those considered morally corruptible of increasingly freely available "pornographic" and violent textual material of the kind found in Brady's library. "We are seeing the most fantastic growth of a semi-literate reading public—semi-literate, as yet no more than that,"[46] Hansford Johnson asserts, contending that "depraved material" like Sade should not be available to "minds educationally and emotionally unprepared."[47] Not only pornography should be banned, however. Hansford Johnson is keen to keep from the poor and unenlightened the works of one Richard von Krafft-Ebing, who, appropriately enough, as we have seen, had himself warned of the dangers to those uneducated and unprepared of reading his medical text, almost a hundred years earlier. Hansford Johnson tells us:

> Not so long ago, I raised a little storm by suggesting, in a letter to the *Guardian*, that it was not desirable for *Krafft-Ebing* [italics *sic*] to be available in a relatively cheap paperback edition on the bookstalls of English railway stations. . . . There are some books that are not fit for all people and some people who are not fit for all books.[48]

To those who would argue that, assuming the problem Hansford Johnson identifies is even legitimate, the solution may be found in a good quality of education for all, rather than the enforced segregation of an elite, educated middle class from an ignorant, illiterate poor, Hansford Johnson has a typically dismissive riposte, delivered in her jolly sensible prose style:

> It might be urged that our only recourse now would be to step up our education in an attempt to bring us all into line with the present *assumption* of our scientific-mindedness—a counsel of perfection, I am afraid, and not one tenable for anybody with the slightest statistical sense.[49]

Pamela Hansford Johnson is not alone in expressing these concerns in such terms. Academic literary critic George Steiner wrote, as an intervention into debates in the press about the role of immoral literature in the Moors Murders case, the following statement, extracted from a letter to the *Times Literary Supplement*:

> What has emerged . . . is the high probability that the reading of Sade and related material was a significant factor in Brady's relations with Hindley. It would appear that the introduction of sadistic literature and certain types of pornography into a mind not previously familiar with the stuff—to the semi-literate print conveys a peculiar authority, a power to neutralize or supersede personal consciousness—can contribute to the total disorientation or "normal" emotional habits and coordinates. Such disorientation may account for

the willingness of a young woman to stand by while a small girl is sexually hu-
miliated and tormented.[50]

He goes on to talk of the

potential of sadistic erotica to bewilder those who do not have counter-cur-
rents of wit, intellectual detachment, literary recognition, and to bewilder
them in a way that creates a pathological consensus in two or more human beings *together*.[51]

The position advanced here can be described as the "corruption hypothesis"—a hypothesis stated as a bald fact, rather than as a contention, by Hansford Johnson when she writes: "Cruelty, like crime, is
imitative."[52]

However, Hansford Johnson and Steiner fail entirely to take into account the fact that the case of the Moors Murders perfectly illustrates
exactly the *opposite tendency* in human beings, with regard to their sus-
ceptibility to corrupting material, to the one the writers assert as true.
Devastating for these paternalistic, pro-censorship arguments is the consequence of Ian Brady's attempt to initiate Myra's brother-in-law, David Smith, into their secret realm of radical freedom by introducing him
to the Sade worldview. Although Smith obediently copied out passages
from the books Ian lent him, to the effect that "rape is not a crime it is
a state of mind" and "murder is a hobby and a supreme pleasure" (JG,
p. 76), when the young man witnessed Ian Brady brutally slay Edward
Evans, and then joke about it with Myra Hindley, his response was to
feel nothing but revulsion, horror, and pity. And, at six the next morning, he telephoned the police station at Hyde to report having witnessed
a violent crime, setting in motion the legal machinery that would condemn Hindley and Brady, despite their vindictive attempts to frame
Smith himself for the crimes.[53] Thus, the exposure of Smith, an uneducated and unemployed petty criminal from a much less privileged background than either Brady or Hindley, to "corrupting material" proved to
have a very different outcome than the one feared by the conservative
commentators.

Similarly, erroneous logic abounds in Hansford Johnson's comments
on sadomasochism. She conflates an interest in Sade qua writer, the sexual practice of what today we would call BDSM, and the historical phenomenon of Nazism liberally throughout her book. Presumably, since

Brady and Hindley had a documented interest in all three, she assumes that they are causally linked and selfsame. We are instructed that we "mustn't forget the Moors Murders case any more than we dare forget Belsen or Auschwitz,"[54] and that "they [Brady and Hindley] were no more mad than the S.S. guards at Auschwitz, and there were hundreds of the latter: when we begin to think about sadomasochistic behaviour which results in murder, by people in the mass, then we have to stop using the word 'mad.'"[55] While I would in no way take issue with Hansford Johnson's last point, her careless conflation of the phenomena she describes is a problem. Pro-sadomasochism historian Alison Moore has explored the tendency to collapse SM onto Nazism in a number of articles. She argues that "in heterosexual pornography of the 1960s and 1970s [Brady and Hindley's era], Nazi imagery acted as the means to express sado-masochistic fantasies in lieu of a developed language for doing so in any other way. Popular and historical representations of Nazism as perverse fed into this tendency."[56] A lack of specific historical and cultural understanding of both nonnormative sexual preferences and the idea of Nazism leads to clumsy and inaccurate confusion between two, only superficially similar, phenomena. The point Moore makes is one with wider application for us here. The tendency of the 1960s British upper classes to posit causality between socioeconomic deprivation; low educational achievement; gender, sexual, and social nonconformity ("kinky" practices, a refusal of marriage and childbearing); and a criminality which—to quote Wyndham—is "mediocre" and "mean" leads to some overly simplistic conclusions. And it moves the concerned moral majority no closer whatsoever to understanding Brady and Hindley, whose desperate and ill-fated desire to escape the destinies that their working-class births held for them lies entirely beyond the ken of the chattering upper-class commentariat.

Afterlife

Until the publication of *The Gates of Janus* in 2001, the incarcerated Ian Brady—sentenced to serve three concurrent life sentences—fell silent and disappeared, somewhat, from public consciousness. When he did speak out it was to express remorse and acceptance of his sentence in 1978, and to confess to two further murders in 1985—those of Pauline Reade and Keith Bennett, for which the pair had not originally been tried.[57] Additionally, Brady undertook a hunger strike and petitioned to be allowed to die. Myra, on the other hand, retained a high-profile presence in the cultural consciousness, partly owing to the exaggerated, sexist media interest in her that I have described above, which began with her arrest and never ceased, but also owing to her visible attempts to campaign for early release; her friendship with high-profile Peers and writers (including, most famously, Lord Longford); and her foiled escape from Holloway prison in 1974, assisted by her prison officer lover, Tricia Cairns. Myra broke her ties with Brady in 1972.

The fact that Myra seemed to want to remain in the public spotlight has been used as confirmation of her wickedness. Journalist Yvonne Roberts wrote that she fully suspected that Hindley "would rather have gone down in history as 'Myra Hindley, Child Murderer' than not go down at all," a position that, to Roberts, suggested that Myra "was a psychopath."[58] But, after being sentenced, *identifying as a murderer* was indeed the only possible subject position open to her and this figure of infamy is such a well-rehearsed and archetypal one, as we have been exploring, that its lure must have been irresistible. What Myra Hindley perhaps failed to grasp, however, was that—being a woman—she was never going to be allowed the ambivalent notoriety of her male sex killer counterparts. The public response would always be one of unadulterated hate.

The infamous blonde head and shoulders photograph discussed previously continued to appear as the accompaniment to almost every story about Myra from her trial until her demise (with the exception of her graduation photo in 1989, showing a smiling woman with short dark hair, which instead provoked outrage that she had been allowed to study for a bachelor's degree in prison). However, she was in life, and remains in death, perpetually fixed in time in the public imaginary at 23 years old, with an extravagant time-warp, beehive hairdo. In an open letter to the *Guardian* in 1995, Myra wrote: "The truth of this continuing Gothic soap opera is that most people don't want to accept that people like myself can change. They prefer to keep me frozen in time, together with that awful mug shot so that their attitudes, beliefs and perceptions can remain intact."[59]

"That awful mug shot" transcended its origins as a stiff, grainy police photograph the very same year, when young British artist Marcus Harvey produced a portrait approximating the photograph, created from the mold of a child's handprint reproduced and overlaid to resemble pixi-

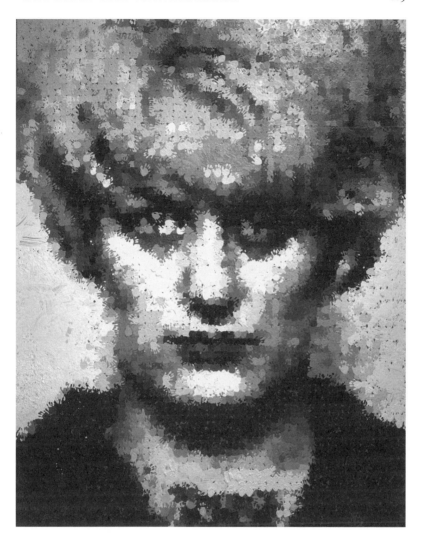

FIGURE 2. Marcus Harvey, *Myra*, 1995. Acrylic on canvas. Photographer: Stephen White, courtesy White Cube. Copyright Marcus Harvey. All Rights Reserved, DACS 2012.

lation, that would become a prominently displayed exhibit at the 1997 *Sensation* exhibition at the Royal Academy of Art in London (fig. 2). The painting had to be removed for repair twice during the exhibition, when artists and the public attacked it. The fact that an artwork depicting Hindley attracted such public violence testifies to the extent to which representing the hated figure was seen as morally reprehensible on the part of the gallery and the artist, and as implicitly legitimizing and promoting her fame/infamy. It also suggests, as Birch has argued, the synecdochic power of that image: its capacity to stand in for all that Myra symbolizes. The affair of Harvey's painting is, perhaps, apt as the afterlife of a murder case in which debate about the morality of art and literature played such a significant part.[60]

The outcry recalls also the negative reaction to the release, in 1984, of a song featured on the debut album of Manchester Indie band the Smiths, entitled "Suffer Little Children." The song treats the case of the Moors Murders and includes the lyrics "Hindley wakes and Hindley says: Hindley wakes, Hindley wakes, Hindley wakes, and says: 'Oh, whatever he has done, I have done.'" Brady is not named in the song. The band's lyricist/vocalist, Steven Patrick Morrissey is reported to have written the song after reading Emlyn Williams's *Beyond Belief*. ("Hindley Wakes" is the title of a chapter of Williams's book, while what Myra says in the lyrics is a quotation from the transcribed police interview.) While Ann West (Lesley Ann Downey's mother) initially decried Morrissey's song, because it mentioned three victims by name and showed on the single cover a woman who superficially resembled Myra, West and Morrissey later became friends and the grieving mother accepted the singer-songwriter's account of the song as a compassionate tribute to the victims, and an attempt at reconciliation with an unresolved part of Manchester's past.[61] The reactions to Marcus Harvey's painting and the Smiths' song underline the continuing difficulty of establishing the moral effects—the corrupting or edifying influence—of artistic and cultural objects, suggesting the need for critical analyses that highlight the kinds of nuances that were simply not admitted when discussing Brady and Hindley's reading of Sade et al. in court back in 1966.

In the case of Harvey's *Myra*, as Lacanian visual studies scholar Jennifer Friedlander has pointed out, it is ironic that the outcry against the painting that issued from victims' families, the campaign group Kidscape, and certain Royal Academicians was echoed vociferously by none other than Myra Hindley herself. Fearing, perhaps, that the negative publicity would harm her already struggling release campaign, Hindley described the artwork as "repugnant and repulsive" and "totally abhorrent," decrying the Royal Academy for showing it since they ignored "not only the emotional pain and trauma that would inevitably be experienced by the families of the victims . . . but also the families of any child victim."[62] Harvey maintains, along the lines of Morrissey, that the aim of his creation was sympathetic to the victims and offered a condemnatory comment on the press's overexposure of the image, rather than an attempt to increase or celebrate its infamy. Cultural critic Marina Warner has argued that the portrait succeeds in defaming rather than morbidly celebrating its subject matter, as the infant handprints "literally brand Hindley with her crime."[63]

Friedlander speculates on the nationally specific effect of Harvey's *Myra*, arguing in particular that the explosive reaction to the painting in Britain, in comparison with the lack of reaction when the exhibit traveled to the United States, demonstrates how images rely for their meaning and affective power on accrued cultural associations. Myra's iconic image existed within, and moved between, "three visual systems: (1) surveillance (where it emerged as a mug shot in 1966); (2) the popular press . . . ; (3) the gallery."[64] To a public lacking familiarity with the meanings of the image accrued in contexts (1) and (2), the artwork has no power; Myra's image is not really, *in itself*, transcendentally evil. It gains meaning only within its "inscription into the currency of other discourses; its intertextuality."[65] In this way, *Myra*'s reception illustrates McDonagh's point that the *idea* of child murder—symbolized here by the blonde cameo of Myra Hindley that stands in for it—"is invested with a bewildering excess of meanings."[66]

The particular nexus of meanings that the idea of Hindley's version of child murder conveys has to do with a destruction of the (socially prescribed) "natural order", the figure who should be the child-bearer being instead the bringer of mortality. Myra's first biographer, ex-*Sun* journalist Jean Ritchie, states baldly: "We never expect women to kill children. . . . All our deep-rooted (and biologically sound) conceptions about women come into play."[67] While I find Ritchie's evolutionary psychology–informed statement both scientifically spurious and politically damaging, it is doubtless the case that she reiterates the common view of the matter—and not only the tabloid attitude. In similar vein, in an article in the *Independent* in 1993, Geraldine Bedell wrote: "Higher standards are expected of women when it comes to the care of children: Myra betrayed her sex and exploited her sex so that children could be sexually assaulted, tortured and killed."[68] Not only is Myra's own sexual excitement in such brutality *literally unthinkable*, but Bedell implies that she also failed in her duty to have been the gatekeeper of *Brady's* sexuality. Both Birch and Lee have pointed out the way in which the tabloid press, arch arbiter of norms, pitted grieving Ann West against Myra Hindley—using West's publicly expressed hatred of Myra and vow to kill her should she ever be released—as a particularly stark way of juxtaposing the archetypes of the good woman and the evil one or, as Birch puts it in metaphorical psychoanalytic terms, the "good mother" and the "bad mother" (since the idea of "woman" can seemingly not be dissociated from the idea of "mother" for this culture, as Ritchie makes so clear, and as I have been arguing throughout this chapter).[69] Indeed, the fact of refusing normative forms of sexual practice and reproduction and the act of killing children lie on an uneasy and ill-thought-out imaginary continuum that nevertheless clearly underlies much discussion of Myra's special wickedness and the danger that she poses. That Myra had internalized her press and adopted this discourse for understanding herself as a strategy is visible in the controversial letter she wrote to Ann West in 1987, where she describes herself as "an utter disgrace to womankind."[70]

Ritchie's biography, *Myra Hindley: Inside the Mind of a Murderess*, appeared in 1988. It focuses exhaustively on the details of Myra's numerous, serial, and often concurrent lesbian encounters and relationships in Holloway, Durham, and Cookham Wood prisons over the course of her then 23-year-long term of imprisonment. It describes the way in which officers and inmates alike "seemed to be under Myra's spell,"[71] or "were starry-eyed about her."[72] Ritchie reports that one officer "admitted being 'intrigued by the Myra enigma.'"[73] In combination with the already extant speculations about Myra's "kinky" sexual practices with Brady, the idea of the murderous woman as excessively, abnormally sexual was strongly reinforced by these reports. Similarly, the autobiographical *The Devil and Miss Jones* by Janie Jones, which appeared in 1993, is full of salacious details about Myra's sexual behavior in prison. Jones, a singer and dancer convicted for running a call girl ring, was a fellow prisoner and former friend, who turned against Myra when she finally confessed to her part in the killings of Pauline Reade and Keith Bennett, of which she had previously vehemently denied any knowledge.[74] While Ritchie reports that Myra and Jones had been lovers,[75] Jones insists that they were only ever close friends, but that Myra had "longstanding and passionate affairs with other prisoners,"[76] and that "she had them all eating out of her hand."[77] Jones asserts that Myra was passionately attracted to Janie, and sent her frequent erotic and romantic letters, but that Janie was uninterested, as "the thing with Myra is that she's got to possess somebody, body, mind and soul."[78] The metaphor of possession is pointed: the title of Jones's book sets its tone; Myra is not just evil, she is "the Devil." As well as reinforcing that long-standing notion of the female killer as sexual deviant, the publication of books like these compounded public outrage. The idea that, while the victims' surviving families suffered ongoing, lifelong torment, Myra was enjoying lesbian sexual exploits (as well as pursuing educational qualifications) in prison, must have been received as unbearable. When it was announced in 1985 that the increasingly isolated and sick Ian Brady was being transferred to a psychiatric hospital with a diagnosis of paranoid schizophrenia, Ann West is quoted as opining that "at least [Brady] had the decency to go mad," in contradistinction to the apparently sane, excessively sexually active, bewitchingly manipulative—and therefore demonstrably "more evil"—Myra Hindley.[79]

The End of "Evil"

The figure of Myra Hindley, from the time of her arrest in 1965 until her death in 2002, has been described by a gender-specific double bind: the sexually and criminally aberrant woman must be either a victim of the influence of her male lover and immoral literature she is too uneducated to appreciate or else a woman so divorced from "natural" (passive, maternal, caregiving) femininity that her agentic individuality represents a pure form of evil. Carol Ann Lee comments on something that Myra wrote five years before her death: "I know people would have liked for me to be chucked into a pond three times to discover if I sank or swam."[80] "It was a shrewd observation," Lee writes. "The nature of her crimes and their unfathomable source tapped into old, unspoken fears."[81] The "old unspoken fears" have a name: pure and unadulterated misogyny. The male fear of women who would not stay in their place was the motivation for witch-burning in the first place. As Germaine Greer, one of the few feminists to speak out for Myra, puts it: "May God have mercy on you, Myra Hindley, for ungodly men will have none."[82] For, as we have seen abundantly, the woman who kills is *never* allowed to be a complex, conflicted person who has committed violent, criminal, immoral acts that she may or may not later regret. She is not allowed, in the representations made of her in the press, documentaries, or books, that human three-dimensionality. Even more than the male murderers explored in this book, her acts define her essence once and for all.

To summarize and to put it schematically: male murderers are "special" in modern Western culture because they are seen to have something *extra*; they are superhuman in the Nietzschean sense. (While Ian Brady took this coda literally and consciously applied it, mainstream culture has it as an unconscious fantasy, as has been shown in the previous chapter by analyzing discourses about male sex murderers.) Female murderers are special, on the other hand, because they are seen to *lack* something that is perceived as being essential to femininity. While (white, heteronormative) maleness stands in for the default human being, femaleness equates to something other to, and less than, maleness, but with culturally ascribed saving virtues such as a capacity for nurturing and an affinity with an ethics of care. Female murderers, if we study closely the ways they are represented, not only disturb this system, but also show up very clearly the workings of its beliefs and values. As Helen Birch puts it: "The mythology of Myra Hindley reveals, above all, that we do not have a language to represent female killing, and that a case like this disrupts the very terms which hold gender in place."[83] What I have further shown is that, when a case of exceptionality threatens those "terms which hold gender in place," mainstream culture seeks to suture the gaps in these terms more tightly than ever before, shoring up a more constraining ideal of female normality against the aberrant outsider.

The backlash against gender-trouble of the kind occasioned by a violent woman—and especially a child-killer—is characterized by moral panic and excessive censure. Lawyer Edward Fitzgerald, who had previously represented murderesses Mary Bell and Maxine Carr, and who took over the fight for Myra's release shortly before her death, believed strongly—echoing Germaine Greer—that "women are not forgiven for their crimes."[84] And, as we have seen, discourses of class function in a similar way. The case of the Moors Murderers served conservative ideology nicely, acting as a particularly emotive incentive for condemnation of the "increasingly permissive society"[85] and allowing commentators such as Hansford Johnson to urge a reinforcement of social-class roles, and increased censorship of the material available to those who issued from "the wrong side of the tracks."

And yet, perhaps even more strongly than either of the conservative attitudes discussed above—the enduring attachment to the innate meanings of socially imposed sex roles and the fear on the part of the dominant classes of those from other social groups attaining autonomy—a comment made by newspaper publisher David Astor in a letter to Myra may help to highlight what is most at stake in the public reaction to the Moors Murderers. Indeed, it hints at a potential explanation for the ambivalent cultural fascination with murderers that this book aims to expose. Astor tells Myra:

> The public associates . . . you with something which they are frightened of in themselves. It is generally admitted that violence towards children is much more prevalent than people generally like to admit. My wife and I think that every parent instinctively knows that the possibility of this happening is present in all parent-child relationships. But of course this is something of which most people are very afraid.[86]

I would extend this telling and insightful analysis to the field of murder, and cultural attitudes toward the murderer, as a whole. The imperative to "other" murderers as either genius criminals or despicably evil, monstrous pariahs, depending on the cultural moment and the sex, class, and sexuality of the killer, issues from a refusal to see clearly "mainstream" society's—and the "normal" individual's—own capacity for more subtle forms of violence and social injustice as a real and ever-present danger. Rather than interrogating the guilty motivations underlying the cultural sentimentalization of children and motherhood, it is easier simply to keep asking the unanswerable question of the exceptional figure: *"Miss Hindley, why?"*

CHAPTER FIVE

"Monochrome Man"

Dennis Nilsen

And I said: Ok. Who is this really? And the voice said:
This is the hand, the hand that takes.
This is the hand, the hand that takes.
This is the hand, the hand that takes.
....
'Cause when love is gone, there's always justice.
And when justice is gone, there's always force.

—(Laurie Anderson, "O Superman [For Massenet]," 1981)[1]

Dennis Nilsen (1945–), a civil servant who strangled to death at least 15 young men between 1978 and 1983 in North London, and kept their bodies around his flat for long periods of time,[2] is one of the most represented faces of serial killing in a contemporary British culture fascinated by the figure of the murderer. As well as spawning the usual tabloid-esque true-crime volumes, Nilsen's case and persona have been the basis for an avant-garde physical theatre piece, an award-winning feature-length "docudrama," an oil painting, and a postmodern Gothic novel.[3] He is therefore notable among twentieth-century murderers for being associated with alternative and high art. Added to this, Nilsen is unusual, though by no means unique, among convicted murderers in terms of the amount of self-representation and creative production, in the form of both confessional and fiction writing, classical music, and images, which he himself has produced.[4] In April 1983, while on remand in Brixton Prison, Nilsen was approached by Brian Masters, a scholar of French literature turned student of murder, who offered to write Nilsen's biography with the murderer's help. Nilsen produced hundreds of pages of detailed confession about his childhood, sexual life, political inclinations, and crimes for Masters, as well as a collection of visual recollections of the death and disposal scenes entitled "Sad Sketches." These textual and visual memoirs are discussed and cited at length in Masters's study *Killing for Company* and have been commented on by numerous scholars.[5]

Since then, while serving a life sentence in prison, Nilsen has written a multivolume autobiography entitled *The History of a Drowning Boy* in an attempt to explicate as fully as possible the circumstances that led to his crimes. While acknowledging that Masters's account does its best to understand his situation, the killer writes that, in the sections of the book focusing on psychology and motive, "I vanish into a muddled array of psychobabble. The human is never explained or answered."[6] Nilsen has, however, been legally prevented from publishing his work, a decision which he has appealed to the European Court of Human Rights to have overturned.[7] In what follows, I will investigate some potential cultural meanings of Dennis Nilsen's inexhaustible desire to represent himself and his crimes, and I will attempt to account for the wealth of critical and artistic production that has been inspired by the persona of this particular murderer. Additionally, in a second section, I explore the discourses of homophobia that accrue to reportage of Nilsen's case and suggest that it may not be coincidental that a murderer who is also a homosexual has been strongly associated with both "the artistic" and "the monstrous." As shown in the introduction, the discourse of the murderer and the homosexual as a "creative degenerate" has strong roots in the nineteenth-century taxonomy of abnormality.

Beyond "Ordinary" and "Extraordinary"

I claimed above that the excessive representation and self-representation of and by Nilsen was "unusual yet by no means unique," and it is this pair of ideas—exceptionality and the rule, deviation and cultural expectation—that lies at the heart of this book and that is particularly well illustrated by the case of Dennis Nilsen. The eminently nineteenth-century intertwined ideas about the killer, the artist, the degenerate, and the sexually abnormal individual explored in the first section of this book with reference to Lacenaire, Lafarge, and Jack the Ripper do not disappear in the twentieth and twenty-first centuries, but rather they form the imaginary means by which artists and commentators understand and represent murderers *and* by which killers themselves construct their identities and their deeds in writing and images. I have been investigating so far what is at stake in the continued cultural investment in making the assumption that the killer is a radically different type of person than the so-called ordinary man or woman, rather than being simply a man or woman who happens to have committed acts that we consider immoral, illegal, and transgressive. Dennis Nilsen himself, perhaps, comes closer to expressing concern with this very question than any published scholar of murder. In the notes prepared for Masters, in which he agonizes about how to provide an answer to the riddle that is himself and his acts (and fails to do so conclusively, or in a way that satisfies him), he writes: "No one wants to believe ever that I am just an ordinary man come to an extraordinary and overwhelming conclusion."[8]

However, this adoption of the label "ordinary" is only fleeting. In most of his discourse, Nilsen preserves for himself the status of the outsider. At times, this comes in the context of abjection and self-hatred, as when he envisions himself as "a national receptacle into which all the nation will urinate."[9] At other times he is the exceptional, superior subject, cut off from the common mass, as when he writes of himself in the third person: "The loner has to achieve fulfillment alone within himself. All he has are his own extreme acts. People are merely supplementary to the achievement of these acts. He is abnormal and he knows it."[10] The mystery of individuality, subjectivity, and "specialness" continues to preoccupy Nilsen's thinking. In his unpublished autobiography he has recently written of the conditions by which we enter the world precisely in terms of uniqueness:

> As the unique amalgam, in a new genetic configuration of contributions from a man and a woman, one is born into the world, as different from other people, in much the same way as my fingerprints were different from other people's.[11]

Despite his claims to ordinariness at rare moments, then, the discourses I have been sketching throughout this book that draw the murderer as special, as exceptional, and that lend a sheen of transcendence to his antisocial acts, are extremely visible throughout Nilsen's own writerly production. And a poetical and metaphysical grandiosity that aligns him with forebears such as Lacenaire, the poet-murderer, is present in his drawings and writings. Nilsen has also composed symphonies while in prison and labels himself a "creative artist." The incompatibility of the assertion of "ordinariness" with the perception of (artistic and criminal) exceptionality produces a schismatic quality in Nilsen's self-representation. As well as being understandable as the symptom of Nilsen's individual psychological peculiarities, or the division wrought by the tension between remorse and self-justification, this contradiction needs to be read as a reflection of the very particular discourses that are available for talking about being a person who kills in a culture in which acts are seen as commensurate with identity.

In *Killing for Company*, Masters reproduces a selection of Nilsen's "Sad Sketches" without analyzing them closely.[12] These ink-on-paper drawings of Nilsen's murder victims embody precisely the schismatic qualities I have described above. Some sketches are sexualized images of the whole corpse; some are representations of partly dismembered bodies. One particular sketch shows the dead body of a blond young man, naked and lying facedown, visualized from above. In the margins of the page, around the figure of the corpse, are two textual excerpts. By the victim's head, Nilsen quotes from Alfred Tennyson's *Maud* of 1855:

Faultily faultless, icily regular,
Splendidly null
Dead Perfection, no more.

The aestheticization of the corpse, suggested for Nilsen by Tennyson's formulation "dead perfection," is present throughout Nilsen's recollection of his crimes. Nilsen describes in detail his attempts to render the corpses he had created aesthetically pleasing as objects: positioning them, washing them, and dressing them. Then, he created secondary objects to represent the primary objects that would inevitably decay, drawing and photographing the bodies (though he ultimately burnt the Polaroids on the same garden bonfires he built to destroy victims' remains). Because of his professed aesthetic appreciation of, and attraction to, dead matter, the label of "necrophiliac" has been considered with regard to his diagnosis by a number of psychiatric experts and cultural commentators alike.[13] Yet what is again crucial here is that Nilsen draws not, or not only, on the resources of a personal, internal psychological pathology, but also on an artistic tradition: the Romantic contemplation of death as beautiful, a form of culturally permissible necrophilia.[14] Cameron and Frazer have termed Dennis Nilsen "the incurable romantic," meaning this both in the sense of "romantic" with a lowercase *r*, since he is the lover who kills to keep the object of his desire with him, and in the sense of exponent of the Romantic aesthetic tradition.[15] Nilsen's acts literalize, and his retroactive representations endorse, reinforce, and reify, this culturally available set of associations.

Yet, in the other margin of his drawing, discursively far from the rarefied citation from Tennyson, Nilsen writes:

> I stripped the body of its clothing. The vest and pants had been soiled with his urine and excrement. I carried him into the bathroom and washed him in the bath. I dried him, put him over my shoulder, and laid him on the bed. He was very clean and looked sublimely at peace. I sat smoking looking at him mesmerized.

The contrast is striking. The sanitized, beautiful, "faultily faultless, icily perfect" version of death is tempered here by the mention of the abject physical fact of defecation and urination, byproducts of fatal asphyxiation. And the language of the everyday permeates the recollection too. Nilsen's smoking while looking, "mesmerized," at the body is visually picked up in the detail of a packet of cigarettes that lies by the corpse in the drawn image.

Nilsen represents his acts not only through the prism of memory and its inevitable distortions and idealizations, then, but also by drawing on a cultural repository of representations of the act of killing as a unique form of transgression, and the appearance of death as sublime. As we have seen, these run from Sade through Dostoyevsky, whose *Crime and Punishment* Nilsen greatly admired, to Nietzsche's idea of a Superman above ordinary moral codes, and finally, in the twentieth century, they are articulated in Bataille's philosophy of eroticism and death as "limit experiences."[16] The experience of killing, often asserted to be unrepresentable, is actually one of the most heavily codified in our culture, as Cameron and Frazer and Josephine McDonagh have argued, both using Nilsen's case as illustrative material.[17] And, as I am arguing here, the experience of *identifying as* a killer is similarly discursively overdetermined. Alongside the Romantic elements of the extraordinary situation that Nilsen describes and draws, however, are aspects of the ordinary, the contemporary, and the practical (if not exactly the commonplace).

The detail of Nilsen's smoking and the necessity to wash the body because of its leaky, permeable nature threaten to break the illusion of a perfect Romantic alabaster corpse and the too-neat idea of corpse as artwork/murderer-as-artist, showing them up as a fantasy.

Viennese-born, London-based artist Dieter Rossi's oil painting entitled *Dennis Nilsen* of 1993 (fig. 3) picks up on this same juxtaposition

FIGURE 3. Dieter Rossi, *Dennis Nilsen*, 1993. Oil on canvas. Copyright Dieter Rossi.

and dislocation of art object and corporeal excess; "extraordinary" situation, yet "ordinary" man that I have discussed above with regard to Nilsen's own images. The painting appears in a series of oil-on-canvas paintings entitled *On Violence*, which also includes a nightmarish abstract painting depicting a face made up of disarticulated body parts called *Jeffrey Dahmer*. Rossi's *Dennis Nilsen* is dominated by the red and orange tones of flesh, the flesh both of the victim—reduced here to meat, to a headless torso aloft on the killer's shoulders—and of the naked Dennis Nilsen. Nilsen has written in his prison diaries that he would often strip to his underpants for the "clinically ordinary task" of body disposal.[18] While the act of creating a "sublime" corpse thrilled him sexually and aesthetically, he claimed to find disposal of "the dirty platter" an unpleasant chore.[19] The meeting point between the perceived extraordinary and the ordinary, or between the sublime and the social, which I identified in Nilsen's drawing in the instance of the cigarettes, can be found within Rossi's image in the detail of Nilsen's glasses, the one manmade, practical, instrumental, and inorganic object in the image. In this detail, Rossi thematizes Nilsen's articulation of himself as the meeting point of ordinary and extraordinary. The unremarkable nature of Nilsen's appearance, perfectly represented in his bespectacled, grimacing, civil servant's face, is perhaps what makes his persona—and this painting—so striking, since we are conditioned to view the killer through the lens of exceptionality rather than considering the counterdiscursive possibility that the man or woman who commits acts that are beyond the pale is not ontologically definable by the nature of the acts.

Portraying the coexistence in the figure of Nilsen of exceptionality and ordinariness seems also to be the aim of Fhiona Louise's *Cold Light of Day* (1989), a fictionalized "docudrama" about Nilsen's case. Bob Flag plays a thinly disguised Dennis Nilsen, renamed "Jorden March." The film exploits camera work to create a cloying, claustrophobic atmosphere. Internal spaces (March's somewhat squalid flat and the house in which it is situated) are filmed using close-ups and narrow camera angles. Sometimes the actors' heads and feet fall outside of the cluttered frames, suggesting the difficulty for the nonnormative subject of "fitting in," of being contained within ordinary life. The images are overlaid with sound effects of heavy breathing, heartbeats, ticking and chiming clocks, evoking regularity and the quotidian, while at the same time creating a sinister sense of expectation (or perhaps revealing that the sinister lives at the heart of the everyday). On the one hand, the film plays on the stereotype of Nilsen as the "Kindly Killer," showing the Jorden character preparing meals for an elderly fellow tenant and taking in a neighbor's cat; on the other, these sequences are juxtaposed incongruously with scenes showing March's brutal strangulation of his male guests and shockingly bloody dismemberment of dead bodies. (Images of body parts and red viscera, resembling the color scheme of Rossi's painting, predominate in such scenes.)

One reviewer writing on the Internet Movie Database (IMDb), Nigel Edwards, opines:

> It tries for realism as a documentary with the everyday scenes . . . and tries for dramatic scenes with the murders and the ensuing aftermath. But really works as neither as both parts come across as dull and boring. Perhaps most killers are as uninteresting as this and maybe that is the point the film is trying to make. Sadly it doesn't make it very entertaining.[20]

While the film may not be "entertaining" as such, it evokes extremely well the "ordinary" man come to "an extraordinary and overwhelming conclusion" that Nilsen describes and embodies. The reviewer's words evince disappointment at the idea that killers might possibly be dull, suggesting the pervasiveness of the myth of exceptionality.

Intriguingly, at the end of the film, just before the credits roll, there is a dedication: "For those too sensitive for this world—Fhiona." It is unclear whether this is meant to refer to Nilsen or to his victims—or, indeed, to both. While it is possible to object that Louise's sympathetic or sentimental treatment is distasteful, *Cold Light of Day* otherwise seems to wish us to see beyond the simplistic portrayal of the killer as a monster or a hero, restoring a measure of humanity—and indeed of *banality*—to March/Nilsen. And it is possible to understand the terms of the IMDb reviewer's negative response, cited above, precisely in light of the film's refusal to deliver a version of the familiar stereotype of the murderer as an exotic, extravagant, wholly "other" individual, prioritizing instead complexity and multidimensionality.

In another of his "Sad Sketches," Nilsen depicts himself standing above a strangled victim lying before him on a bed. Again, a poem and a personal recollection are written in the margins. This time, the poem is authored by Nilsen. It reads:

The monochrome man is a dream
It is the black and it is the white of life.
There he stands, near himself and distant
He is the cameo who activates now and then
Can't cope with metropolitania
Taking him, sometimes, to this numbing chant.
In the waste he laid before him
Peaceful, pale flesh on a bed
Real and beautiful—and dead.

The poem lends itself perfectly to psychoanalytic and psychiatric analysis. The idea of a cameo or mask that Nilsen wears in everyday life, that occasionally slips and is activated into violence, supports Dr. Patrick Gallwey's psychiatric testimony for the defense at Nilsen's trial, in which he claimed the defendant was suffering from a personality disorder characterized by "False Self" syndrome. The psychiatric idea of "false self" originates with R. D. Laing's antipsychiatry and it is a borrowing from existential philosophy. The person allegedly suffering from the syndrome constructs a socially acceptable veneer that is "worn" to hide a disintegrated personality. The individual functions adequately on a daily basis behind the mask of normality, but the mask risks slipping under conditions of stress or extreme stimulation. It will be clear by now that my interest does not lie in the "accuracy" or otherwise of psychiatric diagnoses, but rather in tracing the discursive and ideological beliefs that contribute to them. However, the social and philosophical aspects of the diagnosis merit brief consideration, as the idea of "false self" points to the necessity to conform to a narrow series of socially defined "norms" that have as their inevitable corollary for nonnormative subjects a form of illness that enables survival.

Brian Masters has commented that Nilsen's self-designation as "monochrome man," which Masters takes to mean capable of both good and evil, reflects a post-death-of-God philosophical and literary tradition in which moral polarity is found in the individual, rather than in external deific forces. Masters does not mention in the context of the "Monochrome Man" poem the obvious parallels with Charles Baudelaire, whose poems from the 1850s explore the oxymoronic nature of beauty, which he termed "fangeuse grandeur" or "filthy grandeur." Baudelaire also wrote in striking terms of the duality of human nature, opining: "It would perhaps be sweet to be alternately victim and executioner."[21] This is a theme he expands in his poem "L'Héautontimorouménos' or "The Self-Executioner":

> I am the wound and the knife!
> I am the slap and the cheek!
> I am the limbs and the wheel
> And the victim and the executioner![22]

It is possible that the black-and-white of the "monochrome man" image in Nilsen's poem too refers not only to the human capacity for possessing simultaneously qualities of good and evil, as Masters suggests, but also to the wishful possibility of being at once the killer and victim, the fantasy explored by Baudelaire's poem. Again, this must be read not only as a personal psychological or sexual fantasy on Nilsen's part (though it is no doubt that too), but also as a received discursive trope, something that *belongs* to the culture as a whole, rather than being entirely outside of it, hermetically confined in the figure of the exceptional murderer-pervert. It is this gesture of othering, of pushing outside, that constitutes the mechanism by which the murderer or other "abnormal" subject is constituted as exceptional.

In the prose that sits on the other side of the image of Nilsen beholding the corpse, he writes:

> I stood in great grief and a wave of utter sadness as if someone very dear to me had just died. I knew that I had brought/wrought[23] this result but like life itself that scene looked right and at the same time I was amazed that such a tragedy could not be averted in this day and age. Like a ritual the body had to be undressed and washed. After each one I waited and prepared myself for my arrest. I sometimes wondered if anyone cared for me or for them. *That could easily be me lying there. In fact a lot of the time it was.* (My italics.)

The last two sentences suggest the wishful/wistful identification with the victim's corpse that I have been discussing. In *Killing for Company*, Masters traces the etiology of Nilsen's fantasies prior to his killing career, which involved constructing visual tableaux of himself as a dead body, using talcum powder to erase the traces of color from his cheeks and viewing himself in a mirror as a prelude to masturbating, sometimes filming the scene. In these early versions of the fantasy, Nilsen was able to become both subject and object of sexual desire and homicidal lust. Elsewhere in his prison memoirs, Nilsen writes explicitly that his murders were a way of killing himself: "I wanted to live and be strangled at the same time."[24] And expanding more fully on this theme:

> I did it all for me. Purely selfishly . . . I worshipped the art and the act of death. Over and over. . . . I killed them as I would like to be killed myself . . . enjoying the extremity of the death act itself. If I did it to myself I could only experience it once. If I did it to others I could experience the death act over and over again.[25]

The monochrome man, then, who is capable of embodying both killer and victim, is an impossible phantasmic figure of power and powerlessness—the myth of the exceptional subject writ large.

Speculations on the Killer's Sexuality

The homoeroticism implicit in Nilsen's fantasies and acts, and the fact that most of his victims were young gay men, have not gone unnoticed by commentators and artists drawn to Nilsen's case and figure. In his book, which examines British serial killers from a victim-related sociological perspective, in an attempt to avoid taking for granted the discourse of the killer-as-exceptional-individual that the current book also scrutinizes, David Wilson chooses to discuss Nilsen's case in the chapter dedicated to killers of "gay men," rather than in the chapter treating murderers of "runaways and throwaways," though, as he states, either would be an equally accurate description of Nilsen's victims.

The ways in which the killing of men by a gay man is represented in a heteronormative culture demand careful analysis. Loyal to his aim of showing up how certain classes of person are more readily perceived as—and rendered—victims, David Wilson writes: "That some gay men themselves kill other gay men should not deflect our attention away from the fact that homophobia has created the circumstances in which gay men have become one of the prime targets of serial killers in this country."[26] Neil McKenna, writing in the *Independent* in 1993 about tabloid journalism's coverage of a spate of killings of gay men in London that year, points out the homophobia underpinning the sensationalism with which killings involving a suspected homosexual motive are treated.[27] He cites Simon Watney, writer and AIDs activist, who opines:

> The reporting of the murders has been bizarrely sensationalist. . . . The way coverage has dwelt on intimate details of the victims' sex lives shows that these men are not seen as human beings, but merely as fetishists whose picturesque perversion has led them to this terrible end.[28]

McKenna also quotes cultural studies scholar Richard Dyer, who has made a study of filmic representations of both gay men and serial killers. Dyer states: "Films about gay murders tend to be a semi-prurient, anthropological excursion into this peculiar, other, dangerous world, with endless scenes of gay bars. . . . It's an imaginary, anonymous, fetishistic, sexually-driven and very violent world."[29]

The cultural fantasy that conflates male homosexuality and violence—or, to cite Richard Tithecott, that "confuse[s] "sexual homicide" with homosex"[30]—has a long history. In a poem written in prison, after reading Oscar Wilde's "Ballad of Reading Gaol" (1897), which famously proclaims that "each man kills the thing he loves," Dennis Nilsen collapses criminal guilt onto feelings of homosexual guilt in the final lines of the first and last stanzas. He writes:

> Confusion in the fact of being evil,
> "Born into evil all the time?"
> When evil is the produce
> Can there be a doubt?
> When killing men has always been a crime.
> . . . .
> Sentencing the fact of being evil,
> Dying of evil all the time.
> When love is the produce
> Can there be a doubt?
> When loving men has always been a crime.[31]

That Nilsen's sexual orientation is aligned with his crimes, not only in his own poetry, but also in the public and legal discourse produced about him, is a feature of the homophobia—both internalized and institutional—that Wilson, McKenna, and Dyer draw to our attention. A further facet of this deployment of Nilsen's crimes for political ends comes in the fact that his killings and arrest coincided historically with the outbreak of the AIDS panic in the conservative climate of 1980s Thatcherite Britain. His case could therefore be used implicitly or explicitly to reinforce moral panic about the "gay disease" by suggesting that the killer's modus operandi and homicidal activities paralleled the means of transmission of AIDS.

In *House of Horror,* a book-length, tabloid-esque treatment of the Nilsen case by Fleet Street reporter John Lisners, for example, this homophobic logic is found in abundance. Discussing Nilsen's habit of picking up men, some of whom became his victims, in Soho's gay bars, Lisners collapses homosexuality onto violent predation. He writes: "Gays take the attitude of predators. They are unashamedly open about their ambitions. That suited Dennis Nilsen."[32] The tendency both to vilify the gay killer and to blame the gay victims is exemplified by this callous statement. In his discussion of Nilsen's American gay serial-killing counterpart, Jeffrey Dahmer, David Schmid has explored similar discourses, such as that by true-crime writer Anne E. Schwartz, who writes: "The youths who left gay bars with men they didn't know were leading lives full of risks and, in the end, were killed as a result of their own negligence and recklessness. . . . Their life-styles and unnecessary risk-taking contributed to their deaths."[33] The Nilsen killings, like those carried out by Dahmer on the other side of the Atlantic, have too often been reduced to a product of the predatory nature of gay sexuality as fantasized by the heteronormative perspective.

By a sleight of logic then, Dennis Nilsen is called to embody extreme, unique aberration (the necrophiliac, the killer) on the one hand, and yet is scapegoated as a symptom of the broader perceived dangers of his orientation and "lifestyle" (the promiscuous, cruising gay man) on the other. And this call to embody both fantasies entails an elision of the difference between them: these stigmatized types of "otherness" are collapsed onto each other as if the collapsing does not necessitate a stretch. One of the central tenets of homophobia, as analyzed brilliantly by gay and lesbian studies scholars such as Leo Bersani and queer theorists such as Lee Edelman, is the idea that same-sex sexuality is aligned with death, distanced as it is from the biological possibility of "natural" reproduction. Edelman argues that the figure of "the queer" is always-already positioned as the threat to, and enemy of, the future, as the one who "comes to figure the bar to every realization of futurity, the resistance, internal to the social, to every social structure or form."[34] Thus, it is a small step in what Foucault calls biopolitical terms from this idea of homosexuality as sterile to a fantasy of it as murderous. Responses to such discourses may consist of two broad strategic ploys. The first adopts the rhetoric of assimilation, the assertion of the good queer citizen, in arguing for legislative rights for gay unions and same-sex parenting. The second involves, in Leo Bersani's words, "accept[ing] the pain of embracing, at least provisionally, a homophobic representation of homosexuality."[35] Edelman argues along similar lines as Bersani that the fantasies underlying homophobia, which involve a threat to the social order from sexually dissident subjects, may become the means of using queerness to challenge that very set of norms. He writes: "Queerness . . . figures . . . the place of the social order's death drive" and "queerness attains its ethical value precisely insofar as it accedes to that place."[36]

Some literary and artistic responses to Nilsen's case have taken the homophobia of Nilsen's society as impossible to dissociate from representations of his acts and subjectivity, and their working through of this issue seems to address similar questions to those posed by Bersani and Edelman. Poppy Z. Brite's novel *Exquisite Corpse* (1996) explicitly links AIDS and serial killing. Although in many ways a controversial text, and one which has been critiqued by some reviewers for its prurient objectification of gay male sexuality by its female author,[37] it is possible to read the novel as having taken up the queer challenge of embracing the negativity that homophobia ascribes to male homosexuality for counter-discursive ends. *Exquisite Corpse* is a melodramatic, overblown parody of the Gothic horror genre that, in its postmodern form, suggests an acknowledgment of the hybrid discourses, shorn now of historical specificity, that continue to make up the figures of the contemporary killer and the gay man. The novel features as its first person narrator a figure based on Nilsen, a HIV-positive serial killer named Andrew Compton (Andrew is Nilsen's middle name, Old Compton Street a gay district of London where Nilsen met many of his victims), who has a love affair and engages in a murder spree with a fictionalized Jeffrey Dahmer (called Jay Byrne), in a drugs-and-AIDS-ridden San Francisco underworld. The text resignifies HIV-transmission and interpersonal violence as aspects of erotic encounters, risks worth taking. At a certain moment, Jay comments: "HIV? If it finds me, I accept it with my blessing. Maybe it's already found me. If so, I welcome it."[38] Similarly, the cruelty of the world of encounters that is described in the novel is intercut with romance and intimacy, as in the following conversation between Andrew and Jay in which the discourse of "love" is aligned with destruction:

> "I love you, Jay."
>
> "I can't say that. If I loved you, I don't think we'd both still be alive. But I know you, Andrew, and that's something I've never said to anyone else."
>
> "I know you too."
>
> I felt him shiver.[39]

Brite also uses features of Nilsen's case and submits them to fantastical transformations for the purposes of novelistic (melo)drama. Compton identifies with the diagnostic labels that have accrued to him (to Nilsen), poeticizing them in acknowledgment of their Romantic heritage:

> At the trial they called me *necrophiliac* without considering the ancient roots of the word, or its profound resonance. I was friend of the dead, lover of the dead. And I was my own first friend and lover.[40]

The killer is also given the ability to still his own heartbeat and breath and so appear in a dead state, a fanciful interpretation of Nilsen's reported identification with corpses and a device that allows this fictional killer to escape from prison in the opening chapter:

> I achieved a hovering state between consciousness and void, a state where my lungs seemed to stop pulling in air and my heart to cease beating. I could still sense a subliminal murmur of bodily function, but no pulse, no breath. I thought I could feel my skin loosening from the connective tissue, my eyes drying out behind blue-tinged lids, my molten core beginning to cool.[41]

One criticism that can be leveled at Brite's novel—and that does not fall back on spurious identity-politics-based arguments about the kinds of subject matter that women authors have the legitimacy to treat—is that the fictional Compton is not a refutation of the discourse of the killer as an exceptional figure. Indeed, in the passages cited above, the killer is reified as supernaturally powerful, as a master of life and death.

However, it can be argued that in placing at the surface of the text the oddly Romantic tone that accrues to representations and self-representations of Nilsen, Brite effectively shows up the cultural tradition in which murderers are interpreted as Romantic heroes. In the following extract voiced by Compton, moreover, Brite shows that she understands the potency of the discursive myth of the murderer and, without shattering that power, she draws attention to its very discursivity and long history:

> Some may think killing is easy for men like me, that it is a thing we murderers do as casually and callously as brushing our teeth. Hedonists see us as grotesque cult heroes performing mutilations for kicks. Moralists will not even grant us a position in the human race, can only rationalize our existence by calling us monsters. But monster is a medical term, describing a freak too grossly deformed to belong anywhere but the grave. Murderers, skilled at belonging everywhere, seed the world.[42]

Similarly, *Exquisite Corpse* uses the cultural fiction of Nilsen's perceived uniqueness and aberration against the shame and abjection of the most homophobic readings of his killings. Brite describes her fictional gay male killers as capable of affection in stark rejection of the quiet, everyday despair and loneliness that always forms the counterpoint to borrowed discourses of unique grandiosity in Nilsen's own writing and art, as well as in the homophobic renderings of him in mainstream media production. If the book glorifies the violent sovereign subject for the reader in ways that are ethically problematic, it also offers a challenge to the hypocritical homophobia that would lionize certain types of heterosexual destructive masculinity as heroic while casting queer sexuality as, in Edelman's words, "the place of the social order's death drive."

Lloyd Newson's *Dead Dreams of Monochrome Men*, performed by physical theatre company DV8, and filmed in 1989 by David Hinton, addresses similar concerns, but adopts a very different strategy. The piece is "founded upon the conviction that societal homophobia is bound to result in tragic consequences."[43] While the creator states that the piece is based on Masters's account of the Nilsen case in *Killing for Company*, it is rare in avoiding some of the historically ingrained tropes of both homophobia and the stereotype of the killer that I have been tracing. Unlike Poppy Z. Brite's—in other ways equally radical—account, it departs from the "killer as exception" trope by pluralizing Dennis Nilsen's fantasies and acts across four male performers. (The "monochrome man" becomes the "monochrome men" of the title.) In the course of the physical theatrical experience (neither dance nor a play), these four performers are in turn positioned as predators, seducers, lovers, killers, necrophiles, and victims, moving through a series of sets designed to suggest barrooms and private domestic spaces. As one reviewer comments, writing on the live performance at the ICA (Institute of Contemporary Arts in London) in 1988, "It is the especial distinction of this production that the links between the "ordinary" of brief sexual encounters and the "extraordinary" of necrophilia—that ultimate unreason in a relationship—are subtly suggested."[44] In short, the production suspends the pathologizing logic that places clear and distinct boundaries around normal and abnormal sexual preferences and practices for the space of a physical performance in a theatre of desire. And because the world presented in the performance is an all-male homotopia, a world in which male-male desire becomes, for those watching the spectacle, the "norm," it is possible to show the subtle links between the most "ordinary" and the most "extreme" desires without resorting to homophobic othering or heteropatriarchal taxonomy to do so. It is only in the final scene, which reveals a lone figure in a bedsit, surrounded by three male "corpses," one of which is hanging from the ceiling, that we return to the recognizable figure of Dennis Nilsen qua individual. But the logic of the compelling, strangely sympathetic performance is that the individual has ended up here by chance, not by dint of some inborn taint, some uniqueness. Nor, however, does the performance reinforce the homophobic idea of gay sexuality as intrinsically perverse and murderous—an elision in which killer and victim are conflated as morally reprehensible. Rather, it enacts scenes of alienation, loneliness, and desperation regarding the possibility of forming erotic and loving bonds in a culture saturated by homophobia. The effect is to cast the light of critical suspicion on mainstream culture, rather than on gay male sexual subcultures.

Assumptions about gender and sexuality that cluster around discourses about Nilsen in particular, and "queer" murderers in general, are much older and less localized than the AIDS panic that Brite focuses on, or the twentieth-century urban male homosexual subcultures suggested by the tableaux created in *Dead Dreams of Monochrome Men* and *Cold Light of Day*.[45] Just as the codes that construct Nilsen as artist-murderer are rooted in nineteenth-century aesthetic ideas with a wealth of gender and class-bound implications, so the public discourses that operate around Nilsen's sexuality—and that of his victims—rely on often outdated, and always ideological, bodies of knowledge about normality and aberration. That the homosexual and the murderer come into discursive being at historically the same moment as pathologized abnormal types, and that this simultaneity is not innocent or neutral, are insights for which we can thank Foucault.

In a letter to Brian Masters, published by Masters in a *Vanity Fair* article in 1991, Nilsen reflects on his long-held obsession with being both killer and victim in terms that reveal his adoption of a model for understanding (homo)sexuality that Masters has introduced to him, and that is a regressive remnant of nineteenth-century thinking. Nilsen writes:

> Psychologically speaking, [the murderer] becomes both victim and predator (an easy accomplishment in one's imaginary world). Brian, this is what you described in me as "virile male in performance and passive female in spirit."[46]

To talk of the passive partner in the male homosexual act or relationship as "the woman" is a misogynistic and essentialist stereotype based in a crude understanding of binary sex and gender roles. But this is exactly what Masters has done, and what Nilsen dutifully echoes back to him here. To quote Masters from *Killing for Company*:

> If Nilsen's instincts are feminine, this would help to explain why he never pursued a person for whom he felt love, and why in his sexual encounters he was active in performance but passive in spirit. The act of murder could then be a warped act of love, the only way in which he could give his beloved the warm embrace of his body as a woman would and as his confused sexuality would not permit.[47]

The notion of homosexuality understood according to a heterosexual logic (a female soul in a male body), with difference rather than sameness being the condition for attraction, originates, as we have seen, with Ulrichs, the German lawyer and homosexual rights activist who wished to make homosexuality legal and palatable to a repressive society. In strategically claiming that it occurs in nature and is a medical abnormality (and therefore that punishment by law is inappropriate), he unwittingly entrenched an idea that would lead to some of the most damaging stereotypes about the "nature" of gays and lesbians—and about masculinity and femininity, men and women—for decades and centuries to come.

Brian Masters's conservative ideas about the essential nature of male/female, masculine/feminine, and the ways in which these play into forms of nonconsensual sexual behavior based on the domination-subordination paradigm, are amply in evidence throughout his published works. In his biography of Jeffrey Dahmer (in which he makes the convenient argument that Dahmer, like Nilsen, killed as a result of sexual and romantic loneliness), he cites Richard von Krafft-Ebing *as the direct source and authority* for his theorization, rather than as a historically located voice reflecting a series of discursively specific biases and beliefs. Masters writes:

> Krafft-Ebing pointed out that in history a couple's first copulation came about as the direct reward for pursuit and overcoming . . . and to this day cartoons crudely depict the caveman as clubbing his mate and dragging her to his lair. We retain an echo of this ancient rite in the modern Christian marriage, when the bridegroom-predator picks up his "conquest" and carries her off to his domain.[48]

This is not a critique of patriarchy, but an earnest assertion of the "naturalness" of male-over-female dominance, readable as a veiled justification for rape culture. It is the selfsame discourse that we have seen in late nineteenth-century studies of the beastly nature of male desire gone awry. And again, in that letter to Masters published in 1991, Nilsen uses almost the same language to discuss the same question:

> A common view of the Stone Age depicts a potent male clubbing a sexually desirable female into unconsciousness and "wedding" her by an act of copulation with her passive body. Here we have the ingredients of power/violence rendering the desired person into a state of extreme passivity followed by sexual release for the conqueror. . . . This is constant in the serial-killing conundrum whether the victim is male, female or child.[49]

Nilsen and Masters adopt the outdated sexological logic of natural polarities between males and females / masculinity and femininity mapped along axes of aggressivity and passivity. This means that Masters's interpretation of Nilsen's case, which carries the stamp of authority and expertise, as well as Nilsen's own self-descriptions and self-justifications, incorporate (in a noncritical or historicizing way) not only nineteenth-century Romantic discourses about the aesthete-murderer, but also nineteenth-century psychological and sexological orthodoxies, based on ideologically inflected assumptions about the nature of sex and gender that contain homophobic and misogynistic implications. That the killer—inevitably—shares his culture's narratives is a significant point and an illustration of the extent to which the pervasive fantasy of the "exceptional individual" fails to account for the extent to which the killer is a natural extension of, not a deviation from, his or her culture.

The ways in which the gender and sexuality of murderers are discursively constructed have resonances far beyond the specific treatment of "exceptional" individuals. It is not accidental that Myra Hindley was probably the most publicly reviled of twentieth-century British killers. A woman who could countenance and participate in violence against children risks shattering patriarchal society's self-interested belief in the natural law of femininity: maternal instinct. It is also not innocent or accidental that Dennis Nilsen's homosexuality, necrophilia, and murderousness appear as facets of each other in discourses produced by the killer himself and in accounts from mainstream homophobic culture. Discourses of the exception and of the monstrous, projected on to the figure of the killer, are used to shore up the comforting façade of social normality. The use of these discourses keeps the majority righteous, and isolates the deviant few.

Keeping the Killer Apart

The idea of the isolated killer, totally unique but therefore wholly separate from communal humanity, is expressed in one of Dennis Nilsen's prison artworks, an oil painting, *Bacardi Sunrise*, painted in 1995, in which the subject of the portrait, a lone, naked, seated man, is cut off from the garish sunshine brightness around him by a thick red line (see fig. 4.)

Despite his many flirtations with grandiose discourses about his own uniqueness, Nilsen seems, at moments, to have grasped the emotional fantasy investments of culture at large in the specificity of the figure of the killer—the extent to which we want and need killers to be exceptional. Following the arrest of Dahmer in the United States, Brian Masters wrote to ask Nilsen if he thought he could shed light on the crimes of Dahmer, which seemed to Masters to resemble Nilsen's own. Richard Tithecott in his book on Dahmer has noted that this move, of asking an incarcerated killer to comment on the motivations and modus operandi of another murderer, bears a striking real-life analogy with Thomas Har-

FIGURE 4. Dennis Nilsen, *Bacardi Sunrise*, 1995. Oil on canvas. Copyright Dennis Nilsen.

ris's novels *Red Dragon* and the *Silence of the Lambs*, in which the incarcerated multiple murderer and genius Hannibal Lecter is enlisted in police investigations into cases of serial killers at large.[50] Before Tithecott, however, Dennis Nilsen himself remarked on this very parallel—on life imitating fiction in this way—and noted:

> [Hannibal Lecter] is shown as a potent figure, which is pure myth. It is his power and manipulation which please the public. But it's not at all like that. My offences arose from a feeling of inadequacy, not potency. I never had any power in my life.[51]

In his description of the idealized killer-figure who serves a fantasy of omnipotence for culture, Nilsen could be describing some of the fictionalized characters based on him, especially Poppy Z. Brite's Andrew Compton, whose Superman-like powers I have discussed, as accurately as he describes Hannibal Lecter.

I have argued here that the representations created by Nilsen and those created *of* Nilsen exist in a recognizable continuum in ways that are particularly striking. Nilsen's citations of Romantic poetry and imitation of Romantic poetic conventions in his own writings suggest an identification with the very discourses that birthed the modern figure of the killer as both exceptional, aesthetic subject and as monster beyond good and evil. That discursive identification is the only way to represent the killer, I argue, because that figure only exists as a discourse. Proponents of this discourse range historically from Pierre-François Lacenaire to twentieth-century authors and murder experts. The idea that art is murder and the idea that murder is art are insistently repeated dual falsities—wishful fantasies of a culture obsessed with the figure of exceptionality. This figure functions both as an endlessly fascinating cipher of alterity and as a moral scapegoat. Add to this the extent to which internalized and societal homophobia feature in the meaning-making that occurs with regard to the crimes of Dennis Nilsen, and it becomes clear that the significance of the tragedy wrought by Nilsen may be rooted not in his terrible separateness from the culture in which he lived, but rather in the extent to which he shared—and brought to life—the very fantasies of the culture that dreamed him.

CHAPTER SIX

Serial Killing and the Dissident Woman

Aileen Wuornos

Wuornos: "Hey, by the way, I'm going down in history."
Moore: "What a way to go down in history."
—(Recorded telephone conversation between Aileen Wuornos and her partner
Tyria Moore, 1991)

A raped woman got executed and was used for books and movies and shit.
—(Aileen Wuornos in interview with Nick Broomfield, 2002)

I want the world to know I killed these men, as cold as ice. I've hated humans for a long
time. I am a serial killer. I killed them in cold blood. Real nasty.
—(Aileen Wuornos cited in Oliver Burkman, "Florida Executes Woman Serial Killer,"
Guardian, 10 October 2002)

In this chapter, I explore ways in which the available discourses of the
exceptional murdering subject that have been sketched out so far in
this book are a particularly problematic fit in the case of Aileen "Lee"
Wuornos (1956–2002), a lesbian, prostitute, and victim of sexual abuse,
who killed seven men in Florida between 1989 and 1990.[1] I examine how
the label of "serial killer" was debated with regard to Wuornos, and how
it was at times rejected; at times adopted as a badge of agency and of selfhood by Wuornos herself who continually sought, like those around her,
to make sense of herself through her crimes. Her discourse alternated, as
seen in the chapter epigraphs, between assertions that her killings were
acts of self-defense and statements that interpret them as a proud bid for
recognition via the evocation of the "cold-blooded" serial killer.

Wuornos was frequently described in the media as "the first female text-book case of a serial killer," after the pronouncement of an FBI spokesperson to this effect.[2] In fact, it may well have been the *method of killing* used by Wuornos that earned her this label. Commenting on the FBI's description of Wuornos, Candice Skrapec writes: "This is patently false, unless one uses a definition of a female serial killer as a female who kills a number of people over time using 'male' methods of killing."[3] As Skrapec points out,[4] there had, in fact, been numerous female multiple killers prior to Wuornos (women allegedly representing 10–17 percent of all known serial murderers).[5] Wuornos's crimes, then, are unusual because they defy the norms established for the way in which members of the sexes murder. They certainly fail to match up with Robert Ressler's observed pattern for specifically female homicides: "When there is violence involving women, it's usually in the home, with husbands and boyfriends. It's a close in, personal crime."[6] The difficulty in defining Aileen Wuornos, then, seems to lie in the fact that the modus operandi of her multiple murders was problematically "masculine": she killed alone; she killed strangers, in public spaces, using a gun (rather than the "feminine" methods of poison or smothering); and her habit of hitchhiking as a means of soliciting clients for paid sex was interpreted as a predatory method of hunting for victims.[7] The perception that Wuornos killed "like a man"[8] was additionally doubtless reinforced by the factors of her lesbianism and her aggressive, hostile, "unfeminine" attitude in court. In her feminist study of prostitute-killer Peter Sutcliffe, Nicole Ward Jouve writes: "Why is it that no women go about murdering 'punters,' convinced they're on a God-given mission to rid the city of its litter? It's not just that the case is never reversed: we can't even imagine it being reversed."[9] In some ways, then, Aileen Wuornos did the unthinkable; she brought about this reversal, allegedly taking revenge on physically abusive "punters" by shooting them dead, and professed a continuing belief that she would go to Heaven while those who condemned her to multiple death sentences would rot in Hell.[10]

Aileen's contradictory self-presentation is complicated by the ways in which the commercially viable myth of the extraordinary "first female serial killer" was utilized by her friends, including her lover Tyria Moore; her "adopted mother," born-again Christian Arlene Pralle; and her lawyer-turned-agent, Steven Glazer, in order to market her story and her persona. (This is the central thesis of Nick Broomfield's 1993 documentary, *Aileen Wuornos: The Selling of a Serial Killer*.) The very marketable

Wuornos has certainly been extensively represented on celluloid: Broomfield went on to release a second documentary, *Aileen: Life and Death of a Serial Killer*, in 2003, after Wuornos's execution. She has also been the subject of several narrative films, including the made-for-TV *Overkill: The Aileen Wuornos Story* (Peter Levin, 1992). This film was controversial, as the rights to her story were sold to the production company by Tyria Moore in conjunction with members of the arresting police force (leading to the officers' dismissal from service).[11] Additionally, the award-winning *Monster* (Patty Jenkins, 2003) saw Aileen played by highly paid, glamorous Hollywood actress Charlize Theron, transformed by makeup and prosthetic teeth to resemble the real-life killer, and who reportedly studied Broomfield's documentaries between takes to aid the widely commented-upon verisimilitude of her performance. The commercial mine that was the persona and story of Aileen Wuornos also resulted in numerous true-crime books on the case, the first of which was Michael Reynolds's unsympathetic and often misogynistic *Dead Ends* (1992). These also include Christopher Berry-Dee's *Monster: My True Story*, a biographical work allegedly coauthored with Wuornos, but which disingenuously passes itself off as Aileen's "true" story on the tenuous grounds that transcriptions of her trial testimonies and of recorded conversations are inserted between the chapters in bold uppercase type. Finally, she has, like Dennis Nilsen, been the subject of avant-garde queer artworks that resist the mainstreaming of the killer's story, such as Millie Wilson's 1994 installation *Not a Serial Killer* and Tammy Rae Carland's video *Lady Outlaws and Faggot Wannabes* (1995). Both works critique the media's overexposure and exploitation of Wuornos.[12]

As the titles of both Jenkins's biopic and Berry-Dee's book suggest (though the film is rather sympathetic to its fictionalized Aileen, whereas the book is not), Wuornos was portrayed primarily as a "monstrous" figure, that construction which Foucault tells us was one of the discourses that went to make up the modern subject of criminality and assure its "othering" from the norm.[13] Patty Jenkins has commented in a documentary made for the release of the 2006 DVD box set of *Monster* and the Broomfield films that she wanted to show how "some people don't have a choice but to become a monster."[14] While Jenkins seems to have approached the subject matter of *Monster* sensitively, it has been noted that coverage of the film's success did not focus much on the real-life plight of Aileen herself. Kyra Pearson comments that "in her acceptance speeches for three separate best actress awards for portraying Wuornos in the film, Charlize Theron never acknowledged Wuornos, nor did she use these occasions to raise awareness of violence sex workers commonly face."[15] Nick Broomfield has also expressed the sentiment that "on the night of the Oscars there was very little discussion about Aileen. . . . It made me rather angry."[16] The real-life figure behind Theron's role was made to disappear as attention was—in typical Hollywood fashion—entirely brought to bear on the audacious uglification of Theron for her role (the temporary making monstrous of an exemplum of ideal femininity). Fascination with Theron's transformation thereby overshadowed the story that Jenkins wished to tell: how society made of Aileen Wuornos a monster (see figs. 5 and 6).

Wuornos's identity as a "monster" is constructed with reference to her divergence from cultural norms (or ideals) of class-bound and heterosexual femininity, not only in her lifestyle as prostitute and lesbian, but also—as we have seen—in having killed in a "masculine" way. Although 100 years after Lombroso's account of the criminal woman, the extent to which violence, lesbianism, and prostitution, as three forms of dissident female behavior, intersect to produce the figure of the inappropriately "masculine" woman is visible in portrayals of Wuornos. It is instructive to compare the othered representation of lesbian killer

FIGURE 5. Charlize Theron as Aileen Wuornos in *Monster* (Patty Jenkins, 2003).

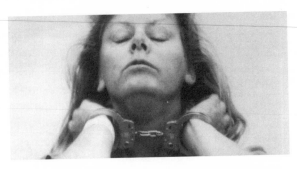

FIGURE 6. Iconic image of Aileen Wuornos in court, attempting to push back her hair while cuffed. *Aileen: Life and Death of a Serial Killer* (Nick Broomfield and Joan Churchill, 2003).

Wuornos with representations of gay male murderer Nilsen, who, while also subject to homophobic discursive treatment, as we have seen, is more closely aligned in creative (if not true-crime or mass media) texts with the nineteenth-century Romantic figure of the artist-murderer that he too cites in his own writings. Wuornos, on the other hand, is relegated the role of serial-killing monster, an improperly gendered peg in the cultural slot marked "sex-beast."

In what follows, I will explore the range of responses to this "rare specimen."[17] As Helen Birch has written, many media discourses about Wuornos assume that she was "self-conscious about what being a serial killer means; in other words, murdering men was her way of courting celebrity."[18] Other sources insist that Wuornos was a troubled, traumatized survivor of past abuse, and/or mentally ill. By reading feminist defenses of Wuornos that claim she is inaccurately described by the label "serial killer" and more accurately served by that of "victim," alongside the vilifying and misogynistic media reports of her crimes, sentence, and execution, I will assess what is really at stake in claiming that Wuornos, a socially disenfranchised woman, used the availability of the archetypal figure of the exceptional-killer-as-celebrity to stake a claim to fame/infamy. I will pay attention to how signifiers of economic deprivation and mental illness intersect with discourses of gender and sexuality in rendering representations of Wuornos exceptional as a killer and monstrous as a woman. In a second section, I will argue that Wuornos's acts and self-presentation need to be considered not only within the dichotomy of the feminist framework of victimhood and the media presentation of serial-killing criminality, but also as acts of radical dissent in and of themselves, intelligible alongside a consideration of radical feminist Valerie Solanas's attempted murder of Andy Warhol in 1968 as a political statement. In such a reading, Wuornos would be a reactive social agent not a passive, defensive victim. Finally, I will argue that the presence of this seldom-articulated, discursively underrepresented figure of a "radical feminist serial killer" nevertheless haunted the Wuornos case and may be responsible for the particularly harsh sentencing and treatment meted out to Aileen. The North American criminal justice system has been argued to be generally more lenient in sentencing women than in sentencing men, but *considerably* more punitive in cases of violent female homicides than in those of their male counterparts, especially when the murdering woman can be seen to flout blatantly other cultural expectations of femininity.[19]

Reading the Violent Woman—Monster, Victim, or Mad Woman?

Criminologists Elizabeth Comack and Salena Brickey have recently argued that "efforts to make sense of the Violent Woman" tend to do so according to three related, but distinct, categories: those of "the bad," "the mad," and "the victim."[20] These three (simplistic) constructions for attempting to reduce nonstereotypical female behavior to the comprehensible are the primary conflicting ways in which Aileen's behavior has been debated and explained.

As David Schmid has asserted, true-crime books, along with lowbrow media, tend to focus on the most sensationalist aspects of a crime and the most stereotypical myths of the murderer, in order to ensure an avid readership.[21] Additionally, their commonly conservative view of gender norms and defense of a right-wing social order tend toward the production of a straightforward moral tale (often in tandem with a hypocritical focus on tantalizing details of the lurid or sexual aspects of a case). Accordingly, and as we would expect, it is here that we find some of the most virulent expressions of misogyny and monstrous othering directed at Wuornos. In an interesting article, Megan Sweeney comments on the, perhaps unexpected, fact that true crime is a popular genre of reading material with incarcerated prisoners, especially women. This perhaps helps us to understand one means by which subjects who will go on to be criminals, or who are already criminals, might self-construct using the vilifying (yet also sometimes mythologizing and therefore aggrandizing) discourses found in these books.[22] Sweeney likewise views this phenomenon through a Foucauldian lens as "self-disciplining" and as a mechanism by which the female criminal is encouraged to adopt "a normalizing gaze that compels her to confess to her character weaknesses."[23] Sweeney makes mention of Michael Reynolds's *Dead Ends*, commenting that it "elides any mention of Wuornos's myriad and profound experiences of social injury, including years of sexual abuse, rape, and homelessness."[24] She further comments that an incarcerated woman she interviewed, whom she calls "Audrey," had read *Dead Ends* and contested strongly Reynolds's account of Wuornos as "a villain that was just out with a gun slingin' it around like a cowboy, just shootin' people for no reason,"[25] as that was not consistent with "Audrey's" own experiences of committing crimes as a woman. This demonstrates that the reading of true crime can promote, for the female reader, the production of reverse-discourse and a questioning of the normative moral perspective presented therein, as a counterweight to the self-loathing identification to which it may also lead.

This counterreading depends on an empathy with the criminalized female perspective and, as is amply evidenced, most of the true-crime and mass media discourse produced about Wuornos (as was seen in the case of Hindley) is from a mainstream, establishment (masculine) perspective and presumably targeted at a readership from a similar demographic. In this, it says more about male expectations of women in general and female criminals in particular than about female experience, as "Audrey's" comments illustrate. Indeed, in an interview with Broomfield in his 1993 documentary, *Dead Ends* author Reynolds expresses blatantly judgmental and misogynist views about Aileen and, by extension, sex workers. He tells Broomfield that Aileen was lazy throughout her life. She didn't apply herself as a prostitute *or* as a criminal. She didn't even make the effort to wear makeup to attract her "punters."[26] Christopher Berry-Dee's fraudulently subtitled *Monster: My True Story* is similarly biased in its perspective. About her childhood abuse, Berry-Dee writes: "We . . . know that Lee was having full sex from around the age of nine. *We cannot even think that she was some kind of 'slut' at that age, as so many observers feel content to believe.*"[27] That he uses the phrase "having sex," rather than "being raped," to apply to a nine-year-old girl is as telling as the implication that "slut" would be a perfectly reasonable label to apply to an older girl or woman. Similarly, describing Wuornos's time as a prostitute and killer, he writes, "The true nature of Lee's psychopathic personality was . . . unleashed . . . in a car *with a vulnerable man at some lonely place.*"[28] That Berry-Dee can twist the gendered power dynamic such that the male "john" appears as the default vulnerable party in any encounter between a man paying for sex and a prostitute—an encounter that, moreover, takes place in the former's car—is again telling. The (perceived) facts of Wuornos's exceptional case provide an alibi for gleeful distortion of the statistical reality of gendered violence in the case of prostitutes.[29]

Such examples of garden-variety misogyny aside, Berry-Dee soon gets into his stride of vilifying Wuornos as an exceptional woman, worse even than those other sluts and nonmurderous predatory hookers for whom he so casually reveals contempt. He writes: "Sometimes society and circumstance throw up a female killer who, because of her crimes and, indeed, because she is a woman, stuns and sickens us all. Lee Wuornos was that very rare specimen."[30] The "sickening" rare specimen is soon named "monster" by Berry-Dee. This comes in the context of Lee's perceived relinquishment of a façade of remorse and desire for forgiveness. "She [originally] wanted to 'make it good with God' before she died," Berry-Dee writes. However, "this would soon change as the months passed inexorably by during which Aileen Wuornos would metamorphose into *the true monster that she really was.*"[31] This exemplifies the mechanism with which we are by now familiar: in the construction of the murdering subject, the true essence of evil is always understood to have been hiding beneath the façade of normality, waiting to emerge. Finally, Aileen's turning her back on both God and her lover are read as signs of her egotism and increasing obsession with fame:

> She had been allowed newspapers and she avidly poured [*sic*]over the notoriety she was now receiving from the world's media. Her emotions, which had originally centered around Tyria, started to take a back seat. Religion and turning to God was way back in the past. She was becoming a celebrity—a person of some import and, for the first time in her life, she felt she had at least achieved something of value.[32]

What is not admitted of in this condemnation is the fact that Tyria had betrayed her, both by taking part in a recorded telephone call in which she entrapped Aileen into incriminating herself at the behest of the police, and in mercilessly selling her story to the highest bidder. As Nick

Broomfield points out, while Aileen Wuornos's persona is not immediately easy to sympathize with, the pathos of her position lies in the fact that everyone she had trusted in her life ultimately betrayed her.[33]

The recourse to the "monster" figure and the meaning of the repeated ascription to Aileen of the "serial killer" label in the media and true-crime may be explained by the fact that these discourses obviate the necessity to look for deeper explanations of motive—and therefore for the possibility of mitigation or moral complexity. "Monster" is the ontological essence of otherness, inexplicable by its very nature. And, as I hypothesized in the introduction to this book, that ascribed quality of the serial killer's crimes that consists in randomness and motivelessness carries on a tradition of belief in a subject who is in no way like the rest of us, who is capable of an acte gratuit. It ensures one-dimensionality and removes from us the responsibility even to *try* to understand. Feminist critics of criminology Lynda Hart and Belinda Morrissey concur. Hart points out that inserting Wuornos's murders into the serial killer narrative casts them as enigmatic and inexplicable,[34] while Morrissey theorizes that, in the guise of "monster" and "serial killer," Aileen "no longer challenges because she now has more in common with a celluloid or literary icon than with flesh and blood women who harbour legitimate grievances."[35]

Lynda Hart's position perhaps best exemplifies the feminist defense of Wuornos. It focuses on the institutional violence and exploitation she suffered and shores up Wuornos's own original defense that she was an abused prostitute defending herself from violent clients who raped and injured, or attempted to rape and injure, her. Indeed, Hart's *Fatal Women* is dedicated "to Aileen Wuornos" and "to all the women who have been vilified, pathologized, and murdered for defending themselves by whatever means necessary." This casts Wuornos very far from the serial killer mold, and in the discourse of victim, despite her obvious capacity for violence (exemplified by the fact that she shot her first victim repeatedly, leading to the sound bite "overkill" being used in relation to her crimes and becoming the title of her first biopic). Comack and Brickey further clarify the systemic nature of the need for female self-defense asserted by Hart: "The Violent Woman of feminist discourse . . . emerged as the 'Victimized Woman.' Her violence was not of her own making but a response to her 'victim' status under conditions of patriarchy."[36]

However, this (feminist) view of self-defense and victimhood is slightly different from the one that was used in court by Aileen's attorney. The case for the defense too relied on Wuornos's status as victim, but focused principally on the facts of the extensive sexual abuse and neglect she had suffered as a child:

> Her early life . . . included her abandonment at three months of age. Her father, in prison for sexually abusing a young girl, committed suicide when Wuornos was seven. She was raised by an alcoholic grandfather who sadistically beat her. Wuornos began life on the streets at 15 and was raped at least five times before she was 18 years old. Her life of drinking, drugs, and abuse eventually led to prostitution.[37]

According to Morrissey, this focus on the past abuse she suffered risks taking attention away from the idea that she really was defending herself against harmful attacks by her clients at the time of the crimes. It makes her instead into a damaged, traumatized woman and suggests the idea that she could have been projecting the abuse of the past onto her "clients" in the present. Morrissey sums up: "Aileen Wuornos was at the mercy of either inhuman lusts or of previous abuse; at no time did her story of reasonable self-defense receive anything but scant consideration."[38] And, moreover, the focus on the past abuse perversely contributed to confirming the "serial killer" diagnosis, "since a disturbed childhood is a feature of many serial killers."[39] What was obviously not taken into account is the extent to which abuse in childhood is rather likely to have a different adult outcome for women than for men, owing to the former group being socialized to internalize trauma and the latter to externalize it as self-assertion and aggression.

Moreover, where in the case of male serial killers who murder female sex workers, the victims' biographies and occupations are often evoked by defense counsels in the service of victim-blaming,[40] in the Wuornos case, the victims were elevated to saintly status, despite the first victim's (Mallory's) prior 10-year sentence for attempted rape, a fact that was not revealed to the jury during Wuornos's original trial. Wuornos's sex, sexuality, and class are doubtless responsible for the reversal that operates in her case. Claudia Card writes:

> Those who have come to be known as serial killers in the past have been relatively powerful or privileged men who preyed upon women, especially powerless women (such as the prostitutes murdered by Jack the Ripper, or college students murdered by Ted Bundy), or upon relatively powerless men (such

as the young gay men of color murdered by Jeffrey Dahmer). Aileen Wuornos has never been socially powerful or privileged, and those she killed were white, heterosexual, middle-class men who would easily have had social protection for doing to her what she said they would have done had she not defended herself.[41]

Indeed, as Pearson has pointed out, the dubbing of Wuornos in the press as "Damsel of Death" is designed to suggest proximity to the idea of a "damsel in distress": the hitchhiking Wuornos, by the roadside, armed with a hard-luck story. In this narrative, her johns/victims can be elevated from punters to chivalrous gentlemen who would never normally have thought of paying a prostitute and were merely helping out a woman apparently in trouble.[42] Contrast Mallory's wife's genteel and gender-conforming description of her husband, the convicted attempted rapist: "He was so sweet . . . if he saw a woman in distress, he would stop and help her"[43] with Aileen Wuornos's vitriolic testimonial: "Mallory . . . was a mean motherfucker. . . . He starts to get violent. The son of a bitch. He's holding me down. He's going to try and rape me. . . . I shot him."[44] Wuornos's account sounds callous, yet it has a directness; it is stripped of any social niceties and reveals the very bones of her truth. Wuornos is, however, damned by her class-marked vernacular, her anger, and her "unladylike" use of profanities here, as when she snarls at the judge following her first death sentence: "I hope your wife and kids get raped in the ass."[45] Juxtaposing Wuornos's social-sexual dissidence with the perceived respectable, middle-class, family-oriented heterosexual maleness of her victims (including a former police chief), the court and the media worked, as Schmid puts it, to "demonize [Wuornos's] lesbianism" while "exonerat[ing] her victims."[46] In response to Wuornos's outburst following her sentencing, the judge remorselessly retorted "may God have mercy on your corpse." Unlike male sentenced killers, Wuornos is presumably not even assumed to have a soul.[47]

The stark socioeconomic disenfranchisement of Aileen Wuornos combined with her appearance as a "masculine" lesbian served to dehumanize the female killer who robbed the lives of "family men" and threatened middle-class standards in the eyes of a gender-normative America reared on family values. In Carland's video, *Lady Outlaws and Faggot Wannabes*, Carland's voice-over, heard against a backdrop of footage of Wuornos speaking in court and in police custody, emphasizes

the markers of working-class poverty and butch mannerisms that drew
the media's attention to her:

> Every time she swears, swaggers or snarls they take a picture. Her skin is ev-
> idence. The way it hangs on her thick bones like gravity prematurely got the
> best of her. Too much sun and cheap soap. Never enough protection. Her
> hands are evidence. Hands that have trailed the bodies of women—looking
> for the place that makes breath halt. . . . The chain that hangs from her belt
> loop is evidence. Low and on the left.[48]

Yet Aileen's erratic speech and behavior in court were not only considered rude and gender nonconformist. They hinted at a mental distur-
bance. She had a diagnosis of borderline personality disorder, but was
considered technically sane. (A personality disorder, as distinct from a
psychosis, is less likely to qualify for an adjudication of legal insanity, as
those diagnosed as suffering from the former are felt to be able to understand the "nature and quality" of the act they commit.)[49]

The question mark around Wuornos's sanity (the "mad" as distinct
from "bad" discourse) intersects with arguments about her status as a
victim, and therefore was subject to the same suspicion from those determined to condemn her as evil. Despite the multiple abuses she had
suffered in childhood and adulthood, despite visible symptoms of post-
traumatic stress disorder and personality disorder, the court could find
no compassion for Aileen Wuornos. Even Berry-Dee who, as we have
seen, is far from being Wuornos's biggest champion, hints at the spite inherent in the multiple death sentence verdict, stating that, despite hearing expert psychiatric testimonies that Aileen was mentally ill, "the jurors neither forgot nor forgave the woman they had come to know during
the trial."[50]

Nick Broomfield believed as early as 1992 that Aileen was telling the
truth about the violent assault by Mallory and that his attack, and her
initial defensive killing of him, prompted a mental breakdown that led to
the other murders. By the time of Wuornos's execution, some 10 years after her first trial, the signs of a troubled, fragmented person had strongly
increased, such that indications of delusion and dissociation consistent
with what is called psychosis were present. Broomfield was anxious for
Aileen to appeal her sentence on the grounds of self-defense and diminished responsibility one final time. The footage he recorded of a conver-

sation with her the day before her execution shows a Wuornos no longer interested in proclaiming self-defense, but possessed of a delusional
conviction that the police had "set her up" to become a serial killer. She
claimed that officials knew that she had killed Mallory from the beginning, as her DNA was all over the crime scene, and that they had left her
at large in order both to "clean up the streets" and to birth a sensational
serial killer whose story would make them money. Moreover, her belief
that the authorities were sending sonic-waves into her cell to penetrate
and control her thoughts suggests a degree of paranoia hardly consistent
with the fact that, a day prior to the taping of this conversation, she was
considered in an interview with a psychiatrist to be sane enough to be
executed. What is worthy of note, however, is that Aileen's fantasy that
the police "created" her as a serial killer has a grain of truth, if not *literally*, as a premeditated ruse, then certainly on the level of the workings
of discursive construction and commercial entrepreneurship. Aileen was
indeed set up, constructed, made subject, and sold as serial killer, but
retroactively—not prior to—her crimes. Her delusion lies only in assuming intention before the fact on the part of the authorities.

Aileen's relationship to her common categorization as either monster or victim is a schizoid one that mirrors the division within the society in which she was tried. At times echoing the feminist line of self-
defense, at other times adopting the serial killer label, Aileen plays with
various discourses, but the only one she never takes up is that which engages with the possibility of her own madness. In 1992, Aileen claimed,
lucidly and logically, to Nick Broomfield that she was not a classic serial
killer, and that counting the number of crimes committed is a red herring when trying to understand her case. Each killing had been a case
of self-defense, she states, and a principle—the right to defend oneself
from harm—should count for more than the number of times one has
had to do so. "It's not about a number, but about a principle," she repeatedly tells Broomfield.[51] By the time of the 2002 interview, when Aileen
was depressed, obviously delusional, and ready to die, Broomfield commented in an interview made for the 2006 DVD box set release of the
film that "she very much acted the part of the serial killer," proclaiming:
"I killed those seven men in cold blood. I'm coming clean. There was no
self-defense."[52] The press picked up on such statements, made repeatedly
in Wuornos's petitions to have her death sentence hastened by the state
of Florida. "I am a serial killer. I would kill again," she is reported as say-

ing in the *Advocate*.[53] And, in the *Chicago Sun-Times*: "I just flat robbed [and] killed them, and there was a lot of hatred behind everything."[54]

David Schmid comments on such stark proclamations by Aileen that "Wuornos's almost parodically vicious assertion of her extreme, inhuman deviance represents her attempt to seize control of the narratives about her."[55]

It is possible that Aileen had merely grown sick of her life on death row and, desperately seeking release via execution, concurred with the identity that others so clearly expected of her. It is also possible, however, that her proud boasts had a rebellious function and that she was genuinely trying to articulate a type of agency and subjectivity that are not identical in meaning with those of the male "serial killer," the profile by which she was being understood. As Pearson has argued, for profilers, media, and judiciary "the process of making her intelligible as a female serial killer depended on labeling her male and masculine."[56] Yet what if Aileen's specific kind of serial-killing monstrosity lay in personifying the threat of the man-hating, castrating, feminist lesbian that, as was amply seen in the course of her trials and media coverage, is patriarchal America's disavowed bogeywoman?

The Female "Serial Killer" as Radical Feminist Terrorist?

In addition to the three explanatory categories applied to Aileen's subjectivity and crimes discussed in the previous section: feminine evil (the supposition implied in the superstitious and gender-conservative true-crime narrative); the instinct for self-defense (argued by feminist commentators and by Nick Broomfield); and insanity (a further mitigating factor in Aileen's defense for Broomfield, confirmed by psychiatric defense witnesses at the original trial), David Schmid suggests a fourth possibility that deserves further investigation: that of political resistance. He writes: "Being honest about Wournos's status as a violent woman and locating Wuornos's murders within a tradition of resistance to violence against women open up a consideration of her murders as a political act, as an act of protest."[57] Moreover, Seltzer has suggested that it makes sense to think of serial killing more generally "as a sort of subpolitical class protest,"[58] an idea that makes particular sense in the cases of female murderers Myra Hindley and Aileen Wuornos, both alienated in different ways from the intersecting economic, cultural, and gendered classes to which they belonged.

That Wuornos was killing as a more or less conscious gesture of defiance of the patriarchy is corroborated by some of the statements she has made, such as the following cited in Reynolds: "I feel like a hero. 'Cause I've done some good. I'm a killer of rapists."[59] Patty Jenkins's biopic also suggests, at moments, this reading of Wuornos, especially in one striking sequence of dialogue between Lee (Theron) and "Selby" (Ricci). (Interestingly, this powerful scene is abridged in the released version and appears in full only in the "extras" of the 2006 DVD box set.) Lee's speech is as follows:

> People kill each other every day and for what? For politics. For religion. And they're heroes. No. There's a lot of shit I can't do any more. But killing's not one of them. And letting those fucking bastards out there go and rape somebody else isn't either. . . . There's a whole world of people out there killing and raping, Selby. But I am the only one killing them. . . . Look at me, Sel. You know me. You do. Do you think I could do it otherwise? I'm not a bad person. I'm a real good person.[60]

The notion of a "real good person" who removes rapists and killers from the streets before they can attack women transforms Aileen from mad/ sad victim into a feminist avenger, uncannily answering Ward Jouve's question about the existence of the murderous prostitute cleansing the streets of aggressive "punters" in revolt against systemic male violence.

Like Valerie Solanas, author of the *SCUM Manifesto* ("Society for Cutting Up Men"), Wuornos at times casts herself as responding to violent men in the only language they understand. Killing, violence, and rape are their currency—and Wuornos obliges by becoming proficient in that language. When Valerie Solanas writes that "the male likes death— it excites him sexually and, already dead inside, he wants to die,"[61] and then attempts to deliver annihilation to men, she follows a joined-up logic that appears (within the system of that logic) expedient rather than cruel, since, according to her, men will in any case ultimately self-destruct. Like Aileen Wuornos, Valerie Solanas had been a prostitute. Like Valerie Solanas, Wuornos wrote and spoke in angry, exclamatory tones. Like Aileen Wuornos, who "killed like a man," Solanas raised her gun and shot Andy Warhol.

However, following her crime, Solanas was recognized as an activist

by fellow feminists who rallied to her defense. Florynce Kennedy, a radical feminist lawyer, declared Solanas "one of the most important spokes-
women of the feminist movement," and Ti-Grace Atkinson named her
the "first outstanding champion of women's rights."[62] For reasons that,
we might hypothesize, are related to class, cultural capital, and education (Solanas having had status within the bohemian subculture she in-
habited in the 1960s that Aileen certainly lacked), Wuornos's crimes
were not received in this spirit by feminists. In an article in 1994, Richard
Greiner actually dubbed Wuornos "feminism's first serial killer," stating
in his title that "Feminists Should Gloat over Their Serial Killer."[63] Yet
feminists very definitely did not gloat, champion, or even defend Wuornos's acts *in these terms*. Pearson has pointed out the lack of concerted
support on the part of sex workers', lesbians', and women's rights groups
for Wuornos:

> [While] the Coalition to Free Aileen Wuornos displayed a banner encourag-
> ing participants at the 1993 March on Washington for lesbian and gay rights
> to "Support Dykes who Fight Back," some members of the Lesbian Aveng-
> ers in New York presumably hesitated to advocate for Wuornos, believing ei-
> ther that she was not a lesbian or that "there were women more worthy of the
> group's support."[64]

Those few that rose to champion her from a feminist standpoint, then,
did so only on the grounds that she was a victim of abuse and rape acting
in self-defense: a victim of the patriarchy not a voluble, violent, and agentic opponent of it. It is as if there is an unwillingness on the part of many
feminist groups to accept women's capacity for violence, which is an odd
political contradiction as one might expect that feminism would oppose
the essentialist gender stereotyping which holds that women are gentle
and peaceful while men are naturally violent. Skrapec has stated that
this is a deeply ingrained belief of Western culture, which may explain
why even most feminists might have trouble deconstructing it: "The public is at once fearful of and fascinated by the individual who lives by his
or her own rules. The notion so violates the idea of femaleness, tied to
her traditional nurturing role, that *a woman is denied her identity as a
multiple murderer*."[65]

It is in recognition of the general lack of willingness to see her on her
own terms, perhaps, that Wuornos's defiant insistence both on being recognized as a victim of male violence *and* seen as a "serial killer" be-

gins to make sense. The subjectifying discourse of "radical lesbian feminist serial killer," which might be closer to the subject position she would
have wished to occupy in the public eye, is not a culturally available one,
despite Greiner's acerbic coining of a similar label. Where the (male)
serial killer is an unlikely hero, a bad boy celebrity, the feminist warrior is not even articulable. Even Valerie Solanas, for all her cult status
and following, was similarly considered mentally ill, and her acts provoked no major feminist uprising. Avital Ronell states that Solanas "was
not meant to have disciples or spawn a new breed of revolutionaries. . . .
She had no followers. She offered the uniquely American dead-end-one-
warrior-revolution spinning on its own determined axis."[66]

Yet there is evidence to suggest that the figure of the murderous radical feminist lesbian *is* a specter haunting both Aileen's discourse and that
of her culture, as seen in the following anecdote recounted to Reynolds by
Tyria, about an evening when Aileen and Tyria were watching *Roseanne*:

> Roseanne was a hoot. She was doing this routine about serial killers, about
> how they were always men who were psychos; but if one of them turned out
> to be a woman, everybody would just call her a man-hater, and Lee has just
> burst out "that's me she's talking about."[67]

A different way of looking at the much-touted accusation of the misogynist stereotype of the "man-hating lesbian" in the case of Wuornos
might, in fact, be to consider it as a proudly adopted identity and form of
political subjectivity, in the face of few alternatives. Yet here, in the *Roseanne* example, the putative threatening figure is neutralized as a sick joke
rather than accorded the reverence meted out to the male serial killer.

Women's anger, as we have seen, is not permitted in mainstream discourse. Wuornos's anger has, in the discourses observed in the first section, been supplanted with madness or with victimhood, even by her
would-be defenders, or obfuscated with metaphysical notions of evil by
those who wish to put her beyond the reach of sympathy or human understanding. Much less can the notion that women might enjoy the violence they commit be countenanced. Schmid writes:

> In order to demonstrate that Wuornos was not an "ordinary" female multi-
> ple murderer . . . but something much more dangerous and threatening, a fe-
> male serial murderer, true-crime accounts of the case must demonstrate that
> Wuornos not only killed the seven men but enjoyed doing so.[68]

Where the patriarchal view reads evidence that Lee may have enjoyed killing men as proof of her monstrous evil, a feminist reading may hold it up as evidence of her *humanness*. Why on earth would it be that male killers might derive some sort of satisfaction from committing a violent act against a hated figure, but no woman ever would? If the role of "serial-killing woman" were to become, even theoretically, one of empowerment and resistance for women in patriarchy, it becomes clear why there would be a strong investment in silencing that interpretation. It becomes clear too what is at stake in the strategy of *turning the female serial killer into a man*, following philosopher Jeffner Allen's assertion that "a woman is not violent, and if violent, a female is not a woman."[69] Just as feminist ideas about the meaningful genderedness of the predominantly male serial-killing phenomenon, such as Jane Caputi's argument that it is "sexually political murder . . . functional phallic terrorism,"[70] are dismissed in favor of the idea of the serial killer as "random" and "motiveless," so Wuornos must be an anomaly, a monster rather than a symptom. The stakes are high when it comes to maintaining that serial killing be understood as an individual aberration rather than an inevitable product of culture. For society to accept otherwise would mean acknowledging the very existence of patriarchy.

"Victim feminism" alone may be no more politically useful or accurate in accounting for Lee's crimes than misogynistic accounts of her as "evil whore and callous thief."[71] Following Schmid's lead, I think it behooves us to "be honest about Wuornos's status as a violent woman." This involves refusing to interpret the exceptional female figure who kills as a cipher of "randomness," of nihilistic meaninglessness, as is implied in the actions of the subject labeled the "serial killer" (that label so contested in relation to Wuornos), and seeing her, in the wake of Valerie Solanas perhaps, as a "dead-end-one-warrior-revolution" without the education or opportunity to articulate a political position that she nevertheless embodied and enacted.

Backlash: Punishing the Violent Woman

Even if Wuornos did not explicitly articulate her subject position as that of a "feminist terrorist," the threat offered by the specter of this figure was nevertheless evidently felt in the speculations surrounding her figure and case. Broomfield comments in a voice-over at the beginning of the 2003 documentary that "the idea of a woman killing men, a man-hating lesbian prostitute who tarnished the reputation of all her victims, brought Aileen Wuornos a special kind of hatred." And Miriam Basilio has commented that Wuornos's killings may be obliquely linked to a backlash against the gains of feminism at the end of the last century and the beginning of this one: "The use of Wuornos to redefine the category of criminal deviance known as the serial killer to include women occurs at a time when women's greater social mobility is causing anxiety in conservative sectors of American society."[72] In light of the fearful, conservative attitudes that, as I have been exploring, were elicited by the case of Aileen Wuornos, it is perhaps not surprising that her sentencing was so harsh and that appeals for the overturning of her multiple death sentences unsuccessful. As Broomfield has pointed out, Aileen was clearly made to pay for having committed violent crimes while female, since more sadistic male serial killers have been treated with greater clemency: "Even Ted Bundy was offered life imprisonment. This was never offered to Aileen Wuornos. At the time I met her she had three death sentences."[73]

Aileen's sentencing was, statistically, unusual. As Renée Heberle writes in 1999 (so prior to Aileen's death, but not to her sentencing), "only 533 women have been among the 19,161 confirmed executions since 1632, and only three women have been among the 437 offenders executed since 1973."[74] However, she goes on to explain that

> some women convicted of capital murder are more likely to land on death row than others not because their crimes are worse, as defined by statutory law, but because they do not enact a properly feminine gender identity. Subject to a social order that requires a certain complementary, dualistic gendered economy, the women on death row are those marked as monstrous, as beyond the pale of not just human but, particularly, feminine behavior.[75]

As has been demonstrated throughout this chapter, this is obviously especially pertinent to the case of Wuornos. Yet, unsurprisingly, the fact that there is a particularly punitive attitude to gender nonconforming women (as well as to socioeconomically disenfranchised individuals and people of color) in operation in death-sentencing is disavowed in juridical discourse. Justice Kogan, writing to support the upholding of Aileen's death sentence by the Florida Supreme Court, states:

Some might characterize trials such as Wuornos' as social awareness cases, because Wuornos herself unquestionably has been victimized throughout her life. I am aware that some sentiment has arisen to portray Wuornos in this light. Nevertheless, "social awareness" does not dispose of the strictly legal issues, beyond which this Court must be absolutely blind. Whether Wuornos were male or female, the facts remain that the State's theory of this case is sufficiently supported by the record.[76]

Kogan's insistence on justice's gender-blindness and desperate attempt to play down the extraordinarily relevant factor of the intersection of Wuornos's sex, gender, and behavior in determining the treatment she received in custody, in media representations, and in sentencing are supreme examples of patriarchy-denial. Wuornos has to be killed it seems because otherwise, as Heberle points out, Kogan might have had to admit that Wuornos's actions were "a rational response to the concrete knowledge available to her about the world and about men."[77]

The idea that Wuornos not only was a killer who, like Myra Hindley, was "monstrous" by dint of flouting the dictates of "natural" femininity, but also offered the fantasy figure of a "radical lesbian feminist serial killer" may have been instrumental, at least at the level of American society's collective unconscious, in ensuring the vengeful death of Aileen Wuornos. However, instead of acknowledging this possibility, most discourses emphasize Wuornos's similarity to a male serial killer, since the male serial killer is a lone wolf, a random exceptional individual who strikes at will and whose exceptionality keeps his acts safely meaningless. The very idea that Wuornos's crimes *may mean something*—that she may be a prophet of female revolt, a member of a dissatisfied class—provokes too much anxiety to be borne. As Claudia Card has put it, with reference to Wuornos's sentencing: "The message to other women is clear: violent women are abnormal, criminal, and *will not be tolerated*."[78]

CHAPTER SEVEN

Kids Who Kill

Defying the Stereotype of the Murderer

Childhood is the sleep of reason.
—(Jean-Jacques Rousseau, *Emile*, 1762)

"I murder so that I may come back"
"Murder isn't that bad. We all die sometime anyway."
—(Mary Bell, aged 11, 1968)

"it"ll be like the LA riots, the oklahoma bombing, WWII, Vietnam, duke and doom all
mixed together. maybe we will even start a little rebellion or revolution to fuck things up as
much as we can. i want to leave a lasting impression on the world."
—(Personal journal of Eric Harris, one of the Columbine killers)

Late twentieth-century cases in the UK and the United States have
brought to prominent public attention the phenomenon of the child
or adolescent who kills. Among these cases, particularly widely discussed is that of the two British 10-year-olds (11 at the time of coming
to trial), Robert Thompson and Jon Venables, who abducted and murdered 2-year-old James Bulger in Liverpool in 1993. On the other side of
the Atlantic, the high school mass shooting perpetrated by 18-year-old
Eric Harris and 17-year-old Dylan Klebold at Columbine High School
in Colorado in 1999 gave a collective name to a particularly American
style of murder, while not being the first example of the phenomenon.
Although specifically turn-of-the-millennium fears about broken soci-
eties and a culture of violence cluster to the coverage of both of these
very different cases, the existence of very young murderers is far from
unique to the turn of the twenty-first century. In his popular true-crime
book, *When Kids Kill*, Jonathan Paul cites the execution of a 12-year-old

girl for murder in England as early as 1774;[1] the serial poisoner Graham Young killed his first victim—his stepmother—when he was aged 15 in 1962; and, in 1969 11-year-old Mary Bell was tried in the North of England for the murder of two younger boys. These precedents, especially that of Bell, reveal as a fallacy the idea that the Bulger case—a case of children killing other children—was a "first" for Britain and a symptom of something particular to the culture of the 1990s. Similarly, the Columbine "craze" that peaked in the 1990s has an early precedent in 1979 when 16-year-old Brenda Spencer opened fire at an elementary school opposite her home in San Diego, California, killing two and wounding nine, because she "did not like Mondays."[2]

This chapter explores a range of discourses treating the underage killers in the Bulger and Columbine cases and, to lesser extent, in the case of Mary Bell, including media reports, true-crime and fiction books, and films.[3] The cases and texts discussed in this chapter stand as testimonies to the extent to which our modern construction of the killer as an ambivalently monstrous/heroic figure of adult masculinity fails to be fit for purpose when applied to the actual demographic diversity of subjects who kill. There is no available discourse for talking about the child who kills other than that of the failure of childhood innocence (a relatively recent construction, as we will see) or the older mythic figure of the "monstrous child." Discourses about kids who kill reflect this lack of adequate representational language, often borrowing unsatisfactorily from the lexicon of the exceptional murdering subject (by default an adult male one). Poet, journalist, and author of a book on the Bulger case Blake Morrison wrote of his arrival at the highly publicized and sensationalized trial of Thompson and Venables that "I had come up the night before—Halloween—expecting monsters dripping blood, Hindleys and Sutcliffes in all but stature."[4] The mystification of Sutcliffe and Hindley is, as we have seen, a cultural strategy for relocating masculine violence and female nonconformity into scapegoated loci of monstrous otherness. Here, the two names stand in metonymically for the exceptional murdering subject of modern Western culture. Their "evil," almost on a par with that of demons and bogeymen, as seen by the pointed reference to the trial taking place at Halloween, is our shorthand for describing the murderer. We will see that there are some attempts to do likewise with children who kill. As Alison Young points out, the monstrous stereotype of evil is often used to stand in place of critical analysis in such cases. In the words of one policeman, speaking of Thompson and Venables: "I believe human nature spurts out freaks. . . . These two were freaks who just found each other. You should not compare these two boys with other boys; they were evil."[5] The idea of the "ordinary child" can remain intact if children who kill can be proven to be sufficiently other.

However, as we shall also see, there is perhaps a greater readiness on the part of commentators in the cases of kids who kill, than in those of their adult counterparts, to look for explanations for the shocking events in the surrounding culture. In the cases of both James Bulger's killers and Harris and Klebold, parental influence, the "loose" morals of society, and violent representation—especially computer games and what were often termed in the UK in the 1980s "video nasties" —came under the lens of moral scrutiny in ways that are less often seen when the killer is an adult—especially an adult male. In what follows, I shall explore in detail how discourses of individual otherness (whether dressed as "evil" or as "psychopathy") on the one hand and discourses of social decay and contagion on the other are constantly evoked, juxtaposed, and placed in dialogue with each other, in an unending—and ultimately unresolved— attempt to find the "why?" in the cases of these young killers.

Child's Play: The Killing of James Bulger

James Bulger's murder, which was repeatedly named in end-of-year roundups on British TV and in the print media as "one of the most significant events of 1993,"[6] was perhaps so shocking and disorienting because it fundamentally threw into question our beliefs about what a 10-year-old is capable of doing and—by extension—about what a 10-year-old *is*, since, as we have seen, acts are thought to reflect ontology in the case of murder. The details of the case are certainly horrible: the two assailants, Robert Thompson and Jon Venables, abducted James while his mother, Denise, was temporarily distracted in a butcher's shop in the Strand Shopping Precinct in Bootle, Liverpool. The abduction was captured in grainy CCTV images, one of which—showing James holding Jon's hand and being led away, the sign displaying the name of the popular chain store Mothercare ironically filling the upper portion of the frame like a title—was repeatedly shown on TV and in newspapers throughout the course of the trial and after (see fig. 7).[7]

The toddler was then marched around town for several hours, in a state of dishevelment and distress. Thirty-eight separate eyewitnesses

FIGURE 7. CCTV footage showing Jon Venables leading James Bulger by the hand. Robert Thompson walks ahead.

later claimed to have seen the party, but nobody intervened. The older boys firstly attempted to push James into a canal, but he refused to kneel down at the edge of the water as they instructed. Eventually Thompson and Venables led Bulger to the railway. They took off his trousers and underpants; pelted him with stones, batteries, and bricks; beat him; and threw blue paint, which they had earlier stolen from the shopping center, in his eyes. When he was dead, they placed his body on the railways lines and covered his face with bricks. The corpse was later cut in two by a train. When the body was discovered, police initially suspected a registered sex offender who was known to have been in the area on the day of James's disappearance, but he had a watertight alibi. The identity of the killers, when revealed, was a national shock.

Reactions to the identity of James Bulger's killers highlight the confusion that results from the intersection of the cultural fiction of "murderer" and the cultural construction of "child." It is arguably the case that these two modern figures emerge at a similar period of history, namely the nineteenth century. Philippe Ariès has suggested that prior to late modernity, the concept of childhood as we know it did not exist.[8] Ariès argues that before the emergence of the Romantic nineteenth-century figure of the child, children were not thought to possess any particular "nature," but simply to be miniature adults. Once youngsters proved themselves strong enough for manual labor, they were incorporated into the adult world, regardless of actual age. Similarly, according to Ariès, the idea of the family, and its current Western model, the nuclear family, did not exist prior to the Victorian age. Other historians agree that our current conception of childhood is a modern invention, but have taken issue with Ariès's claim that prior to the nineteenth century children were not assumed to have any particular nature. Chris Jenks and Gill Valentine both highlight historically specific discourses about the nature of children, such as the pre-seventeenth-century belief that children as a class are bearers of evil, being weak and susceptible to sin.[9] Foucault claims that the nineteenth century marked the point at which children were no longer seen as "knowing," but were marked by a dual Romantic discourse of innocence and a concomitant medical discourse of protection/intrusion. Prior to the psychiatric and sexological "specification of individuals," adults would have behaved bawdily around children, Foucault claims, without this having any sinister or pathological meaning. The demarcation of children as innocents placed lines of surveillance and scrutiny around them, guarding against behaviors capable of spoiling their innocence, such as masturbation,[10] and, as Anneke Meyer argues in her excellent constructionist reading of the social problem of pedophilia, simultaneously casting sexual suspicion on the adults who interacted with them.[11]

Despite our current conception of children, which is the inheritance of the nineteenth-century understanding that they embody innocence, the killers of James Bulger, at 11 years old, were tried in an adult court, in front of a jury (a procedure that obtains only for the crimes of rape and murder). The age of criminal responsibility in England is 10 years old.[12] However, the presumption of *doli incapax*—the notion that a child is incapable of understanding the meaning and consequences of his or her actions—first had to be legally rebutted in the case of Thompson and Venables. (Following the introduction of the Law and Disorder Act in 1998, this safeguard was abolished and anyone over 10 is now assumed to have the same degree of awareness of right and wrong as an adult.) The psychologists who testified at the trial understood the two boys to be of normal intelligence, and therefore capable of embodying the fictive rational subject of law. I should make it clear that my attempt in this chapter to highlight the constructed nature of childhood and "the child" is not to be understood as the equivalent of claiming that I believe there to be no difference between those we call "children" and those we call "adults," and that the treatment of children who kill as rational adults is therefore right and justified. Rather, it is my contention that the way in which culture currently constructs children—not as individual subjects, future adults with developing cognitive, emotional, and intellectual skills, but as a class apart (the class signifying *those whose nature is innocence*)—is damaging for both those children who emerge as social agents, as Venables and Thompson did, *and* for those who emerge as the victims of tragedies such as this one. In the former case, they appear considerably more aberrant and evil than would an adult, who is not presumed to embody perfect innocence. In the latter, their victimhood appears regrettably as an inevitable extension of their "nature," making oppression of children appear natural too.

As Young points out in her reading of the Bulger case, coverage of the crime rests upon establishing the distinction between James Bulger as an "ideal child" and the two killers as not quite children. She argues that in newspaper coverage of the case, "James Bulger was represented as the quintessential child: small, affectionate, trusting, dependent, vulnerable, high-spirited,"[13] whereas his killers, in light of what we know about them, are defined by their divergence from this stereotype. Bulger looked "essentially child-like, an ideal child, or an *idea* of a child,"[14] whereas Thompson and Venables, in the words of one journalist, "did not look like ordinary boys *even before the murder.*"[15] Young further posits, following reports that the sale of child reins increased rapidly in the months following the trial, that parents were "anxious that their child could be a James Bulger (that is a victim) and not a Jon Venables or a Robert Thompson (a murderer)."[16]

Similar discourses were much in evidence in the case of Mary Bell, tried in Newcastle in 1968, alongside a friend, Norma Bell (no relation), for the fatal strangulation of two small boys, Martin Brown and Brian Howe. Norma was acquitted, in part, it is felt, owing to her sympathetic persona as an educationally slow child who seemed afraid, upset, and vulnerable in court.[17] Mary, on the other hand, whose manner in court was markedly non-childlike, being one of attentiveness and precocious intellectual combativeness, was found guilty of manslaughter in both cases. Her crime was reduced from murder to manslaughter because of the presumption of diminished responsibility, since she was found to be suffering from a psychopathic personality disorder. Gitta Sereny, who has written two books about the case of Bell, describes the attitude to the child killer in the courtroom and the media: "Irrespective of medical evidence [that she suffered from psychopathic personality disorder] what we had here was *not* a "sick" child, but a clever little MONSTER."[18] The diagnosis of "psychopathy," moreover—that ultimate otherness in a human personality, characterized by an incapacity to empathize with others and a cunning manipulativeness—often seems to end up serving the same discursive function and eliciting the same emotional reaction as the unscientific idea of evil, while appearing rational since it issues from the discipline of psychiatry. Unlike psychotic illnesses such as schizophrenia, in which the person's relationship with reality is felt to be damaged, psychopathy often seems to function as no more than a shorthand, psy-sciences term to describe human monstrosity. Given the construction of children as innocent and vulnerable, a psychopathic child is a particularly horrifying idea, accounting, perhaps, as Sereny goes on to describe, for the epithets ascribed to Mary:

> Thus labeled [as a psychopath], the prosecutor would go on to describe Mary as "vicious," "cruel," "terrifying"; even the judge was to allow the word "wicked" to slip into one of his perorations. Was it surprising that the media, not so much creating as responding to the tone set by the court and to the public outrage and fear, called Mary "a freak of nature," "evil born" and . . . "a bad seed."[19]

Perhaps disappointingly for those who drew attention to Robert Thompson's "mad staring eyes" in court,[20] the two killers of James Bulger were not found to be suffering from psychopathy or any other discernable psychiatric abnormality. They were therefore found guilty of murder rather than manslaughter and sentenced to be detained at her Majesty's pleasure. This meant that the label of "evil," unmitigated even by a psychiatric diagnosis, was universally applied to the two boys.

If Bell, and later Venables and Thompson, were capable of doing what they did, the logic seems to go, then by definition they *cannot be children*. This idea is implicitly addressed and challenged in Morrison's sensitive study of the Bulger case, *As If*. The text is a plea for understanding, if not forgiveness, of the actions of Thompson and Venables. It constitutes an explicit rebuttal of then British prime minister John Major's anti-intellectual statement in response to the case that "we must condemn a little more and understand a little less."[21] It attempts to break down the barrier between "ordinary" childhood instances of violence and cruelty (Morrison uses examples from his own childhood and adolescence) and those carried out by Thompson and Venables, to show that they exist on a continuum, rather than as ontologically separate. The reason that they are constructed as ontologically unrelated has precisely to do with cultural investment in the idea of "the child" and its alleged incompatibility with that of "the murderer" (ignoring entirely the view of such experts as psychoanalyst Melanie Klein who demonstrated that young children feel anger as all-consuming rage and are homicidal in the intensity of their emotions, if not their actions).

Morrison writes: "If child-killings are the worst killings, then a child child-killing must be worse than worst, a new superlative in horror."[22] He then juxtaposes this idea with the violent public reaction to Thompson and Venables, two 11-year-olds, including the gathering outside court of vigilantes baying for the killers' blood, captured in press photographs: "The men in the photograph had come wanting to kill the kids who'd killed the kid, because there's nothing worse than killing a kid."[23] He wittily shows up the faultiness of the taxonomical logic that prevents the same person occupying both the box marked "child" and that marked "killer." Children who kill another child forfeit their membership of the category of childhood and become ripe for being killed in turn as an abjected outsider. The failure of the individual child to match the epithets culturally designated for him or her results in a greater moral response than a violent (especially male) adult would provoke, as a supposed natural feature of adult masculinity is violence. Yet while trying to maintain that there is a relative, rather than absolute, gap between children who are "ordinarily" cruel and/or violent and those who kill, Morrison still maintains the fiction of the *recognizably other* adult murdering subject. He, like the policemen and journalists cited above, *looks at* Robert and Jon in court in the hope that how they look will reveal their essence. He writes: "Those children in court didn't appear evil or psychopathic: there are only looks to go on, but they didn't look *the real thing.*"[24] Although Morrison finds, unlike the policemen and journalist I have cited above, that the two boys *do* look ordinary, the enduring expectation that murderers are special and recognizable is still present here.

In her new preface to the latest edition of *The Case of Mary Bell*, produced after attending the Bulger trial, Sereny writes:

> When the other child (Nancy Bell) was acquitted, the whole country seemed to breathe a sigh of relief. The older girl being found innocent created an equation acceptable and even welcome to society: fate, or some terrible wrath

of God, had produced a freak: one monstrous child, a "bad seed," the uniqueness of whose evil could be seen as confirming the probity and virtue of society at large.[25]

Sereny describes the scapegoating function served by the exceptional
murderer, here the exceptional murdering child, whose role, in being
sacrificed, is to ensure the shoring up of the world order we understand.
The discourse of monstrosity leveled at Mary Bell and at Venables and
Thompson prevents us having to wonder how similar these children
might be to the ones we designate "ours."

As we have seen, Mary Bell and James Bulger's killers manage to
transcend the social category to which their age would commit them and
become monsters. Yet there is clearly a more pervasive fear underlying
all of these polarized discourses about child-killers and their victims or
potential victims, which is the fantasy that the violent monstrous child
(Bell, Venables, Thompson), rather than the innocent cherub (Martin,
Brian, James), may in fact be the "real" face of childhood. The determined relegation of children to a class that is different from adults signifies, at base, like all instances of othering, a fear of the othered group.
Coverage of the Bulger case, for all its attempts to suture over this fear
by asserting the unassailable difference between James on the one hand
and Jon and Robert on the other, reveals the fantasy clearly. Young concludes her chapter on the Bulger case with the assertion that behind the
public discourse lurks a suspicion that "even though 'our' children look
(to us) like 'James Bulgers,' . . . they might be the non-children that Robert Thompson and Jon Venables are taken to embody."[26] And a headline
in the *Sunday Times*—excessively sensationalist in its choice of vocabulary for this particular publication—seems to bear this out. "We will
never be able to look at our children in the same way again," it declares,
and goes on: "Parents everywhere are asking themselves if the *Mark of
the Beast* might not also be imprinted on their offspring."[27]

Yet parallel to these attempts to make the child who murders into
an innately evil exceptional subject, discourses about kids who kill, as
I mooted in the introduction to this chapter, are generally likely to look
also to cultural and environmental factors in the children's background,
interrogating the child's interests and hobbies (with a special eye to exposure to violent television, films, and video/computer games) and the
parenting they have received (with particular suspicion reserved for single parents—and overwhelmingly for single mothers). Such attempts,

however, often fail to expose the actual roots of potential trauma, as in the case of Bell, whose protracted and horrendous childhood physical and sexual abuse at the hands of her mother was eventually documented by Sereny in 1998, following extensive interviews with the then-released Mary. Sereny assumes that the abuse and the killings were causally linked, and blames British law for the failure to understand Mary's actions and traumatized state. The nature of the British judicial system admits of no interest in discovering what might have led a child to kill, only in establishing whether or not that child did in fact kill. Similarly, the aim of much media attention that clusters to the parents and backgrounds of young murderers is often not to seek to explain or understand the tragedy, but rather to confirm conservative cultural prejudices about "appropriate" child rearing and to condemn further those who have been shown to fail.

Blake Morrison has demonstrated how discourses of permissiveness were applied to the parents of Thompson and Venables, children of the "swinging sixties," and how these are part of a tissue of prejudices regarding social structures and families. He writes: "Single mothers, absent fathers, school indiscipline, the decline of churchgoing, the 60s, the pill—all were blamed for the emergence of a new generation of child-hoodlums."[28] And Young asserts that "the press discourse thoroughly interrogates the relationship between the three children involved . . . and their mothers."[29] Just as James Bulger and his killers are represented as polar opposites, as almost different species, so "an enormous divide is opened up between Denise Bulger and the mothers of the other two children."[30] It is not only because Denise is the mother of the victim rather than of the killers—and as we have seen, sympathizing with the mothers of the killers would involve an identification that has to remain culturally disavowed, that would be too risky, since their situation constitutes "the prohibited and the repellent"[31]—it is also that Denise represents a normative idea of maternal respectability. Both of the killers' parents were separated. Robert's father, Robert Thompson senior, an alcoholic, left his wife Ann when Robert was six; Jon's parents, Susan and Neil, divorced but maintained an amicable relationship, living only streets apart so that Jon could go between their houses at will, and often holidaying together as a family. Denise was not only in a supportive, conventional marriage, but also heavily pregnant with a new baby at the time of the trial, providing the image of a perfect "maternal archetype."[32] (The same press that implicitly blamed divorced parents for the murder later made much of the birth of Denise's baby—another boy—and did not for a moment suggest that her own recent divorce from her husband, subsequent to the trial, might in any way impact negatively on the new child.)

Were such investigations into the home lives of junior killers genuinely in the service of exposing abuse, such as that uncovered by Sereny, they might not be so rebarbative. However, more often than not such discourses merely trade in stereotypical and class-bound assumptions about the "normal"—or rather idealized—family, searching for instances of deviation from this norm in the families of child-killers as corroboration of an already firmly held belief. In her popular true-crime book on children who kill, Carol Anne Davis writes of Thompson and Venables:

> Both boys came from the family backgrounds that make a child most likely to become extremely violent. That is, they had abusive childhoods, had *fathers who were absent in Robert's case and passive in Jon's case*. Both had *dominant mothers*—and Jon's mother was *also overprotective*.[33]

It does not require advanced expertise in the analysis of gender politics to see that what is being perpetuated here is the notion of the unnatural woman and the damage that she does to the males in her life. There is a familiar echo of the misogynistic cultural tendency explored earlier to blame women's sexuality for men's sex killing. And Jane Caputi has pointed out that blaming mothers in particular for their sons' murderousness has a long tradition, as exemplified on celluloid by the ultimate "boy" with a mother who is a "clinging, demanding woman": Norman Bates of Hitchcock's *Psycho*.[34] The killers may be younger in the case of the murder of James Bulger, but the strong inclination to blame women and mothers is identical. The public condemnation here is not of a specific violent, sick, and sexually abusive mother, such as Mary Bell is now known to have had; rather it is a more general condemnation. It is the condemnation of a *dominant* mother, a dominant woman, that is, a woman who fails to be appropriately feminine.

The specter of monstrous mothers haunts the discourse about monstrous children. Young theorizes that the desire for retribution felt in the case of child-murderers—the call for harsh sentencing, for "life to mean life"—reveals a cultural anxiety about the inappropriate mother and the weak or absent father, in short, about the perceived failure of the nuclear family and its traditional, patriarchal gender roles. Young describes the law as playing the part of a "paternal surrogate" in order to "suture the breach in the maternal relation" that has occurred in such cases.[35] She goes on: "The call to watch the mortification and near-erasure through lifetime imprisonment of the two boys [Thompson and Venables] speaks of the will for the father to return."[36] The notion that not only paternity, but also the institution of the family and of blood relations, are unambiguously benign is seen in the testimonies of those 38 eyewitnesses who saw James being led around town by Robert and Jon. Although some of them commented that the older boys were being rough with the younger child, nobody intervened *because they assumed the three children were brothers*. The symbolic authority of the familial relation is visible in this fact. Although the eyewitnesses later attracted criticism, with the *Independent on Sunday* describing "our national guilt that we could be the kind of people who let this sort of thing happen,"[37] their assumption is intelligible and backed up by a pervasive cultural belief. Although we are—increasingly—intellectually aware of the fact that considerably more abuse takes place *within* families than as a result of "stranger danger," a deep-seated assumption that "the family" is both benevolent and desirable persists.

Moreover, as in the trials and media coverage of Myra Hindley and Aileen Wuornos, socioeconomic class clearly plays a role in the cases of child-killers and the treatment of the children and their family in court and in the press. Sereny, who attended the trials of both Mary Bell and Thompson and Venables, comments that in Liverpool in 1993, as in Newcastle in 1968, there was the strong sense that "this was a case of 'them,' the children of the poor, drunk and inadequate, and therefore could never be 'us.'"[38] And, likewise, Morrison comments on the way in which the judge, whose own voice was recognizably "RP" (received pronunciation, characteristic of the British upper middle classes), mimicked Thompson and Venables's diction during his summation:

> He repeats the boys' words and mimics their accents: "on me own," "yeah," "cos," "yeah," "if you want, like," "yeah," "God's honest truth," "yeah," "yeah," "yeah." . . . The impersonations, if not malicious, have a sniff of distaste. Middle-class children would not be mimicked like this.[39]

There is a strong—and prejudicial—perception that both child abuse and resulting child delinquency are the prerogative of the working classes.

Davis summarizes the "ingredients" of child-murderers thus: "The child is physically and emotionally abused by an adult or adults, often the very people that created him . . . in turn, he — or she — goes on to perpetrate violence on someone else."[40] While I do not in any way wish to downplay the significance that child abuse probably had on the making of young killers such as Mary Bell, and *may* have had on Thompson and Venables (speculations that Robert Thompson had been sexually abused abounded, mainly because he was allegedly responsible for removing James's trousers and underwear prior to killing him), one might wonder why the undoubtedly large number of children abused is not even nearly matched by the small number of children who go on to kill. Jonathan Paul poses the question: "Why do some children take their fantasies one step further and turn them into a catastrophic reality?" The answer he offers is provided by Dr. Susan Bailey, OBE, consultant adolescent forensic psychiatrist at the Bolton, Salford and Trafford Mental Health Partnership. It is, quite simply, Dr. Bailey says: "bad luck."[41] With its lack of reliance on the discourse of the exceptionally evil subject (whether mother or child — or both), such an answer, applied to both underage and adult killers, will always fail to satisfy the cultural need for clear delineation between the ordinary and the exceptional: the guarantee that "they" cannot be "us."

Yet the wider society, functioning as what Young would call "paternal surrogate," was also put on trial for failing children in 1993. The fact that the judge in the Bulger case explicitly named "exposure to violent video films"[42] in his final address to the court, as a possible cause of the two boy's actions, led to a renewed moral panic about contagion and corruption, such as those that featured in the 1840s with regard to Marie Lafarge's reading of purple prose, and again in the mid-1960s in the case of the Moors Murderers and their Sade fandom. The specific film that has been linked to the Bulger case is *Child's Play 3* (Bender, 1991), which Jon is thought to have watched at Neil Venables's house, unbeknownst to his father. The film depicts a toddler-sized doll, called Chucky, which is possessed by the soul of an adult serial killer. Eventually, the doll is vanquished. Davis writes:

> It seems that the original idea was Jon's — he'd been so excited at school the day before that his teachers couldn't get any work out of him. The theft of the batteries and blue paint (the latter appearing in the Chucky film *Child's Play*) suggest he may have had some vague plan — based on childish logic — to have access to his very own Chucky-sized living doll.[43]

Significantly, the *Child's Play* films and the reception of the Venables/ Thompson case both reveal a dominant cultural fantasy: that of the small person as evil, as a monster. Literally evil children are represented in popular and acclaimed horror films such as *Rosemary's Baby* (Polanski, 1968), *The Exorcist* (Friedkin, 1973), and *The Omen* (Donner, 1976). That the childlike creature in the less cinematically distinguished *Child's Play* is an automaton, not an actual child, but one with the characteristics and the *essence* of an adult serial killer, *a Sutcliffe or a Hindley in all but stature*, offers an irresistible analogy with how children who kill—those "not-children"—are consistently represented. In a weird reversal, given that it has been theorized that James was to represent Chucky in Jon's fantasy world, Thompson and Venables subsequently *became* Chucky for *us*.

The judge's words led to a series of debates and investigations into the effects on children of exposure to violent material. Professor Elizabeth Newson's report, *Video Violence and the Protection of Children*, signed by 25 child psychologists, found that

> it is now clear that many children watch adult-only videos on a regular basis. . . . There must be special concern when children . . . are repeatedly exposed to images of vicious cruelty in the context of entertainment as amusement.[44]

In contradistinction, however, the Policy Studies Institute's report, *Young Offenders and the Media*, coauthored by Ann Hagell and Tim Newburn, found that "persistent young offenders do not watch more violent films or television than 'ordinary' schoolchildren and they prefer soap operas to video nasties."[45] Young points out that whereas the former was taken up by all sections of the UK parliament and widely cited in the media, the latter, which suggested that such simplistic answers were neither accurate nor satisfactory, was largely ignored.[46]

We Need to Talk about Columbine: High School Killers as "Subjects of Murder"

The debates about the effects of media violence and home environment, juxtaposed with those about the extent to which inherent "evil" (or the phenomenon of "psychopathy") can account for criminal acts by the young, are also central to discourses that surround the Columbine

school massacre and other American high school killing sprees by teen-
agers for which "Columbine" provides a collective label. The details of
Harris's and Klebold's crimes are as follows: on Tuesday, 20 April 1999,
the two boys arrived at Columbine High School in Littleton, Colorado,
armed with rifles, pipe bombs, and two propane bombs (having already
set up a third bomb in a nearby field, that was supposed to explode before the school killing began in order to divert attention from it). When
neither of the propane bombs placed in the school went off at the ap-
pointed time, Eric and Dylan opened fire and began to shoot classmates
and throw pipe bombs. Twelve students and one teacher were killed, and
over 20 others injured.[47] The shootings that took place inside the school
centered especially on the library, where there was a particularly large
concentration of people. After several hours of siege, Harris and Klebold turned their guns on themselves and committed suicide.

Unlike the preadolescent killers discussed in the previous section,
teenage murderers Eric Harris (who had only just turned 18) and Dylan Klebold (still 17) were self-aware and articulate about their acts, and
represented themselves precociously, particularly in the case of Harris,
as the exceptional killing subject of the collective cultural imagination.
They discussed, fantasized about, and planned their massacre in minute detail for more than a year. Both Harris and Klebold kept extensive
journals. Klebold's writing focused mainly on suicidal rather than homicidal impulses and on the pain of unrequited love, but he also talked of
his absolute difference from other people. Harris dwelt on his nihilistic
philosophy, the importance of showmanship and aesthetic perfection in
crime, and the desire to create a legacy through violence. For Dwayne
Fuselier, FBI behavioral expert and father of a Columbine High School
student (not one of the victims), Harris's (unlike Klebold's) writing bore
the classic symptoms of psychopathy: he was "charming, callous, cunning, manipulative, comically grandiose, and egocentric, with an ap-
palling failure of empathy."[48] As Dave Cullen puts it in his comprehensive study of Columbine, "Dylan exceeded even Eric in his belief in his
own singularity, but Eric equated 'unique' with 'superior'—Dylan saw it
mostly as bad."[49] As well as their journals, Harris and Klebold left behind evidence of their intentions and worldview in a series of homemade
videotapes known as "the basement tapes" that they made five weeks
prior to the killings. In these, they make clear that following the murders they will take their own lives, Eric commenting to the camera: "You
all need to die. We need to die too," and Dylan glibly quoting the words

of his dominant partner in crime, Eric: "I've narrowed it. It's humans I hate."[50]

Harris and Klebold are fairly unusual among murderers in terms of the very extent to which their meticulous, premeditated planning was coupled with full and faithful documentation of their feelings about it. One is reminded irresistibly of Foucault's discussion of Pierre Rivière's aesthetic written confession, part of which was constructed in advance, as constitutive and productive of the crimes he committed and the criminal he became. Harris and Klebold similarly designed their personae and explored the aesthetics of the acts they would commit well in advance of the actual killings. Cullen theorizes that, for Eric at least, "Columbine was a performance. Homicidal art."[51] In his journal Eric anticipates with frustration that *what he understood to be* the meaning and motivation behind his acts—the celebration of sheer nihilism, the draw of the abyss—would fail to be apprehended by those left behind. "The majority of the audience wont [sic] even understand my motives," he wrote, in frustration.[52] Cullen opines that Harris "scripted Columbine as a made-for-TV murder, and his chief concern was that we would be too stupid to see the point."[53] The notion of murder-as-art and the ambition to commit crimes that seem "pure" and "motiveless" are, of course, not new. They are two of the tropes we have been tracing throughout this book. The way Cullen describes Harris's project resonates directly, in fact, with De Quincey's idea of murderous art: "The whole point was impressing people. Details mattered. Wardrobe, staging, atmospherics, audio, pyrotechnics, action, suspense, timing, irony, foreshadowing— all the cinematic elements were important."[54] Likewise, for De Quincey, a worthwhile murder requires "design, gentlemen, grouping, light and shade, poetry, sentiment."[55]

The planning and legacy of the Columbine massacre offer a particularly good example of Schmid's concept of the murderer as ultimate celebrity in North America, and the journals and tapes created by Harris and Klebold illustrate how murderers can consciously appeal to cultural tastes and fascinations in order to ensure that (posthumous, in this case) fame. The idea of murderer-as-artist and murder-as-art is, as we know, Romantic in origin, but the appeal to cinematography and the use of the Internet (Harris's journal was originally kept online) demonstrate the adaptation of the transcendental idea of artistic murder to contemporary technological, media, and aesthetic fashions, and the adaptation of adult forms of expression to adolescent ones. In a referential and self-aware gesture, Eric and Dylan's shorthand for their planned event was "NBK," standing for *Natural Born Killers*, the title of Oliver Stone's 1994 satirical film about the media's glorification of psychopathic serial killers and their acts. The idea that Eric was honing his crime and his persona for a filmic audience proved apt, as a spate of high school killing-themed films, perhaps predictably, followed the Columbine massacre.

Michael Moore's 2002 documentary *Bowling for Columbine* was the first film to name Columbine in its title, though it is a broad investigation into gun crime in the United States, rather than a film focusing on the details of the Columbine case and killers. (Indeed, a small inaccuracy occurs in the title and the opening sequence: contrary to Moore's claim, Eric and Dylan did not attend their early morning bowling class on the day of the massacre.) Moore's voice-over asks who is to blame for events such as Columbine. There are quick cuts between a series of talking heads, giving answers such as "*South Park*," "Video games," "Satan," "Society," and then, one after the other, all proclaim: "Marilyn Manson." Fourteen-year-old Andrew Wurst, who shot to death a teacher and wounded a number of classmates at a school dance in Pennsylvania in 1998, had allegedly been a Satanist and a Manson fan. Moore explores how society more readily blames cultural influences such as the music of Marilyn Manson for these killings than the availability of firearms and ammunition in the United States and the normalization of gun ownership and interpersonal aggression. Marilyn Manson appears in the film, and talks about having canceled his planned tour just after the Columbine killings as a mark of respect, since his work had been cited as a possible influence on such events. Moore juxtaposes this with Charlton Heston's refusal to cancel his appearance at a meeting of the National Rifle Association in Colorado shortly after Columbine, despite the mayor's request. Thus, he points out the ready demonization of youth subculture and alternative music at the expense of analyzing the normalization of (nominally defensive) violence as enshrined in the Second Amendment of the Constitution. He also alludes to the fact that on the day of the Columbine killings, "the USA dropped more bombs on Kosovo than at any time previously." And Marilyn Manson remarks on the irony that nobody asked the question of whether *the president* may have had any effect on the actions of the killers.

However, in its attempt to answer the broader implicit question, why is the USA so violent?, the documentary does not draw easy answers. It shows that in Canada, where it is extremely easy to purchase weapons, only 165 people die yearly as a result of gun crime, in comparison with the yearly US figure of 11,127. Moore also cites all the commonly named triggers for violence and shows that they are inconclusive as causes by means of cultural comparison. He points out that people watch violent films in France, listen to Goth music in Germany, play more violent video games in Japan than in the United States; that there are more broken homes in the UK than in the United States; that liberals claim unemployment is responsible for a violent society, but more people are unemployed in Canada than in the United States. None of the available explanations account for the disparity in death figures or the American "popularity" of the school killing spree and its grown-up equivalent, the workplace massacre. Moore concludes that "the American people are conditioned by network news to believe that their communities are much more dangerous than they are," and thereby suggests that the prevalent cultural paranoia about protection of self and property provides an alibi for the normalization of violence. Moore's broad aim is to deflect blame from something "out there": an outsider, an eccentric, an exception. He makes a plea for close scrutiny of the values at the heart of the culture, rather than a demonization of alternative subcultures. Yet when Moore interviews two girls who were bowling classmates of Eric and Dylan at Columbine High and asks them what the two killers were like as people, they answer, quite simply, that Eric and Dylan were "weird." The cult of exceptional personality that Harris so cultivated thus has the last word despite Moore's soul-searching analysis for social causes.

Gus Van Sant's narrative film *Elephant* (2003) clearly references Harris and Klebold's crimes. It depicts a day in the lives of several high school students and teachers that will end with a firearm massacre perpetrated by Alex and Eric. (Confusingly, the "Alex" character is the dominant friend who most closely resembles Eric Harris; while "Eric" is the Dylan Klebold character, the follower. The names of the characters are identical with the names of the actors, Alex Frost and Eric Deulen, young unknowns, adding to the naturalistic feel of the film.) *Elephant* enjoyed a positive critical reception, taking a Palme d'or at Cannes, but later became the target of controversy as it was in turn linked to a real-life shooting. Coverage of the 2005 Red Lake High School massacre made reference to *Elephant*, as gunman Jeff Weise allegedly viewed the film two weeks before committing his crime.[56] Just as high school shootings are often blamed on the effects of media and film, these crimes then inspire films that subsequently attract blame for provoking further copycat crimes. The impossibility of dissociating society from representation is doubtless confirmed by such phenomena, but what remains unproven in this relationship is the presence of causality rather than a mere instance of correlation.

Elephant's title was borrowed from Alan Clarke's 1989 film of the same name, which treated sectarian violence in Northern Ireland. Clarke had in turn drawn on Bernard MacLaverty's description of the Troubles as "the elephant in the room."[57] With this genealogy in mind, Van Sant's title clearly alludes to a large, systemic social problem that is unspoken, that is deliberately disavowed in favor of more local explanations and alibis. Yet the stark, clean film does not propose any explicit analysis or criticism of broader culture, in contradistinction to Moore's documentary. Indeed, Van Sant's film has been criticized for its moral neutrality. It bears witness, but does not offer explanations or condemnation. However, the fact that Eric and Alex are shown in an early scene being bullied by school "jocks" and later embracing naked in the shower before going out to commit their crime references two explanations that have repeatedly been proposed for school shootings: bullying and the alienation felt by "outsiders" such as gay children in the normative environment of high school. Homophobia is further alluded to in the film by the fact that one scene depicts a meeting of the Gay-Straight Alliance, suggesting that heteronormativity may be at least one of the elephants in the room of high school and culture at large. Finally, Alex is shown to be a frustrated artist, a gifted pianist who can find no satisfaction in his music, turning instead to the easier art of murder. These allusions, however, remain subtle and implicit rather than taking on the epistemological status of explanations.

If these films, in different ways, fail to offer conclusive explanations for the Columbine killings—or, in the case of *Elephant*, foreground the very inexplicability of these events as the point of the film text—media discourse and offender-profiling experts are no more successful in their attempts to answer the question, why? In 1999, the Secret Service produced a report on school shooters that concluded that there is no "useful or accurate profile" that can be drawn of this type of offender.[58] Regardless, the media propagated a series of myths of the "type" of the high school killer. The first of these is that such killers are outcasts, loners, often bullied, suspected to be homosexual (as suggested in *Elephant*), or belonging to Gothic subculture. None of these fit in the case of Harris and Klebold. As Cullen points out, "Dylan laughed about picking on the new freshman and 'fags.' Neither one complained about bullies picking on them—they boasted about doing it themselves."[59] And, on the basement tapes, Eric and Dylan can be heard insulting black and Latino people, gay people, and women. "Yes moms, stay home," Eric says, adding: "Fucking make me dinner, bitch."[60] Similarly, despite the apparel chosen for the day of the killings—long black overcoats—neither of the boys was part of the Gothic subculture (which in any case was misrepresented in the press as likely to promote violence. In fact, Goths tend to be melancholic and pacifistic, their aestheticization of death of a distinctly nonviolent hue). Nor were they even members of a group at their school known as the Trench Coat Mafia (TCM). Yet CNN did not hesitate within the first two hours of the occupation of Columbine High School to conflate in their broadcasts the TCM, Goths, gays, and street gangs, and to speculate that the killers inside the school belonged to all of the above.[61] The other popular myth about this type of killer is that he or she "snaps" after a long period of repressed rage or stress. In fact, 93 percent of school shootings were found to have been planned in advance, though few in as minute detail as Harris's and Klebold's crimes.[62] Finally, the home environments of Harris and Klebold were very far from the broken or single-parent family decried by conservative, often religious, factions as responsible for society's ills and cited by FBI experts as indicators for psychopathy.[63] Both sets of parents were middle-class—as are the parents of most high school killers—and in married family units.

As in the cases from the UK described in the first section, consumption of violent media by the young killers was discussed at great length in the press, and yet ultimately found to be inconclusive as a cause for the killings when research was undertaken. Cullen describes an FBI report on incarcerated high school killers which found (similarly to the British Policy Studies Institute's widely ignored report cited at the end of the previous section) that "only a quarter" [of interviewed offenders] "were interested in violent movies, half that number in video games—probably below average for teen boys."[64] The conclusion of the report, then, is that cultural influence appeared weak as an explanation for such events. However, it is possible to argue that the aesthetic/dramatic event of the highly publicized school shooting and the figure of the rebellious, revolutionary high school shooter become in and of themselves a "cultural influence." In the 10 years following Columbine, more than 80 school shootings took place in the United States.[65] Eric and Dylan achieved their dream of leaving a legacy, as seen in the fact that Seung-Hui Cho, who killed 32 people and then committed suicide at Virginia Tech on 16 April 2007, left behind a manifesto that "cited Eric and Dylan at least twice as inspiration. He'd looked up to them."[66] One can argue that violent acts in the world, like violent films, do not *make* further violence happen ex nihilo. At most they determine the form, the aesthetic of the violence. What is copied in a so-called copycat killing is a mode, a style—a historically specific aesthetic. The stylization of the exceptional killing subject to which would-be murderers aspire has, as we have seen, a longer history than is commonly acknowledged, but the local forms the murderer's acts take in order to allow them access to that role differ over time and place.

The question of the original and the copy in the case of high school killings is one of the themes explored in the acclaimed novel by Lionel Shriver *We Need to Talk about Kevin* (2003). The novel is narrated from the point of view of Eva, the mother of the eponymous high school mass killer. The novel is referential of real-life school killings and shows a familiarity with media discourses and psychological theories surrounding child-killers. We are told that Kevin's fictional crossbow massacre in the high school gymnasium takes place only several days before the Columbine killings,[67] and that Kevin is later "obsessed with those Columbine kids who upstaged him . . . with six more fatalities."[68] And, in discussing the influences—or lack thereof—that may have shaped his burgeoning taste for destruction, Eva speculates that "there was little in *Braveheart*—or *Reservoir Dogs*, or *Chucky II*—that Kevin could not have invented for himself."[69] The mention of *Chucky* also brings the discussions surrounding the Bulger case irresistibly and directly to mind.

The character of Kevin is fashioned as a psychopath: lacking empathy, emotionally blank, manipulative—much as Eric Harris is described. His hobby as a teenager is collecting computer viruses, perhaps an allusion to Eric's own passion for hacking into and developing the code of "Doom," a first person shooter video game. The unresolved question at the heart of Shriver's book, then, is whether destructiveness was an innate quality of Kevin's nature, present from birth, or whether it was acquired. Eva, who never bonded with her child, fully believes the former: "He was a singular, unusually cunning individual who had arrived to stay with us and just happened to be very small,"[70] she asserts. As Eva is revealed to be an unreliable narrator, the other suggestion is allowed to emerge that Kevin's character was "made" by the coldness, ambivalence, and emotional rejection of this same mother and, perhaps also, by the contrasting superficial, doting cheeriness of his father, Franklin. (In an unexpected twist that forms the denouement of the novel, it is revealed that, before leaving home to commit his high school massacre, Kevin first killed his despised father and sister once Eva—the intended "audience" for his crimes—had left for work.) The novel depicts Eva being unsuccessfully sued in civil court by the family of one of Kevin's victims for being a negligent mother, suggesting the common perception that the crime of the child *is* the crime of the parent, and echoing the fact that such civil suits against parents did follow from various real-life school massacres. *We Need to Talk about Kevin* thus explores, without resolving, such perpetually aired debates as the one concerning nature and nurture, and seems to conclude that they may well be unanswerable.

It also interrogates, and similarly fails to provide an answer to, the question of why the figure of the high school killer came into vogue. One theory proposed in the novel is that the badge of "high school killer" offers self-definition to those at a notoriously difficult life stage. Shriver has Eva write: "He's *found himself*, as they said in my day. Now he doesn't have to worry about whether he's a freak or a geek, a grind or a jock or a nerd. He doesn't have to worry if he's gay. He's a murderer."[71] The idea is thereby raised that the subjective identity contained in the label of "murderer" has become an option for children, as well as for adults, in the context of the high school killing trend. And, in a culture of peer-regulated obsession with "coolness," the role of murderer is "cooler" than any of the other available roles:

> Every time Kevin takes another bow as Evil Incarnate, he swells a little larger. Each slander slewed in his direction—*nihilistic, morally destitute, depraved, degenerate,* or *debased*—bulks his scrawny frame better than my cheese sandwiches ever did.[72]

School massacres are so shocking, at least in part, because of the idealized notion to which culture clings that school is a safe, protective, nurturing environment. In fact, schools are hothouses of power struggles, iniquities, and class divisions, pretty much mirroring those of culture at large, but with immature and disenfranchised players. Shriver's book does not shy away from challenging our comfortable assumptions about the institutions of childhood, maternity, paternity, and school. It allows for a reading that suggests that questioning the innate benevolence of these institutions may be a more productive endeavor than continuing to attempt to "solve" the secret riddle of the making of the individual aberrant killer. As Eva comments several times in the novel, about a variety of things, "the secret is that there is no secret." At the close of the book, with Kevin about to turn 18 and be transferred from juvenile detention center to adult prison, he finally gives a straight—if inconclusive—answer to his mother's burning question of *why* he committed his crimes. For once he speaks directly and without swagger: "'I used to think I knew,' he said glumly. 'Now I'm not so sure.'"[73]

The End of Innocence

The search for answers to the enigma of the child who kills, however, continues unabated. About the demonizing media treatment of Thompson and Venables, Morrison wrote: "Evil is no answer. That's one of the lessons of the Bulger case. . . . Time to grow up. Evil won't do."[74] Similarly, if the rejection of one-dimensional explanations is in order, it is also the case that the presumption of innocence as the default character of children simply will not do either. Childhood as a construct needs to be freed from the specter of its regressive Victorian framing that conceptualizes children as a class whose nature is defined—and constrained—by their innocence. Children need to emerge as *people*. Thirdly, I would contend that it will simply not do to continue unquestioningly to assume the positive influence of the institution of "the family," if enacted in its current, culturally ideal, nuclear form. The cause of violent behavior in young people is repeatedly laid at the feet of families who fall short of the normative ideal, especially divorced, single-parent, alcoholic, abusive, or economically deprived families. While there may be causative links between abuse and delinquency, this is not the whole picture. Such a charge is proven to be patently inaccurate in the cases of school shooters Harris and Klebold, who both had educated, boundary-setting, financially comfortable, happily married parents—the very opposite of the stereotype of the family that would produce a young killer.

It may be worth considering instead the proposal that the nuclear family *itself* is a problematic institution, based as it is on a paradigm of hierarchy and dominance, and indeed of ownership. (The common perception that children belong to and with their mothers as a matter of both nature and right accounted for Mary Bell's extended family leaving the little girl in her mother's charge, despite their serious worries over the suspicion that, *on at least four occasions*, Betty Bell had tried to kill Mary.) Radical feminist Shulamith Firestone made the liberation of children from ownership by parents one of the central tenets of her imagined postpatriarchal utopia. In a chapter entitled "Down with Childhood," she describes how the "cult of childhood"[75] is not in the interest of children's well-being, as we like to imagine, but rather in the service of shoring up small, self-centered family units in which children are important because they are the "product of that unit, the reason for its maintenance"[76] and the guarantors of the hierarchy on which it rests, since they are by definition at the very bottom of the heap. She further argues, in an audacious move that resonates particularly powerfully with our discussion of kids who kill, that children are so trapped, so oppressed by the wishful fantasies that adults project onto them, and so powerless to resist them owing to their physical weakness and lack of full citizen status, that "childhood is hell" and "the result is the insecure and therefore aggressive/defensive, often obnoxious little person we call a child."[77]

The so common as to be clichéd "what about the children?" or "think of the children" rhetoric beloved of the tabloid press, which made intelligible the discourses about James Bulger as the archetype of "ideal child" and ideal victim, does not benefit actual living young people, but serves instead to shore up conservative beliefs about what society should look like and what childhood means, as queer theorist Lee Edelman has devastatingly argued. What "The Child" signifies, according to Edelman, is a cipher for the preservation of the Anglo-American conservative order.[78] It encourages compulsory heterosexuality and a pro-reproductive social imperative; it ensures homophobia, as discourses of gay male sexuality are so often collapsed onto discourses of pedophilia; and it perpetuates misogyny, promoting a narrow idea about women's social roles and the biological and cultural "rightness" of maternity. Also, as Edelman shows, "The Child" is the symbol of the idea of the Future. The child who kills other children is therefore unbearable to the social order. He or she is the ultimate example of futurity-negation, more "unnatural" even than the murdering woman or the gay murderer, other commonly hated symbols of the destruction of reproductive futurity.

The cases discussed in this chapter show up the necessity to deconstruct and rethink both the category of "the child," with regard to questions of agency, individuality, violence, and citizenship, and the category of "the murderer." As has been seen throughout this book, the myth of the exceptional individual exculpates society and scapegoats the individual in the case of male adult murderers, obviating the need for class-based analysis. Feminists have repeatedly pointed this out, claiming that male-perpetrated murders are in fact extreme symptoms of a mainstream violence/rape culture. Looking at the treatment of women killers and of kids who kill alongside the representation of male adult murderers, as I have been doing, throws into relief an instance of colossal cultural hypocrisy. In the case of the classic male serial killer, his killing is commonly assumed to have no cultural meaning and not to be symptomatic of any larger trend. Words such as "randomness" and "motivelessness"—the latter an inheritance of the nineteenth century—abound in descriptions of the classic male psychopathic serial killer. Men simply exemplify subjectivity, whether normative or abnormal. In the case of women, individual "monstrousness" is evoked, but the unnatural woman is also far more likely to be read as a symptom of cultural degeneration, as she is seen as weaker and more susceptible to corruption because of her child-like nature, as Lombroso wrote. Finally, in the case of children themselves—the most vulnerable and therefore most corruptible of all—either the child-killer must be revealed as bearing, in the words of the *Times* journalist cited earlier, "the Mark of the Beast," and thereby escape the "innocent child" designation, or else deviations from the "ideal" in his or her environment are blamed for the crimes committed. And most often in the latter case, as we have seen, the negative effect of a mother is sought, since, as Firestone puts it, "women and children are always mentioned in the same breath." The child's crime effectively becomes the mother's, as Shriver's fictional narrative so brilliantly shows. For Firestone, the nature of the bond that ties woman and child so closely together "is no more than shared oppression,"[79] an oppression, moreover, that is all the more devastating and hard to rebut for being "couched in the phraseology of 'cute,'"[80] the very projected characteristic that accounts for the excessive vilification of those child and woman killers who fail—or refuse—to live up to it.

By Way of Brief Conclusion . . .

Identification with a psychotic murderer provides gratification of a death wish against others while simultaneously ensuring exculpation through the projection of all guilt onto the self-same cultural anomaly: "the monster of perversion."
—(Diane Fuss, "Monsters of Perversion: Jeffrey Dahmer and *The Silence of the Lambs*," 1993)

Art lets you get away with murder.
—(Pablo Picasso [attributed])

In Florence, city of art and culture, less than a mile from the Uffizi, can be found a Museo Criminale: Serial Killer e Pena di Morte (Criminal Museum of Serial Killers and the Death Penalty). Inside, one can explore re-creations of Cesare Lombroso's late nineteenth-century skull studies of criminal types, visit mock-ups of the crime scenes of North American serial killers Ed Gein and Ted Bundy, and read about the murders of Aileen Wuornos, before observing the gendered statistics of serial murder ("men 87%; women: 13%," a wall display claims—without stating its source). Fact and fiction intermingle in the *museo*, and accuracy is very obviously not the point. Outside, to attract the public, there is a life-sized dummy dressed to resemble Thomas Harris's genius cannibal killer and connoisseur of taste, Dr. Hannibal Lecter, whose residence in Florence in the third eponymous book (*Hannibal*, 1999) might explain the location of the Museo Criminale, established in 2006—but which alone cannot account for its existence and the popularity of the cultural figure it perversely celebrates. The existence of this establishment and the constitution of its contents (a mixture of European medical history, North American reality-become-folklore, and figures from fiction with the status of cultural icons) perfectly reflect how a paradigmatic modern figure of exception—the subject of murder—has found a place in postmodern, globalized culture.

Having gestured toward the indissolubility of fact and fiction in the construction of the subject of murder, it is worth making an observation about the project of writing about murderers. Such subject matter seems, almost inevitably, to spawn textual hybridity, creative license, and narrative dissidence in the texts it inspires. It encourages a blending of myth, "reality," and imagination. Obvious examples of this are fictionalized literary reconstructions of murders, such as Truman Capote's *In Cold Blood*, an account of the events of the quadruple murders by Hickock and Smith, and Emlyn Williams's inventive and highly speculative "biographies" of Dr. Crippen,[1] and of the Moors Murderers (*Beyond Belief*). The appearance of thinly disguised real-life killers as the protagonists of novels, such as Dennis Nilsen's and Jeffrey Dahmer's fantastical incarnations in Poppy Z. Brite's *Exquisite Corpse*, is a different facet of this phenomenon. Also striking is the fact that scholars of literature—particularly of French literature, it seems—are some of the most prolific commentators on murder cases, as seen in Nicole Ward Jouve's study of Peter Sutcliffe (Ward Jouve has also published on Baudelaire), and Brian Masters's popular work on murderers such as Dennis Nilsen and Jeffrey Dahmer (Masters had previously published on Sartre and Saint-Exupéry). My own book is, of course, part of this tradition, as I am currently employed as a professor of French and also publish on Decadent French literature, among other subjects. I would argue that the influence of aesthetic and literary traditions from the European nineteenth century on the codes of representation—and self-representation—that cluster to the persona of the murderer in modernity may account for this trend, to which I first drew attention in the case of Foucault's admitted fascination with Rivière's memoirs and persona.

Even offender profilers admit that their discipline, throughout its history, has "relied more on crime fiction than on crime fact."[2] Acknowledging that real murderers are often understood according to fictional codes is not, of course, to trivialize the very potent harm done by killers to their victims, and to those who love them. Rather, it is to show how banal horror and real suffering are consistently sutured over by the glittering images of personae capable of fascinating us, much in the way that film stars are understandable, according to cinema theory, as "star texts" not identical with the human individual actor who bears the brand.[3] Our fascination with the figure of the killer is enabled by the very literary and

cinematic qualities of our culture's construction of that exceptional figure. I do not pretend for a moment that I am exempt from this attraction; however, it is a willingness to deconstruct that fascination that has
prompted the critical interrogation found in this book. My hope is that
it has encouraged us to look again at our interest in the subject of murder as a symptom of a cultural need to fix violence, dissidence, or resistance in the person of an idealized or demonized "outsider"—Superman or monster—with whom we can convince ourselves that we share no
common identity other than as an extravagant fantasy.

I have contended that murderers (those social subjects who inhabit
this cultural role and are ascribed that label) have the enduring capacity
to hold our attention in part because there exists a long tradition of ex-
ulting the perceived social and metaphysical transgressions that inhere
in their acts as sublime and transcendental. Ian Brady writes:

> It is part of the eternal human psyche and cycle for the normal individual to
> derive cathartic satisfaction and enjoyment from savouring the crimes of oth-
> ers, and from luxuriously dreaming of personally committing them.[4]

Mark Seltzer too draws a distinction between the "psychic killer" (all of
us who, in imagination, and certainly in childhood fantasy if the Klein-
ians are to be believed, are homicidally inclined) and the "psycho killer,"
that figure of exception who passes "from fantasy to act."[5] He also talks
of "the generally murderous but non-murdering public."[6] The appeal of
both of these propositions is that they offer reassurance that the line di-
viding the fantasist from the agent is an absolute and ontological one,
that there is such a thing as the "normal individual" and the "others."
This involves a disingenuous mechanism of disavowal of *our own* potential capacity for violence.

The idea of the murderer thus serves a convenient function for a dis-
honest society. By focusing on the evil that those individual murderers
do, our attention is diverted from our complicity with a broader, systemic culture of symbolic and actual violence characterized by hetero-
patriarchy, homophobia, the "ownership" of children, racial and ethnic
oppression, and economic inequality. As an alternative to the painful
and ethically engaged project of attempting to explain everyday forms
of violence, the extraordinary exploits of the lone killer (or the killing
couple, powered by a destructive folie à deux) capture our imagination
and make resound in the present echoes of the figure of the Romantic

"outsider"—a myth that is fully endorsed by respected murder "experts" such as Colin Wilson and Brian Masters. The exceptionality ascribed to the murderer in a range of discourses from the nineteenth century to the present day works to affirm that it is not merely by chance or circumstance that some individuals come to murder; rather it is because they are *ontologically different types of subject*. Whether that difference is dressed as superiority or inferiority depends on the political provenance of the given discourse and the gender, sexuality, age, and class of the murderer. This fact notwithstanding, much wringing of hands has occurred over the possibility of the corruption of "the weak" by cultural influences—Sade, lurid romance novels, video games, pornography—that can then be made culpable for the moral failing and legal transgression of the few.[7] Suspicion of contagion falls especially on women, those from lower socioeconomic classes, and children, as I have argued throughout, since these barely subjects are seen to possess neither the capacity for rectitude of the moral and rational subject of humanism, nor the godlike qualities of the sovereign killer.

When Ian Brady writes testily that "women's lib prefers to claim less than equality in the field of murder,"[8] he is neither entirely wrong nor quite fair. Feminist analyses of murder have focused on the common tendency of discursive representation to elide the gendered nature of murder, framing the murderer as a "person" who kills "victims" or "people" when, in the overwhelming majority of cases, the person who kills will be male and the victim female. They also point out the patriarchy-denying motives that underlie such an elision. To some extent, however, there may be a grain of accuracy in Brady's accusation, as seen in the general feminist response to Aileen Wuornos, which preferred to defend her as a victim of patriarchal abuse than understand her as an agent bringing violent resistance to bear on a locus of it. My contribution to a gender-aware cultural analysis of murderers has been to point up that those discourses that make of men the default social subject and make of murderers exceptional individuals have no adequate language or logic for talking about women who kill, as we have seen in the cases of Lafarge (dismissed as a hysteric), Hindley (either an incarnation of the devil or Brady's passive, masochistic sidekick), Wuornos (monstrous lesbian or insane victim of childhood abuse), and 11-year-old Bell (a "bad seed" and demonic child), since such females transcend the role allotted them by a binary gender-obsessed culture that indulges in the double think of believing in both the inevitability of female passivity *and* the unspeakable danger of "unnatural" women. This feminist would wish to claim a measure of equality in the field of murder only to the extent that confronting head-on the way in which the discourses about "feminine nature," which both naturalize female victimhood and make the female killer such an epistemological and ontological problem, are detrimental to the full agency and subjectivity of *all* women, who unlike men, appear first as gendered beings and secondly, if at all, as complex human persons.

However, the reduction of complexity in the case of the murdering subject is also a tendency identified in discourses about all of the murders discussed in this book. The artist-killer, the sex-beast, the unnatural child-hating woman, the "random" serial killer: these are archetypes in the history of discourses about the murderer that are seldom challenged, and that function to make the persona of a given murderer fixed, singular, and one-dimensional. On the one hand, then, many of the murderers discussed *are* exceptional. Civil servants and trade union activists are not usually prolific homicidal necrophiles, as Dennis Nilsen was. Women who do sex work do not usually commit the kinds of killings that Wuornos did. Most children do not set out to murder other children. However, focusing on this exceptionality as proof of an incomprehensible "other" type of subjectivity is a red herring. So too is focusing on the unfathomable nature of the crimes as reflections of the nineteenth-century "pure act," often translated into the twentieth-century discourse of "randomness" ascribed to the typical serial killer and the psychopath. (I have argued that the attempt to ensure the label of "serial killer" for Wuornos was designed to render her acts meaningless and obviate the necessity to speak truth to power and consider her crimes in the light of her justifiable anger and social disenfranchisement.) The insistence upon these subjectifying stereotypes is thus a way of obviating what is really exceptional about the cases—that they are aberrant reactions to, *and symptoms of,* normative and normalizing culture, not the acts of wholly incomprehensible monsters, madmen/women, or geniuses. To borrow a term from Jacques Lacan, the murderer may be best understood as an example of "extimacy,"[9] that is, as the kernel of otherness that is interior to—at the heart of—our own culture, intimate but necessarily disavowed in order to maintain a semblance of decency.

I close, then, with the assertion of my solemn and sobering belief that we all, whatever our gender, age, sexuality, ethnicity, or economic class, could, in some circumstances, ourselves become murderers. It is also my conviction that, in such an extreme situation, we would find ourselves treated very differently depending upon our particular status within those hierarchical categories. Both of these propositions, however, are ones that "civilized" culture, which shores up its unassailable rectitude by the creation of abjected "others," refuses absolutely to own.

Notes

Introduction

1. Simone de Beauvoir, *Le Deuxième sexe*, 2 vols. (Paris: Gallimard, 1949).

2. This is, broadly, the argument of Jane Caputi's book: *The Age of Sex Crime* (London: The Women's Press, 1987). See also: Deborah Cameron and Elizabeth Frazer, *The Lust to Kill: A Feminist Investigation of Sexual Murder* (Cambridge, UK: Polity, 1987).

3. David Schmid, *Natural Born Celebrities: Serial Killers in American Culture* (Chicago: University of Chicago Press, 2005), pp. 1–27.

4. Ibid., p. 5.

5. Michel Foucault, *I, Pierre Rivière, Having Slaughtered My Mother, My Sister, and My Brother: A Case of Parricide in the Nineteenth Century* [1973], trans. Frank Jellinek (Lincoln: University of Nebraska Press, 1975), p. xiii.

6. Ibid., p. x.

7. Ibid., p. xiii.

8. As Alison Moore has pointed out, although Sade did not tend to capitalize "nature" in his texts, most English translations of Sade give "nature" an uppercase letter *N*. This has the effect of personifying "her" more than Sade may have intended. See: Moore, "Sadean Nature and Reasoned Morality in Adorno/Horkheimer's *Dialectic of Enlightenment*," *Psychology and Sexuality*, 1, 3, 2010, 250–261, p. 252.

9. D-A-F de Sade, *The Complete Justine, Philosophy in the Bedroom and Other Writings*, trans. Richard Seaver and Austryn Wainhouse (New York: Grove Press, 1965), p. 520.

10. "l'habitude de céder à l'instinct qui nous porte aux plaisirs des sens." Cited in Andrzej Siemek, *La Recherche morale et esthétique dans le roman de Crébillon fils* (Oxford: Oxford University Press, 1981), pp. 34–35. My translation. All translations from French, unless otherwise indicated, are mine.

11. See: Lucienne Frappier-Mazur, "Sadean Libertinage and the Esthetics of Violence," *Yale French Studies*, 94, 1998, 184–198, p. 184.

12. Foucault, "What Is an Author?," [1969] in *Essential Works of Foucault 1954–1984*, vol. 2, ed. James D. Faubion (London: Penguin, 2000), 205–222.

13. Cameron and Frazer, *Lust to Kill*, p. 55.

14. Ibid.

15. Angela Carter, *The Sadeian Woman: An Exercise in Cultural History* [1978] (London: Virago, 1998), p. 27.

16. Ibid.

17. Foucault, *Madness and Civilization: A History of Insanity in the Age of Reason* [1961], trans. Richard Howard (Pantheon: New York, 1965), p. 210.

18. See: Foucault, *The Birth of the Clinic: An Archeology of Medical Perception* [1963], trans. A. M. Sheridan (London: Routledge, 2003).

19. Rux Martin, "Truth, Power, Self: An Interview," in *Technologies of the Self: A Seminar with Michel Foucault*, ed. Luther H. Martin, Huck Gutman, and Patrick H. Hutton (Amherst: University of Massachusetts Press, 1988), 9–15, p. 15.

20. Foucault, *The Will to Knowledge: The History of Sexuality*, vol. 1 [1976], trans. Robert Hurley (Harmondsworth, UK: Penguin, 1990), pp. 42–43.

21. Foucault, *Abnormal: Lectures at the Collège de France 1974–1975*, trans. Graham Burchell (London: Verso, 2003), p. 81.

22. Ibid., p. 19.

23. Ibid., p. 20.

24. Foucault, "Technologies of the Self," in *Technologies of the Self*, ed. Martin, Gutman, and Hutton, 16–49, p. 17.

25. Foucault, *Discipline and Punish: The Birth of the Prison* [1975], trans. Alan Sheridan (Harmondsworth, UK: Penguin, 1991), p. 68.

26. Thomas De Quincey, *On Murder as a Fine Art* [first pub. *Blackwood's Magazine*, 1827] (London: Phillip Allan, 1925), p. 40.

27. Josephine McDonagh has discussed the gendered implications of De Quincey's choice of whole families as the most poetic murder victims, arguing that this constitutes a murder of the feminine. See: "Do or Die: Problems of Agency and Gender in the Aesthetics of Murder," *Genders*, 5, 1989, 120–134.

28. De Quincey, *On Murder*, p. 50.

29. Ibid.

30. Joel Black, *The Aesthetics of Murder: A Study in Romantic Literature and Contemporary Culture* (Baltimore: Johns Hopkins University Press, 1991), p. 14.

31. Immanuel Kant, *Critique of Judgment* [1790], trans. J. H. Bernard (New York: Haffner, 1951), p. 91.

32. Jacques Lacan, "Kant avec Sade," [1962] *Ecrits* (Paris: Seuil, 1966), 765–790.

33. Black, *Aesthetics of Murder*, p. 15.

34. Friedrich Schiller, "Reflections on the Use of the Vulgar and Lowly in Works of Art," 1802, cited in Black, *Aesthetics of Murder*, p. 35.

35. Oscar Wilde, *The Complete Works of Oscar Wilde* (New York: Harper and Rowe, 1989), p. 993. Also of relevance to the aestheticization of murder is Wilde's story "Lord Arthur Savile's Crime" (1887).

36. For an account of how an English Romantic discourse reemerged in specifically French Decadence at the fin de siècle, see: Lisa Downing, "Beyond Reasonable Doubt: Aesthetic Violence and Motiveless Murder in French Decadent Fiction," *French Studies*, 58, 2, 2004, 189–204.

37. W. H. Auden, "The Guilty Vicarage," *The Dyer's Hand and Other Essays* (London: Faber and Faber, 1975), 146–158, p. 152.

38. See: Schmid, *Natural Born Celebrities*, pp. 1–4.

39. Ricarda Vidal, "Murderous Art: The Morbid Attraction of Serial Killers and Their Art," *Desipentia*, 17, 1, April 2010, 12–15.

40. Black, *Aesthetics of Murder*, p. 9.

41. Laurence Senelick, *The Prestige of Evil: The Murderer as Romantic Hero from Sade to Lacenaire*, Harvard Dissertations in Comparative Literature (New York: Garland, 1987).

42. Friedrich Nietzsche, *The Will to Power* [published posthumously], trans. Walter Kaufmann and R. J. Hollingdale (New York: Vintage, 1968), p. 222.

43. Nietzsche, *On the Genealogy of Morals* [1887], trans. Walter Kaufmann and R. J. Hollingdale (New York: Vintage, 1969), p. 66.

44. Jean Genet, *Our Lady of the Flowers* [1943], trans. Bernard Frechtman (New York: Grove Press, 1963), p. 186.

45. See: Christine Battersby, *Gender and Genius: Towards a Feminist Aesthetics* (London: The Women's Press, 1989).

46. For more on French alienism, see: Jan Goldstein, *Console and Classify: The French Psychiatric Profession in the Nineteenth Century* (Cambridge: Cambridge University Press, 1987). For more on the monomania diagnosis, see: Marina Van Zuylen, *Monomania: The Flight from Everyday Life* (Ithaca, NY: Cornell University Press, 2005).

47. For more on this point, see: Downing, "Eros and Thanatos in European and American Sexology," in *Bodies, Sex and Desire from the Renaissance to the Present*, ed. Sarah Toulalan and Kate Fisher (Basingstoke, UK: Palgrave Macmillan, 2011), 201–220.

48. Max Nordau, *Degeneration* [1892], translation of the 2nd edition by George L. Moss (Lincoln: University of Nebraska Press, 1968). For more on degeneration theory see: Daniel Pick, *Faces of Degeneration: A European Disorder, c. 1848–1913* (Cambridge: Cambridge University Press, 1989).

49. See: Cesare Lombroso, *Criminal Man* [1876], trans. Mary Gibson and Nicole Hahn Rafter (Durham, NC: Duke University Press, 2006) and Cesare Lombroso and Guglielmo Ferrero, *Criminal Woman, the Prostitute, and the Nor-*

mal Woman [1893], trans. Mary Gibson and Nicole Hahn Rafter (Durham, NC: Duke University Press, 2004).

50. Krafft-Ebing, *Psychopathia Sexualis with Especial Reference to Contrary Sexual Instinct: A Medico-Legal Study* [1886], translation of the 7th German edition by Charles Gilbert Chaddock (Philadelphia: F. A. Davis, 1892), p. 64.

51. Ibid., p. 59.

52. Nordau, *Degeneration*, p. 119.

53. See: Andrew Elfenbein, *Romantic Genius: The Prehistory of a Homosexual Role* (New York: Columbia University Press, 1998) and M. Gibson, "The Masculine Degenerate: American Doctors' Portrayals of the Lesbian Intellect, 1880–1949," *Journal of Women's History*, 9, 1998, 78–103.

54. See: Thomas Szasz, "The Mad Genius Controversy," *The Freeman: Ideas of Liberty*, December 2005, 22–23, p. 22.

55. Ibid.

56. J. C. Pritchard, *A Treatise on Insanity and Other Disorders Affecting the Mind* (London: Sherwood, Gilbert, and Piper, 1835).

57. Thomas Strentz and Conrad V. Hassel, "The Sociopath: A Criminal Enigma," *Journal of Police Science and Administration*, 6, 1978, 135–140.

58. See: Caputi, *Age of Sex Crime*, p. 10. The Norman Mailer text she refers to is "The White Negro," in *Advertisements for Myself* (New York: Signet, 1959), 302–322.

59. Alan Harrington, *Psychopaths* (New York: Simon and Schuster, 1972), p. 33. My italics.

60. See: G. A Weatherby et al., "The Buller-McGinnis Model of Serial-Homicidal Behavior: An Integrated Approach," *Journal of Criminology and Criminal Justice Research and Education*, 3, 1, 2009.

61. Mark Seltzer, *Serial Killers: Death and Life in America's Wound Culture* (London: Routledge, 1998), p. 16.

62. Ibid., p. 14.

63. Harris sat in on courses at Quantico before beginning the trilogy of stories set in and around the FBI's Behavioral Science Unit, *Red Dragon* (1981), *The Silence of the Lambs* (1988), and *Hannibal* (1999).

64. Seltzer, *Serial Killers*, p. 15.

65. For more, see: Brent Turvey, *Criminal Profiling: An Introduction to Behavioral Evidence Analysis* (San Diego: Academic Press, 1999).

66. Seltzer, *Serial Killers*, p. 17.

67. Ian Brady, *The Gates of Janus: Serial Killing and Its Analysis by the "Moors Murderer"* (Los Angeles: Feral House, 2001), p. 37.

68. Thomas Harris, *The Silence of the Lambs* [1988] (London: Arrow, 1999), p. 10.

69. Robert D. Hare, *Psychopathology Checklist-Revised (PLC-R)* (Toronto: Multi-Health Systems, 2003).

70. Szasz, "The Mad Genius Controversy," pp. 22–23.

71. For more on the insanity defense, and an argument for punishing "evil," see: Lawrie Reznek, *Evil or Ill: Justifying the Insanity Defence* (London: Routledge, 1997).

72. "Diminished responsibility" means that at the time of committing the crime, the perpetrator demonstrated such "abnormality of mind" as to have "substantially impaired his mental responsibility for his act."

73. Cameron and Frazer, *Lust to Kill*, pp. 128–129.

74. Wendy Hollway, " 'I Just Wanted to Kill a Woman.' Why? The Ripper and Male Sexuality," in *Sweeping Statements: Writings from the Women's Liberation Movement, 1981–3*, ed. H. Kanter et al. (London: The Women's Press, 1984), p. 17.

75. For more on Christie's Case, see: Ludovic Kennedy, *10 Rillington Place* (London: Victor Gollancz, 1961) and the film of the same name directed by Richard Fleischer and starring Richard Attenborough (1971).

76. See: Brian Masters, *She Must Have Known: The Trial of Rosemary West* (London: Corgi, 1997), p. 297.

77. Seltzer, *Serial Killers*, p. 34.

78. Hannah Arendt, *Eichmann in Jerusalem: A Report on the Banality of Evil* [1963] (Harmondsworth, UK: Penguin, 1994).

79. "I'll never be able to have a baby now and I would have liked one so much. I'd have loved to have been a mother." Myra Hindley in 1983, cited in Carol Ann Lee, *One of Your Own: The Life and Death of Myra Hindley* (Edinburgh: Mainstream Publishing, 2010), p. 319.

80. Cameron and Frazer, *Lust to Kill*, p. 42.

81. Joan Smith, "Getting Away with Murder," *New Socialist*, May/June 1982, 10–12, p. 12.

82. Lee, *One of Your Own*, p. 10.

83. Peter Sotos, "Afterword," in Brady, *Gates of Janus*, 289–305, p. 293.

84. E.g.: Judith Flanders's recent book, *The Invention of Murder: How the Victorians Revelled in Death and Detection and Created Modern Crime* (London: HarperCollins, 2011), which argues that it was the public appetite for detective fiction and reports of true-life murder cases that arose in tandem with organized policing that gave rise to the fascination with murder. She does not explore the figure of "the murderer" as a specific type as such.

85. Foucault, *I, Pierre Rivière*, p. xiii.

86. See: Downing, *The Cambridge Introduction to Michel Foucault* (Cambridge: Cambridge University Press, 2008), pp. 73–74.

87. Alison Young, *Imagining Crime* (London: Sage, 1996), p. 35.

88. See, for example: Peter Vronsky, *Serial Killers: The Method and Madness of Monsters* (New York: Berkley, 2004) (female killers get a separate Vronsky-authored volume of their own); Colin Wilson, *The Serial Killers: A Study in*

the Psychology of Violence (London: Virgin, 1990) (female killers are included here, but they are very much an afterthought); and Mark Seltzer's intelligent academic study, *Serial Killers*, which argues that contemporary Western culture is fascinated by murder because it has an addiction to trauma, to "torn and open" bodies and psyches. The book discusses numerous murder cases, but none of notable murderous women. In the "Women Who Kill" category are: Ann Jones, *Women Who Kill* (London: Victor Gollancz, 1991); Carol Anne Davis, *Women Who Kill: Profiles of Female Serial Killers* (London: Allison and Busby, 2001); Peter Vronsky, *Female Serial Killers: How and Why Women Become Monsters* (New York: Berkley, 2007); and Belinda Morrissey's very thoughtful *When Women Kill: Questions of Agency and Subjectivity* (London: Routledge, 2003).

89. Two noteworthy exceptions are: Kenneth Polk, *When Men Kill* (Cambridge: Cambridge University Press, 1994), a qualitative study of Australian male-perpetrated homicide and the masculine scripts served by it, and Martin J. Wiener, *Men of Blood: Violence, Manliness and Criminal Justice in Victorian England* (Cambridge: Cambridge University Press, 2004).

90. See, for example: Jonathan Paul, *When Kids Kill* (London: Virgin, 2003) and Carol Anne Davis, *Children Who Kill: Profiles of Pre-Teen and Teenage Killers* (London: Allison and Busby, 2003).

91. See: Lynda Hart, *Fatal Women: Lesbian Sexuality and the Mark of Aggression* (Princeton, NJ: Princeton University Press, 1994) and Lisa Duggan *Sapphic Slashers: Sex, Violence and American Modernity* (Durham, NC: Duke University Press, 2001). Both books in different ways explore the lesbophobia attending many discourses about women who kill, and the fear of female violence and threat to the modern patriarchal order attending many discourses about lesbians. A phenomenon I will not discuss in this book is the tendency in fictional representations of serial killers to ascribe homicidal psychopathy to transgendered subjects. (Harris's *The Silence of the Lambs* was criticized on these grounds for its portrayal of Jame Gumb, the cross-dressing "Buffalo Bill"). The reason for this omission in my book is that I deal with real-life killers as case studies, and the large number of transgendered fictional murderers is in no way borne out by any notable examples of real-life cases. Indeed, trangendered people are much more likely to be the victims than the perpetrators of homicide. My analyses of discourses of gender nonconformity (e.g., the case of Aileen Wuornos, a butch lesbian) will, however, touch on the reasons why those subjects who flout binary gender norms are demonized and criminalized.

92. R. E. L. Masters and Eduard Lea, *Sex Crimes in History* (New York: Julian Press, 1963); Robert A. Nye, *Crime, Madness and Politics in Modern France: The Medical Concept of National Decline* (Princeton, NJ: Princeton University Press, 1984).

93. Cameron and Frazer's feminist account of sex crimes is an exception: it takes onboard the importance of both sets of discourse in making the serial sex murderer, but confines its study to those killers that fit this description.

94. E.g., Susanne Kord, *Murderesses in German Writing, 1720–1860* (Cambridge: Cambridge University Press, 2009); Maria Tatar, *Lustmord: Sexual Murder in Weimar Germany* (Princeton, NJ: Princeton University Press, 1995).

95. E.g., Nicole Ward Jouve, *'The Streetcleaner': The Yorkshire Ripper Case on Trial* (London: Marion Boyars, 1986); Rachel Edwards and Keith Reader, *The Papin Sisters* (Oxford: Oxford University Press, 2001).

96. Richard Tithecott, *Of Men and Monsters: Jeffrey Dahmer and the Construction of the Serial Killer* (Madison: University of Wisconsin Press, 1997).

97. Philippe Ariès, *Centuries of Childhood* [1960], trans. Robert Baldick (New York: Vintage Books, 1962).

Chapter One

1. Voici une saississante et terrible actualité; voici *Lacenaire.*
   Il portait une lyre et un poignard!
   Il était poète et il assassinait!
2. En même temps molle et féroce,
   Sa forme a pour l'observateur
   Je ne sais quelle grâce atroce,
   La grâce du gladiateur!

   Criminelle aristocratie,
   Par la varlope ou le marteau
   Sa pulpe n'est pas endurcie,
   Car son outil fut un couteau.

   Saints calus du travail honnête,
   On y cherche en vain votre sceau.
   Vrai meurtrier et faux poète,
   Il fut le Manfred du ruisseau!

3. *Autopsie physiologique de Lacenaire, mort sur l'échafaud le 9 janvier 1836,* cited in Pierre-François Lacenaire, *Mémoires de Lacenaire avec ses poèmes et ses lectures,* ed. Monique Lebailly (Paris: Albin Michel, 1968), p. 253.

4. Published in *Émaux et Camées* (1852). Reproduced in Lacenaire, *Mémoires,* pp. 293–294.

5. Edward Baron Turk, *Child of Paradise: Marcel Carné and the Golden Age of French Cinema* (Cambridge, MA: Harvard University Press, 1989), p. 269.

6. Foucault, *Discipline and Punish,* p. 284.

7. Louis Chevalier, *Classes laborieuses et classes dangereuses à Paris pendant la première moitié du dix-neuvième siècle* (Paris: Plon, 1958).

8. "une nation à part, au milieu de la nation." Honoré de Balzac, *Codes des honnêtes gens'ou l'art de ne pas être dupe des fripons* [1825] (Paris, Manya, 1990), p. 15.

9. "un veritable don de nature." Lacenaire, *Mémoires*, p. 68.

10. Lacenaire is allegedly the inspiration behind the character of Valbayre in Stendhal's unfinished *Lamiel*, the writing of which was interrupted by the author's death in 1848.

11. The crime committed by Raskolnikov, the protagonist of Dostoyevsky's *Crime and Punishment*, was based on the details of Lacenaire's murders, as revealed at his trial.

12. Charles Baudelaire, "De l'héroisme de la vie moderne," in "Salon de 1846," *Œuvres complètes*, ed. Marcel A. Ruff (Paris: Seuil, 1968), p. 260.

13. For more on this group, see: Théophile Gautier, *Les Jeunes France* [1833] (Paris: Flammarion, 1992) and Enid Starkie, *Pétrus Borel: The Lycanthrope, His Life and Times* (New York: New Directions, 1954).

14. A cette époque funeste,
    Reniant jusqu'à son nom,
    Dans ce Paris qu'on déteste
    S'il regna, quoique Bourbon,
    Je suis sûr que notre roi
    Pense aujourd'hui comme moi,
    Quel malheur!
    Je le dis avec douleur
    Nos trois jours, c'est une horreur!

    Pour rassurer la patrie
    Sur un pareil attentat,
    Contre la presse en furie
    Il nous faut un coup d'état.
    Les amandes, l'interdit,
    N'ont pu nous mettre en credit.
    Quel malheur!
    Je le dis avec douleur
    Nos trois jours, c'est une horreur!
    Lacenaire, *Mémoires*, p. 152.

15. See: Anne-Emmanuelle Demartini, *L'Affaire Lacenaire* (Paris: Aubier, 2001), p. 335.

16. "La presse s'est emparé du procès de Lacenaire pour incriminer soit la société actuelle, soit le pouvoir. Les uns s'en prennent à la corruption du siècle, les autres à ce qu'ils appellent l'immoralité des gouvernants. Il serait plus raisonna-

ble de regarder Lacenaire comme une terrible exception, du genre de celles qui ont apparu sous tous les régimes et dans tous les temps, mais heureusement pour l'humanité, à de rares intervalles." *Journal de Paris*, 19 November 1835.

17. "l'histoire de notre littérature et de nos littérateurs va se trouver bientôt dans notre *Gazette des tribuneaux*." *La Chronique de Paris*, 13 December 1835.

18. "qu'à force de scélératesse et de perversité cynique ils peuvent se racheter de l'horreur qu'ils inspirent et se faire des admirateurs." *La France*, 23 December 1835.

19. "Au moins autrefois, avant Robert Macaire, le vice était d'ordinaire tout souillé et tout fangeux; il faisait peur rien qu'à le voir; aujourd'hui Robert Macaire est habillé comme les plus élégants . . . bien plus, le crime, sur le banc des assesses, cite des vers d'Horace, le poète épicurien. . . . Robert Macaire, à coup sûr, est le père de Lacenaire." Jules Janin, *Œuvres diverses de Jules Janin*, vol. 1 (Paris: Librairie des bibliophiles, 1878), p. 269.

20. "J'ai vu jouer *Robert-Macaire* et *L'Auberge des Adrets*; ces deux ignobles ouvrages m'auraient dégouté de crime, tant Robert travaille par ostentation et l'autre par bêtise." Lacenaire, *Mémoires*, p. 237.

21. Michel Foucault, *I, Pierre Rivière*, p. viii.

22. "aux besoins des générations blasées qui demandent des sensations à tout prix." Charles Nodier, *Mélanges de literature et de critique*, ed. Alexandre Barginet, vol. 1 (Paris: Raymond, 1820), p. 411.

23. "[Un] infanticide. Tant de vierges timides en sont à leur troisième, tant de filles vertueuses comptent leurs printemps par des meurtres . . . Loi barbare! préjugé féroce! honneur infâme! hommes! société! tenez! tenez votre proie . . . Je vous la rends!!!" Pétrus Borel, "Champavert: Le lycanthrope," in *Champavert: Contes immoraux* (Paris, Eugène Renduel, 1833), 397–438, p. 435.

24. "Je préfère le sang que j'ai aux mains à la boue immonde qui les couvre tout entiers." Letter from Lacenaire to Eugène Scribe, cited in Demartini, *L'Affaire Lacenaire*, p. 55.

25. Salut à toi ma belle fiancée
    Qui dans tes bras vas bientot m'enlacer
    A toi ma dernière pensée,
    Je fus à toi dès le berceau.
    Salut ô guillotine! Expiation sublime,
    Dernier article de la loi,
    Qui soustrait l'homme à l'homme et le rends pur de crime
    Dans le sein du néant, mon espoir et ma foi.
    Lacenaire, *Mémoires*, p. 162.

26. Demartini, *L'Affaire Lacenaire*, p. 126.

27. "est un phénomène moderne d'essence démocratique." Ibid., p. 188.

28. "une illustration de la pensée au dix-neuvième siècle." Ibid., p. 346.

29. Peter France (ed.), *New Oxford Companion to Literature in French* (Oxford: Clarendon, 1995), p. 327.

30. "l'homme qui a inventé la métaphyisque de l'assassinat." Cited in Black, *Aesthetics of Murder*, p. 113.

31. Foucault, *Discipline and Punish*, p. 160.

32. "n'a jamais réussi de tuer d'un seul coup." Maxime du Camp, *Paris, ses organes, ses fonctions et sa vie dans la seconde moitié du xixe siècle*, vol. 4 (Paris: Hachette, 1875), p. 491.

33. Margaret Waller, *The Male Malady: Fictions of Impotence in the French Romantic Novel* (New Brunswick, NJ: Rutgers University Press, 1993), p. 16.

34. Senelick, *Prestige of Evil*, p. 289.

35. Waller, *Male Malady*, p. 11.

36. Ibid., p. 21.

37. Demartini, *L'Affaire Lacenaire*, p. 52.

38. Black, *Aesthetics of Murder*, p. 118.

39. "les femmes, avides d'émotion, ont fait le succès de Lacenaire." *La chronique de Paris*, 17 January 1836.

40. *Le Vert-Vert*, 15 February 1836.

41. "le thème de la femme amatrice de procès et de criminels est un *lieu*, au sens rhétorique, du discours sur les femmes au 19ième siècle." Demartini, *L'Affaire Lacenaire*, p. 54.

42. Vautrin was shown throughout those books of the *Comédie humaine* in which he features to have a predilection for his adolescent male protégés. As well as Lacenaire, the figure of Vautrin was allegedly inspired by the figure of Eugène François Vidocq, a criminal turned crime-fighter, for whom Lacenaire too expressed admiration. See: Senelick, *Prestige of Evil*, p. 282.

43. "Tuer les mouchards et les gendarmes, ça n'empêch' [*sic*] pas les sentiments." Cited in ibid., p. 267.

44. "Un homme seul contre tous, mais un homme fort et puissant de son génie, que la société a rejeté dès son berceau, qui a senti sa force et l'a employé au mal; un homme qui a tout étudié, tout approfondi; un homme qui donnerait vingt fois sa vie pour reconnaître un bien-fait; un homme qui sent tort sans pouvoir l'exprimer, mais à l'âme duquel rien de beau et de noble n'est étranger, un homme enfin qui, tout en méprisant ses semblables, a eu plus de violence à se faire pour arriver au mal, que beaucoup d'autres pour arriver a le vertu." Lacenaire, *Mémoires*, p. 95.

45. Rachilde's novels and short stories are littered with aesthetic murder, necrophilia, and lust killing. For more on this female Decadent's treatment of these themes, see: chapter 4 of Downing, *Desiring the Dead: Necrophilia and Nineteenth-Century French Literature* (Oxford: EHRC, 2003) and Downing, "Beyond Reasonable Doubt."

46. Rachilde, *Cynismes: Lacenaire et Monsieur Papon* (n.p.: Collection La Marguerite, 1995), p. 1.

47. Ibid., p. 2.

48. This is a fictional amorality tale we might bear in mind when considering the case of the Moors Murderers, whose sentimental fondness for animals was often used against them at trial as absolutely incommensurate with their killing of children—and was somehow assumed to make their crimes even more monstrous.

49. "Je vois d'ici une nuée de phrénologues, cranologues, physiologists, anatomistes" . . . "les détails les plus minutieux et les plus exacts sur mes goûts, mes passions et même sur les aventures de ma vie." Lacenaire, *Mémoires*, p. 25.

50. Significantly, however, Auteuil would also go on to play the role of the Marquis de Sade in Benoît Jacquot's reverential biopic, *Sade*, 2000. Sade is similarly an antihero of a previous century who has been lionized on celluloid during the twentieth and twenty-first centuries and canonized as a writer by the appearance of the prestigious Pléiade edition of his works in 1990.

51. "Lacenaire s'inscrit dans ce vaste mouvement par lequel, au xixième siecle, le criminel s'installe comme jamais dans le champs du discours, mais il en inverse les modalités et la signification: tandis que le criminel existe dans le discours en tant qu'objet, Lacenaire s'institue sujet du discours qui le concerne." Demartini, *L'Affaire Lacenaire*, p. 339.

52. Ibid., pp. 328–331.

53. "J'agis sans crainte et sans espérance, et par la seule force de ma volonté." Lacenaire, *Mémoires*, p. 93.

54. "Je me suis fait ce que je suis. La nature n'avait rien fait pour moi." Ibid., p. 73.

55. "J'ai lu Diderot, d'Alembert, Jean-Jacques, à un âge où nous ne nous plaisons guère qu'avec Florian ou Robinson Crusoé; eh bien! Dussiez-vous me taxer d'orgueil, je vous dirai qu'en morale et en religion, mes idées étaient tellement les leurs que je croyais déjà les avoir lus quelquefois, et même les avoir appris de mémoire. J'achevais souvent, sans regarder le page, la pensée ou la phrase commencée." Ibid., pp. 236–237.

Chapter Two

1. Lombroso and Ferrero, *Criminal Woman*, p. 279, n. 39.

2. "deux choses: un feu d' artifice donné tous les soirs au peuple, et un procès Lafarge donné tous les matins aux classes éclairées." Edmond and Jules de Goncourt, *Les hommes de lettres (Charles Demailly)* (Paris: E. Dentu, 1860), p. 151.

3. "M. Gamblin lui demanda immédiatement son opinion sur Mme Lafarge. Ce procès, la fureur de l'époque, ne manqua pas d'amener une discussion vio-

lente." Gustave Flaubert, *L'Éducation sentimentale* (1869), ed. René Dumesnil, 2 vols. (Paris: Société les Belles Lettres, 1942), p. 15.

4. Edith Saunders, *The Mystery of Marie Lafarge* (London: Clerke and Cockeran, 1951), pp. 7–8.

5. Janet Beizer, *Ventriloquized Bodies: Narratives of Hysteria in Nineteenth-Century France* (Ithaca, NY: Cornell University Press, 1984).

6. Jann Matlock, *Scenes of Seduction: Prostitution, Hysteria and Reading Difference in Nineteenth-Century France* (New York: Columbia University Press, 1994).

7. Martha Noel Evans, *Fits and Starts: A Genealogy of Hysteria in Modern France* (Ithaca, NY: Cornell University Press, 1991).

8. "Tout ce qu'on a coutume d'attribuer au temperament nerveux de la femme rentre dans le domaine de l'hystérie." Charles Richet, "Les Démoniaques d'aujourd'hui," *Revue des deux mondes*, 37 (15 January 1880), p. 341.

9. Lombroso and Ferrero, *Criminal Woman*, p. 237.

10. Senelick, *Prestige of Evil*, p. 298.

11. Ibid., p. 303.

12. Lombroso and Ferrero, *Criminal Woman*, p. 239.

13. Hilary Neroni, *The Violent Woman: Femininity, Narrative and Violence in Contemporary American Cinema* (Albany: SUNY: 2005), p. 60.

14. Matlock, *Scenes of Seduction*, pp. 249–280.

15. Mary S. Hartman, *Victorian Murderesses: A True History of Thirteen Respectable French and English Women Accused of Unspeakable Crimes* (London: Robson, 1977), p. 19.

16. Matlock, *Scenes of Seduction*, p. 254.

17. Anna Norris, *L'écriture du défi: Textes carcéraux féminins du XIXe et du XXe siècles: entre l'aiguille et la plume* (Birmingham, AL: Summa, 2003).

18. "Les femmes écrivent, écrivent avec une rapidité débordante; leur cœur bavarde à la rame. Elles ne connaissent généralement ni l'art, ni la mesure, ni la logique; leur style ondoie comme leurs vêtements." Charles Baudelaire, "Études sur Poe," in *Œuvres complètes*, ed. Claude Pichois, 2 vols. (Paris: Gallimard/Pléiade, 1975–1976), vol. 2, pp. 282–283.

19. "Elle n'a jamais été artiste. Elle a le fameux style coulant, cher aux bourgeois. Elle est bête. Elle est lourde. Elle est bavarde." Baudelaire, "Mon cœur mis à nu," in *Œuvres complètes*, vol. 1, p. 686.

20. "un souffle de poésie, bien qu'elles abondent de détails minutieux et frivoles." Henri Didier, "Lafarge," in *Biographie universelle ancienne et moderne* (Paris, n.d.), p. xxii.

21. Senelick, *Prestige of Evil*, p. 302.

22. Joseph Shearing, *The Lady and the Arsenic: The Life and Death of a Romantic: Marie Cappelle, Madame Lafarge* (London: Heinemann, 1937), p. 3.

23. "Elle est brune, belle, adorable. Un visage d'un ovale parfait, un teint

d'une blancheur exquise, une voix sublime. Elle est intelligente, cultivée, douée d'un désir fou de vivre et d'aimer." Laure Adler, *L'Amour à l'arsenic: Histoire de Marie Lafarge* (Paris: Denoël, 1985), p. 11.

24. Edward Shorter has argued that the 1840s saw the rise of a "surge of sentiment" in France, with young people, particularly women, focusing on criteria of "affection and compatibility," rather than the traditional matrimonial motive of combining the assets of two powerful families in an advantageous way. Shorter goes so far as to argue that this "surge of sentiment" resulted in a Romantic revolution that materially changed the dynamics of marriage. This may be claiming too much, since this alleged "surge," if it operated in the imaginary and literary sphere, was in stark contrast to the persistence and prevalence of arranged marriages of financial convenience in the period, of the kind of which Lafarge herself was a victim. This meeting of incompatible ideals and realities exacerbated the potential for female unhappiness, in a civic state in which divorce was illegal. See: Edward Shorter, *The Making of the Modern Family* (New York: Basic Books, 1979), pp. 3–21 and pp. 148–161.

25. Louise Kaplan, *Female Perversions* [1991] (Harmondsworth, UK: Penguin, 1993).

26. "Je n'en ai pas même eu la pensée. Je ne comprends pas qu'on invente des nouvelles aussi niaises et aussi peu intéressantes pour le public." Georges Sand, *Correspondance*, ed. Georges Lubin, vol. 5 (April 1840–December 1842) (Paris: Garnier, 1969), p. 69.

27. "Je vous laisserai ma fortune; Dieu permettra qu'elle vous prospère, vous le méritez. Moi, je vivrai du produit de mon travail ou de mes leçons, je vous prie de ne laisser jamais soupçonner que j'existe. Si vous le voulez, je prendrai de l'arsenic, j'en ai . . . mais recevoir mes caresses, jamais!" Marie Cappelle Lafarge, *Correspondance*, ed. Boyer D'Agen, 2 vols. (Paris: Mercure de France, 1913), vol. 2, p. 51.

28. "Fleurs délicates, destinées à rester infécondes; elles se replient sur ellesméme au moindre contact, au moindre souffle d'amour, car un seul souffle en semblerait ternir la blancheur virginale; êtres en un mot, incapables d'aimer autrement que s'aiment les anges; amour de cœur et de pensée sous une forme aérienne et qui ne comporte rien de la grossièrté des organes corporelles." *Revue élémentaire de medicine et de pharmacie domestique* (1848), quoted in Julien Raspail, "L'Affaire Lafarge," *La Revue*, 15 September 1913, p. 181.

29. See: Alison Moore and Peter Cryle, "Frigidity at the Fin de Siècle in France: A Slippery and Capacious Concept," *Journal of the History of Sexuality*, 19, 2, 2010, 243–261.

30. Lombroso and Ferrero, *Criminal Woman*, p. 35.

31. Ibid., p. 183.

32. Ibid., p. 28.

33. Ibid., p. 149.

34. Ibid., p. 171.

35. Ibid., p. 83.

36. Ibid., p. 70.

37. Ibid., pp. 189–190.

38. Ibid., p. 188.

39. See: Shearing, *The Lady and the Arsenic*, p. 100.

40. Lombroso and Ferrero, *Criminal Woman*, p. 35.

41. "Ainsi de la femme criminelle dont la nature ressort comme un élément exacerbant les délits, et dont on dresse une typologie de crimes spécifiques: empoisonnement, vol (domestique ou grands magasins) mais également adultère, prostitution, avortement ou infanticide, tous ces crimes liés à la sexualité, au sexe même de son auteur et qui revèle à travers l'analyse faite le consensus sur le danger du sexe porté par la femme." Martine Kaluszynski, "Aux origines de la criminologie: L'anthropologie criminelle," "crimes," *Frénésie*, 5, Spring 1988, 17–30, p. 23.

42. Lombroso and Ferrero, *Criminal Woman*, p. 98.

43. Alexandre Lacassagne, "Notes statistiques sur l'empoisonnement criminel en France," *Archives d'Anthropologie criminelles et de sciences pénales*, 1, 1886, pp. 260–264.

44. "M. Lombroso a raison, le crime des femmes, le crime feminin, a quelque chose de plus particulièrement odieux et de plus pervers. La femme tue plus volontiers pour se venger, et alors elle apporte là une sorte de raffinement. Le poison lui est une arme comme la lettre anonyme. Et l'empoisonneuse a sa soif comme l'ivrogne, avec cette difference qu'elle verse sa boisson aux autres." Georges Claretie, "Femmes criminelles," *Le Figaro*, 23 July 1904.

45. "Elle est le type du criminel femme, il y avait du félin dans sa nature. . . . Les crimes de femmes ont pour trait essentiel une terrible duplicité. Lombroso les qualifiait de 'diaboliques,' il y a chez elles d'effroyables premeditations. Ce n'est que dans les crimes commis par les femmes que l'on rencontre ce genie de la perversité, cette prodigieuse aisiance dans le mensonge." Jules Marché, *Une vicieuse du grand monde: Madame Lafarge* (Paris: Radot, 1926), p. 8.

46. Matlock, *Scenes of Seduction*.

47. The psychoanalytic interpretations of the insistence on the phallic attributes of Lacenaire—the hand, the knife, and the pen that did the "work" (of killing and writing) are obvious and do not need to be elaborated here. Similarly, the association of Lafarge with poison offers stereotypically feminine imagery. Poison is not only subtle and deceptive, it is invisible and, like the disavowed female sex as opposed to the imaginary of the phallus, a murder by poison does not offer itself to the naked eye; it is mysterious and invisible.

48. Lombroso and Ferrero, *Criminal Woman*, p. 191.

49. Raymond de Ryckère, *La Femme en prison et devant la mort* (Paris: Maloine, 1899), p. 84.

50. Lombroso and Ferrero, *Criminal Woman*, p. 189.

51. Ibid., p. 185.

Chapter Three

1. "Les bêtes sauvages restent des bêtes sauvages, et on aura beau inventer des mécaniques meilleures encore, il y aura quand même des bêtes sauvages dessous."

2. The Ripper's "known" victims (the "canonical five") were Mary Ann "Polly" Nichols, Annie Chapman, Elizabeth Stride, Catherine Eddowes, and Mary Jane Kelly. Other possible victims include Emma Smith, Martha Tabram, Rose Mylett, Alice McKenzie, and Frances Coles.

3. Masters and Lea, in their historical account of sex murder, chronicle the existence of an "infestation" of Rippers between 1885 and 1895, including Vacher, the French Ripper; a Moscow Ripper in 1885; a Texas Ripper who killed black prostitutes; and a Nicaraguan Ripper in 1889. Masters and Lea, *Sex Crimes in History*, pp. 79, 93–94.

4. Alexandra Warwick and Martin Willis, "Introduction," in *Jack the Ripper: Media, Culture, History* (Manchester, UK: Manchester University Press, 2007), p. 2.

5. Seltzer, *Serial Killers*, p. 48.

6. Christopher Frayling, "The House That Jack Built," in *Jack the Ripper*, ed. Warwick and Willis, p. 13.

7. Patricia Cornwell, *Portrait of a Killer: Jack the Ripper—Case Closed* (New York: Penguin Putnam, 2002).

8. See: Caputi, *Age of Sex Crimes*, pp. 124–133.

9. See: Frayling, "The House That Jack Built," p. 18.

10. See: Cameron and Frazer, *Lust to Kill*, p. 124.

11. Jack the Ripper's letter to the Central News Agency, 18 September 1888, cited in Sander Gilman, " 'Who Kills Whores?' 'I Do,' Says Jack: Race and Gender in Victorian London," in *Jack the Ripper*, ed. Warwick and Willis, p. 215.

12. Gilman, " 'Who Kills Whores?,'" p. 215.

13. Ibid., p. 216.

14. Foucault, *Madness and Civilization*, p. 210.

15. Krafft-Ebing, *Psychopathia Sexualis: The Case Histories* (London: Velvet, 1997), p. 32. Hereafter cited as Krafft-Ebing, *Case Histories*. References to Krafft-Ebing, *Psychopathia Sexualis* refer to Krafft-Ebing, *Psychopathia Sexualis with Especial Reference to Contrary Sexual Instinct*, cited in the introduction.

16. Krafft-Ebing, *Psychopathia Sexualis*, p. 1.

17. Ibid., p. 13.

18. Ibid., p. 14.

19. What is striking is that the social gender politics and power structure of patriarchy are taken wholly for granted in Krafft-Ebing's imagined dystopia here. Excessively concupiscent women would become *prostitutes*, not simply women who seek their own sexual gratification. It is a strange sort of "uncontrollable," natural sexual instinct indeed that has a commercial imperative and can adapt itself to servicing a paying client.

20. Krafft-Ebing, *Psychopathia Sexualis*, p. 12.

21. Ibid., p. 67.

22. Ibid., p. 398.

23. Caputi, *Age of Sex Crime*, p. 14.

24. Krafft-Ebing, *Case Histories*, p. 32.

25. Krafft-Ebing, *Psychopathia Sexualis*, p. 62.

26. Ibid., p. 64.

27. Ibid., p. 1.

28. Pick, *Faces of Degeneration*, p. 106.

29. Max Nordau, *Degeneration*, p. 557.

30. Ibid., pp. 141–142.

31. Ibid., p. 557.

32. Ibid., p. 260.

33. Krafft-Ebing, *Psychopathia Sexualis*, p. 87.

34. Ibid., pp. 138, 140.

35. Ibid., p. 137.

36. Ibid., p. 148.

37. Cameron and Frazer, *Lust to Kill*, p. 25.

38. Ibid., p. 164.

39. Pick, *Faces of Degeneration*, p. 74.

40. Geoff Woollen, "Zola: La machine en tous ses effets," *Romantisme*, 41, 1983, and "Des brutes humaines dans *La Bête humaine*," in *Zola: La Bête humaine: Colloque du centenaire à Glasgow*, ed. Geoff Woollen (Glasgow: Glasgow University Press, 1990).

41. Pick, *Faces of Degeneration*, pp. 84–85.

42. Pauline McLynn, "Human Beasts? Criminal Perspectives in *La Bête humaine*," in *Zola: La Bête humaine: Colloque du centenaire à Glasgow*, ed. Geoff Woollen (Glasgow: Glasgow University Press, 1995).

43. "beau garçon au visage rond et régulier, mais que gâtaient des mâchoires trop fortes." Emile Zola, *La Bête humaine* [1890], in *Œuvres complètes*, vol. 6 (Paris: Cercle du livre précieux, 1967), 11–310, p. 48.

44. "le Jacques Lantier a bien quelques caractéristiques anatomiques du criminel né." Cesare Lombroso, "*La Bête humaine* et l'anthropologie criminelle," *La Revue des Revues*, 4–5, 1892, p. 261.

45. Nordau, *Degeneration*, p. 451.

46. See: McLynn, "Human Beasts?," p. 126.

47. "Tuer une femme, tuer une femme! Cela sonnait à ses oreilles, du fond de sa jeunesse, avec la fièvre grandissante, affolante du désir. Comme les autres, sous l'éveil de la puberté, rêvent d'en posséder une, lui s'était enragé à l'idée d'en tuer une." Zola, *La Bête humaine*, p. 61.

48. Cited in Vernon Rosario, *The Erotic Imagination: French Histories of Perversity* (Oxford: Oxford University Press, 1997), pp. 69–70.

49. Geoff Woollen, "Une nouvelle de Camille Lemonnier: De Jack l'Eventreur à *La Bête humaine*," *Les Cahiers naturalistes*, Paris, 1995.

50. Philippe Hamon, *La Bête humaine d'Emile Zola* (Paris: Gallimard, 1994).

51. "Je lègue à la science . . . l'être pervers et compliqué qui pour moi demeura un insondable problème." Cited in ibid., p. 135.

52. "Cela venait-il donc de si loin, du mal que les femmes avaient fait à sa race, de la rancune amassée de male en male depuis la première tromperie?" Zola, *La Bête humaine*, p. 62.

53. Rosario, *Erotic Imagination*, p. 163.

54. Krafft-Ebing, *Psychopathia Sexualis*, p. 13.

55. Ibid., p. 14.

56. "posséder, tuer, cela s'équivalait-il?" Zola, *La Bête humaine*, p. 153.

57. Elle renversa son visage soumis, d'une tendresse suppliante, découvrait son cou nu. . . . Et lui, voyant cette chair blanche, comme dans un éclat d'incendie, leva le poing armé du couteau." Ibid., p. 269.

58. "la jeter sur son dos, morte, ainsi qu'une proie qu'on arrache aux autres." Ibid., p. 151.

59. Rachel Mesch, "The Sex of Science: Medicine, Naturalism and Feminism in Lucie Delarue-Mardrus's *Marie, fille-mère*," *Nineteenth-Century French Studies*, 31, 3&4, 2003, 324–340, p. 327.

60. "Elle ignorait que le désir est un chasseur sans pitié. Elle ne s'était jamais demandé pourquoi toutes les femelles animales, plus intelligentes que les filles, commencent par fuir les males après les avoir appelés à cause qu'une sorte de peur les talonne devant la fatalité de l'amour. . . . Elle ne savait pas qu'il y a de la lutte dans l'amour et de l'assassinat dans la possession, qu'il y a d'un coté l'attaque, et de l'autre la defense, et que l'homme, plus cruel que tout autre bête, est agité dans sa jeunesse par la sourde envie de terrasser la femme comme un adversaire plus faible." Lucie Delarue-Mardrus, *Marie, fille-mère* (Paris: Eugène Fasquelle, 1908), p. 20.

61. Philippe Hamon, *Le Personnel du roman: Le système des personnages dans les "Rougon-Macquart" d'Emile Zola* (Paris: Droz, 1983).

62. Hannah Thompson, *Naturalism Redressed: Identity and Clothing in the Novels of Emile Zola* (Oxford: European Humanities Research Centre, 2004), p. 97.

63. "Elle avait la curiosité des accidents." Zola, *La Bête humaine*, p. 68.

64. "vierge et guerrière; dédaigneuse du mâle." Ibid., p. 58.

65. "Elle avait le besoin de marcher jusqu'au bout, de mourir toute droite, par un instinct de vierge et de guerrière." Ibid., p. 250.

66. l'homme efféminé, délicat, lâche; la femme masculine, violente, sans tendresse." Zola, "Préface au Roman d'un inverti-né," in *Nos ancêtres les pervers: La vie des homosexuels au dix-neuvième siècle*, ed. Pierre Hahn (Paris: Olivier Orban, 1979), 231–235, p. 234.

67. Caputi, *Age of Sex Crime*, p. 5.

68. Donald McCormick, *The Identity of Jack the Ripper* (London: Arrow Books, 1970).

69. Cited in Tom A. Cullen, *When London Walked in Terror* (Boston: Houghton Mifflin, 1965), p. 105.

70. Caputi, *Age of Sex Crime*, p. 21.

71. Cited in Lawrence D. Klausner, *Son of Sam: Based on the Authorized Transcription of the Tapes, Official Documents and Diaries of David Berkowitz* (New York: McGraw-Hill, 1980), p. 168.

72. Cited in ibid., p. 146.

73. Cited in Carol Kennedy, "Striking Again," *Time*, 17 September 1979, p. 49.

74. Joseph Collins, "A New Jack the Ripper Is Terrorizing England," *Us*, October 1979, p. 31. Cited in Caputi, *Age of Sex Crime*, p. 45.

75. Caputi, *Age of Sex Crime*, p. 43.

76. Ibid., p. 45.

77. Cameron and Frazer, *Lust to Kill*, p. 33.

78. Caputi, *Age of Sex Crime*, p. 22.

79. Cited in ibid., pp. 93–94.

80. Cited in John Beattie, *The Yorkshire Ripper Story* (London: Quartet Books, 1981), p. 133.

81. Cited in Cameron and Frazer, *Lust to Kill*, p. 128.

82. Ibid.

83. This is a phenomenon discussed at length by Maria Tatar in *Lustmord*.

84. Cited in Donald Rumbelow, *The Complete Jack the Ripper* (Boston: New York Graphic Society), p. 204.

85. Cameron and Frazer, *Lust to Kill*, p. 166.

86. Ibid., p. 44.

Chapter Four

1. Julien Offray de La Mettrie, *Man a Machine and Man a Plant*, trans. Richard A. Watson and Maya Rabalka (Indianapolis: Hackett, 1994), p. 52.

2. In fact, while Brady was found guilty of all three murders, Hindley was found guilty of murder in the cases of Lesley Ann Downey and Edward Evans and of being accessory to the murder of John Kilbride. In 1985 Brady made a confession that his and Hindley's victims also included Pauline Reade (disappeared aged 16) and Keith Bennett (disappeared aged 12).

3. "Hindley: I Wish I'd Been Hanged," BBC News, Tuesday, 29 February 2000, http://news.bbc.co.uk/1/hi/uk/661139.stm.

4. A telling example of the vehemence and longevity of public hatred of Myra Hindley is the following: the girl's name "Myra," relatively common in England prior to 1966, declined sharply in popularity thereafter. Such is the continuing infamy associated with the case that in 2008, on the well-known website for parents www.mumsnet.com, a thread was devoted to the topic: "I love the name Myra but does it have too many negative connotations?" The majority of the 75 responses said that the name was still too intimately linked to Hindley to be an appropriate choice for a new baby. "CuppaTeaJanice" commented: "I must admit Hindley was the first word that sprung to mind when I read your post." See: http://www.mumsnet.com/Talk/baby_names/624121-i-love-the-name-myra-but/ AllOnOnePage. The name "Ian" has suffered from no such similar rejection.

5. The UK's Murder (Abolition of Death Penalty) Act suspended the death penalty in 1965. In 1969 the act was made permanent. Parallels may be drawn between the high-profile nature of the case of Ruth Ellis, the last woman to be hanged in the UK in 1955, and Myra Hindley. Jacqueline Rose has written that the execution of Ellis was "the event which had brought the enormity of capital punishment home to the country as a whole. It was of course because Ellis was a woman that she aroused this interest." "Margaret Thatcher and Ruth Ellis," *New Formations*, 6, 1988, 3–29, p. 8.

6. Brady is reputed to have read, and to have discussed with Myra, Meyer Levin's *Compulsion*, a fictionalized account of Leopold and Loeb. (See: Lee, *One of Your Own*, pp. 99–100.) This famous case was immortalized on celluloid by Alfred Hitchcock with *Rope* (1948), Richard Fleischer with *Compulsion* (1959) (which Ian Brady saw at the cinema), and Tom Kalin with *Swoon* (1992). In both Hitchcock's and Kalin's films, the (homo)erotic undercurrent of the crime is foregrounded—more explicitly, as would be expected, in the case of the later film which has been considered an example of "new queer cinema."

7. Brian Masters, *On Murder* (London: Coronet, 1994), p. 164.

8. For a full account of the campaign to free Myra and the countercampaign run by the victims' relatives, especially Mrs. Ann West, mother of Lesley, see: Lee, *One of Your Own*, pp. 288–379.

9. Pamela Hansford Johnson, *On Iniquity: Some Personal Reflections Arising out of the Moors Murders Trial* (London: Macmillan, 1967), p. 17.

10. Helen Birch, "If Looks Could Kill: Myra Hindley and the Iconography of Evil," in Birch (ed.), *Moving Targets: Women, Murder and Representation* (Lon-

don: Virago, 1993), 32–61, p. 33. Hindley's first biographer, Jean Ritchie, also asks in 1988 why Myra has celebrity status when other, male, murderers "merit nothing more than a footnote in forensic history books?" and goes on to answer: "the fact that she is a woman." Ritchie, *Myra Hindley: Inside the Mind of a Murderess* (London: Angus and Robertson, 1988), p. viii and, in her conclusion she recaps: "Her notoriety, and that of the whole Moors Murders case, rests upon the fact that she is a woman," p. 286.

11. Birch, "If Looks Could Kill," p. 33.

12. Conversely, two years later in 1968, at the trial of 11-year-old child-murderer Mary Bell, 5 of the 12 jurors were female, and the trial judge commented on the "assistance of women jurors" as being "of very great importance." Cited in Gitta Sereny, *The Case of Mary Bell: A Portrait of a Child Who Murdered* [1972] (London: Pimlico, 1995), p. 84. One wonders if the difference in attitude stems from the fact that in the latter case, the accused was herself a (female) child—and dealing with children is what women are supposed to do "naturally."

13. See, for example: Catherine McKinnon, *Toward a Feminist Theory of the State* (Cambridge, MA: Harvard University Press, 1989).

14. Hansford Johnson, *On Iniquity*, p. 10.

15. Hindley termed it "the most obnoxious piece of lies and fabrications that I have ever read" (Lee, p. 288) and Brady, a life-long animal-lover, was particularly upset by Williams's depiction of him as an adolescent cat-torturer.

16. Emlyn Williams, *Beyond Belief* [1967] (London: Pan, 1968), p. 115.

17. Birch, "If Looks Could Kill," p. 39. The full reference to Elizabeth Wilson's book is *Only Halfway to Paradise: Women in Postwar Britain 1945–1968* (London: Tavistock, 1980).

18. Williams, *Beyond Belief*, p. 127.

19. Ibid., pp. 75–76. Even more ironic is that Myra, unlike Ian, was actually gifted at sports and had played for her school teams. But it is unimaginable in the 1950s and '60s that a Gorton girl might aspire to a professional sports career.

20. It has, however, been posited that this was a ploy, agreed upon by the pair, to increase the chances of Myra being acquitted. Indeed, following their estrangement in 1972, Brady wrote from prison that Myra had been an active, sadistic protagonist in all of the crimes, killing Lesley Ann Downey herself with a silk cord. The truth will never be known; what is telling is the way in which the killers played to social perceptions and expectations: it would be believed that an unknown woman in 1966 might have been manipulated by her violent male partner but, once the mythic figure of Myra Hindley had been created, Brady could easily and credibly appeal to her public infamy when he wished to tell a different tale. It is suggestive that he pins the killing of Lesley in particular on Myra, given the very public campaign against Hindley led by Lesley's mother, Ann West. (See: Lee, *One of Your Own*, p. 175.)

21. All dialogue from police interviews and cross-examinations in court are from the trial transcript by Jonathan Goodman, *The Moors Murders: The Trial of Myra Hindley and Ian Brady* (1973; London: Magpie, 1994), p. 179. (Hereafter JG.)

22. Cited in Williams, *Beyond Belief*, p. 144.

23. The term originates with Laura Mulvey's much-cited essay "Narrative Cinema and Visual Pleasure," *Screen*, 16, 3, 1975, 6–18.

24. Lee, *One of Your Own*, p. 270.

25. Hansford Johnson, *On Iniquity*, p. 22.

26. Ibid., p. 89.

27. Birch, "If Looks Could Kill," p. 52.

28. Hansford Johnson, *On Iniquity*, p. 23.

29. Ibid.

30. Ibid., p. 90. Italics mine.

31. Cited in Lee, *One of Your Own*, p. 243.

32. Ibid., p. 228.

33. Lee, *One of Your Own*, p. 228.

34. Cited in ibid., p. 243.

35. Lee, *One of Your Own*, pp. 370–371.

36. McDonagh, *Child Murder and British Culture 1720–1900* (Cambridge: Cambridge University Press, 2003), p. 6.

37. Hansford Johnson, *On Iniquity*, p. 18.

38. Williams, *Beyond Belief*, p. 112.

39. Ian Brady, open letter to the press, cited in Lee, *One of Your Own*, p. 343.

40. Williams, *Beyond Belief*, p. 179.

41. Francis Wyndham, *Sunday Times*, 8 May 1966, cited in Hansford Johnson, *On Iniquity*, pp. 74–75.

42. Duncan Staff, "Myra Hindley in Her Own Words," *Guardian*, 29 February 2000, cited in Lee, *One of Your Own*, p. 94.

43. Hindley, cited in Lee, *One of Your Own*, p. 98.

44. Hansford Johnson, *On Iniquity*, p. 23.

45. Ibid., p. 27.

46. Ibid., p. 29.

47. Ibid., p. 33.

48. Ibid., p. 28.

49. Ibid., p. 29.

50. George Steiner, Letter, *Times Literary Supplement*, 26 May 1966. Cited in ibid., p. 115.

51. Ibid.

52. Hansford Johnson, *On Iniquity*, p. 126.

53. The acclaimed made-for-TV two-part docudrama *See No Evil: The Moors*

Murders (Chris Menaul, 2006) pays sensitive close attention to the story of David and Maureen Smith and the negative impact their proximity to Brady and Hindley had upon their lives and reputations subsequent to the trial.

54. Hansford Johnson, *On Iniquity*, p. 134.

55. Ibid.

56. Alison M. Moore, "Visions of Sadomasochism as a Nazi Aesthetic," *Lesbian and Gay Psychology Review*, 6, 3, 2005, p. 172.

57. Myra refused to admit involvement in the murders of Reade and Bennett until 1987.

58. Cited in Lee, *One of Your Own*, p. 341.

59. David Rowan and Duncan Campbell, "Myra Hindley: My Life, My Guilt, My Weakness," *Guardian*, 18 December 1995.

60. Other uses to which Myra's mug shot have been put include the cover image of Gordon Burn's 1991 Whitbread Prize–winning novel *Alma Cogan*, a decision which Helen Birch describes as "a cynical marketing ploy" (Birch, "If Looks Could Kill," p. 46), and a portrait of Myra made from bloodstained carpet and ropes by Gary Cartwright hangs in the Greater Manchester Police Museum (Lee, *One of Your Own*, p. 444, n.19).

61. See: Mick Middles, *The Smiths: The Complete Story* (Omnibus, 1985). See also: Birch, "If Looks Could Kill," p. 46.

62. Jennifer Friedlander, *Feminine Look: Sexuation, Spectatorship, Subversion* (New York: SUNY, 2008), p. 84.

63. Marina Warner, "Peroxide Mug Shot," *London Review of Books*, 1 January 1998.

64. Friedlander, *Feminine Look*, p. 78.

65. Ibid., p. 80.

66. McDonagh, *Child Murder and British Culture*, p. 8.

67. Ritchie, *Myra Hindley*, p. 286.

68. Geraldine Bedell, "Profile: Beyond Forgiveness? Myra Hindley," *Independent*, 18 April 1993.

69. Birch, "If Looks Could Kill," p. 54.

70. Cited in Ritchie, *Myra Hindley*, p. 279. In this much-discussed letter, which West sold to the press, Hindley confides to West that Lesley was not "physically tortured" before being killed "as is widely believed." For more discussion, see: Lee, p. 333.

71. Ritchie, *Myra Hindley*, p. 142.

72. Ibid., p. 170.

73. Ibid.

74. Like many of Hindley's prison friends, Jones felt duped at this revelation, having previously believed Myra's version of events: that Ian Brady was the dominant partner and Myra an innocent stooge who knew no more about the crimes than she had admitted in court. David Smith had been Ian's real accomplice—

and possibly his lover: "I had succumbed to her charm and fallen for all of her tearful accounts of herself as a victim." Janie Jones with Carol Clerk, *The Devil and Miss Jones: The Twisted Mind of Myra Hindley* (London: Smith Griffon, 1993), p.109.

75. Ritchie, *Myra Hindley*, pp. 188–189.

76. Jones, *The Devil and Miss Jones*, p. 163.

77. Ibid., p. 115.

78. Ibid., p. 110.

79. Birch, "If Looks Could Kill," p. 55.

80. Cited in Lee, *One of Your Own*, p. 18.

81. Lee, *One of Your Own*, p. 18.

82. Cited in ibid., p. 349.

83. Birch, "If Looks Could Kill," p. 61.

84. Cited in Lee, *One of Your Own*, p. 364.

85. Hansford Johnson, *On Iniquity*, p. 7.

86. Cited in Lee, *One of Your Own*, pp. 315–316.

Chapter Five

1. Nilsen listened repeatedly to Anderson's experimental song through headphones prior to committing his murders. Brian Masters, *Killing for Company: The Case of Dennis Nilsen* (London: Jonathan Cape, 1985), p. 7.

2. Dennis Nilsen's victims were, in chronological order: Stephen Dean Holmes, Kenneth Ockendon, Martyn Duffey, Billy Sutherland, an unidentified Asian man, the "unknown Irishman," an unidentified homeless Caucasian "hippy," an unidentified man (Nilsen can remember nothing about him other than that he kept him under the floorboards for a long time), an unidentified Scotsman, another unidentified Scotsman, an unidentified English skinhead with the words "cut here" across his throat, Malcolm Barlow, John Howlett ("John the Guardsman"), Graham Allan, and Stephen Sinclair. His known attempted victims include Paul Nobbs, Douglas Stewart, and Carl Stottor.

3. The physical theatre piece is Lloyd Newson's *Dead Dreams of Monochrome Men* (1988), performed by physical theatre company DV8 and filmed in 1989 by David Hinton; the film is Fhiona Louise's 1990 Venice Film Festival award-winning biopic *Cold Light of Day* (1989); the oil painting is Dieter Rossi's *Dennis Nilsen* (1993); the novel is Poppy Z. Brite, *Exquisite Corpse* (1996).

4. This assertion is intended to correct claims such as those by Russ Coffey, a journalist who has recently been allowed access to Nilsen's writings, and who writes that Nilsen "is the only serial killer to have attempted this kind of self-analysis." Coffey, "Inside the Mind of a Serial Killer," *Sunday Times Magazine*, 7 September 2003, 34–43, p. 36.

5. Masters, *Killing for Company*. See also: Cameron and Frazer, *Lust to Kill* and McDonagh, "Do or Die."

6. Coffey, "Inside the Mind of a Serial Killer," p. 39.

7. Ian Brady was permitted, with Colin Wilson's support, to publish his study of the philosophy and psychology of serial killing, *The Gates of Janus*, under his own name in 2001. However, the book was released in the United States, not in the UK. Also, it was a condition of publication that Brady not discuss the details of his own murders in the book.

8. Masters, *Killing for Company*, p. 26.

9. Ibid., p. 184.

10. Ibid., p. 242.

11. Cited in David Wilson, *Serial Killers: Hunting Britons and Their Victims 1960–2006* (Winchester, UK: Waterside Press, 2007), p. 13.

12. The sketches and accompanying poems and fragments of prose handwritten in the margins of them are reproduced at the end of Masters, *Killing for Company*, on unnumbered pages. References to these sketches and quotations from Nilsen's handwritten poems and notes are taken from here.

13. See: ibid., pp. 267–279; Cameron and Frazer, *Lust to Kill*, pp. 148–155.

14. This is the subject of my earlier book, Downing, *Desiring the Dead*. See also: Elisabeth Bronfen, *Over Her Dead Body: Death, Femininity and the Aesthetic* (Manchester, UK: Manchester Press, 2002). Bronfen makes the feminist argument that the socially acceptable necrophilic image is that of the dead or dying female body, which enables the male artist/writer or viewer/reader to locate weakness, passivity, and death in the realm of the feminine.

15. Cameron and Frazer, *Lust to Kill*, p. 152.

16. Georges Bataille, *L'Érotisme*, in *Œuvres complètes* (Paris: Gallimard, 1987), x, 7–270.

17. Cameron and Frazer, *Lust to Kill*; McDonagh, "Do or Die."

18. Masters, *Killing for Company*, p. 161.

19. Ibid.

20. See: http://www.imdb.com/title/tt0356476/reviews.

21. "Il serait peut-être doux d'être alternativement victime et bourreau." Baudelaire, *Œuvres complètes*, vol. 2, p. 676.

22. Je suis la plaie et le couteau !
    Je suis le soufflet et la joue !
    Je suis les membres et la roue,
    Et la victime et le bourreau !
    Ibid., vol. 1, p. 79.

23. I cannot decipher Nilsen's handwriting here.

24. Masters, *Killing for Company*, p. 277.

25. Ibid. This quotation is used, word for word, in the film *Cold Light of Day*.

It is spoken by "March" as a monologue and provides the climactic moment of his confession to the police detectives. Despite Fhiona Louise's decision to change the names of the characters and places in her film "to protect the innocent" (as a disclaimer tells us after the opening credits), and the inclusion of fictitious incidents, the use of Nilsen's own words leaves in no doubt the extent to which the film is intended as an exploration of Nilsen's case.

26. Wilson, *Serial Killers*, p. 125.

27. Neil McKenna, "Fleet Street's Perverse Cocktail of Kinky Sex and a Serial Killer: Neil McKenna Berates the Reporting of a Series of Homosexual Murders," *Independent*, 20 June 1993, http://www.independent.co.uk/news/uk/fleet-streets-perverse-cocktail-of-kinky-sex-and-a-serial-killer-neil-mckenna-berates-the-reporting-of-a-series-of-homosexual-murders-1492873.html.

28. Cited in ibid.

29. Ibid.

30. Tithecott, *Of Men and Monsters*, p. 73.

31. Cited in Masters, *Killing for Company*, p. 145.

32. John Lisners, *House of Horror* (London: Corgi Books, 1983), p. 101.

33. Anne E. Schwartz, *The Man Who Could Not Kill Enough: The Secret Murders of Milwaukee's Jeffrey Dahmer* (New York: Carol, 1992), p. 115, cited in Schmid, *Natural Born Celebrities*, p. 227.

34. Lee Edelman, *No Future: Queer Theory and the Death Drive* (Durham, NC: Duke University Press: 2004), p. 4.

35. Leo Bersani, "Is the Rectum a Grave?," in *AIDS: Cultural Analysis/Cultural Activism*, ed. Douglas Crimp (Cambridge, MA: MIT Press, 1988), 197–222, p. 209.

36. Edelman, *No Future*, p. 3.

37. Mark Richardson writes: "My suspicion is that the problem lies with Poppy Z. Brite's gender. For many, Brite's artistic motives are far from transparent." Such critiques center on the question of whether a woman has any business penning "hyper-erotic, sometimes gratuitous, descriptions of gay male sex." http://www.spikemagazine.com/0704bloodsuckers.php.

38. Poppy Z. Brite, *Exquisite Corpse* (1996) (Guernsey, UK: Phoenix Press, 1998), p. 186.

39. Ibid., p. 188.

40. Ibid., p. 7.

41. Ibid.

42. Ibid., p. 77.

43. Cover notes, DVD, *Dead Dreams of Monochrome Men*, 1989.

44. Clement Crisp, "Dead Dreams," Review, *Financial Times*, Friday, 4 November 1988.

45. Very few academic or critical studies of *Exquisite Corpse* interrogate the

historical longevity of the idea of the murderer-and-homosexual as exceptional/ monstrous. See, for example: Susan E. Cook, "Subversion without Limits: From *Secretary*'s Transgressive S/M to *Exquisite Corpse*'s Subversive Sadomasochism," *Discourses*, 28,1, 2006, 121–141. (This article fails too to link Andrew's and Jay's "identities" to those of Nilsen and Dahmer, meaning that it lacks both profound historical understanding and local contextual specificity.)

46. Cited in Brian Masters, "Dahmer's Inferno," *Vanity Fair*, November 1991, 182–189 and 264–269, p. 186.

47. Masters, *Killing for Company*, p. 275.

48. Masters, *The Shrine of Jeffrey Dahmer* (London: Hodder and Stoughton, 1993), p. 201.

49. Cited in Masters, "Dahmer's Inferno," p. 186.

50. Tithecott, *Of Men and Monsters*, p. 6.

51. Cited in Masters, "Dahmer's Inferno," p. 265.

Chapter Six

1. The victims were Richard Mallory (whose prior conviction for attempted rape was suppressed in the evidence presented at Wuornos's trial), David Spears, Charles Carskaddon, Peter Siems, Troy Burress, Charles "Dick" Humphreys (a retired chief of police), and Walter Jeno Antonio (a police reservist).

2. See: Michael Reynolds, *Dead Ends* (New York: Warner Books, 1992), p. 238.

3. Candice Skrapec, "The Female Serial Killer: An Evolving Criminality," in *Moving Targets: Women, Murder and Representation*, ed. Helen Birch (London: Virago Press, 1993), 241–268, pp. 266–267.

4. Ibid., p. 266.

5. Eric Hickey, *Serial Murderers and Their Victims* (Pacific Grove, CA: Brooks/Cole, 1991), p. 107.

6. Cited in Kyra Pearson, "The Trouble with Aileen Wuornos, Feminism's 'First Serial Killer,'" *Communication and Critical/Cultural Studies*, 4, 3, 2007, 256–275, p. 259.

7. "Once labeled a serial killer, Wuornos was transformed into a predator whose hitchhiking is read as an act of enticing innocent and good-hearted men who think they are stopping for a 'Damsel in Distress' stranded on the highway, when, as *Time* put it, they meet the 'Damsel of Death.'" Schmid, *Natural Born Celebrities*, p. 261.

8. Reynolds, *Dead Ends*, p. 232.

9. Ward Jouve, *Streetcleaner*, p. 34. See also: Cameron and Frazer, *Lust to Kill*: "This book began from a simple observation: there has never been a female Peter Sutcliffe," p. 1.

10. Footage in Nick Broomfield and Joan Churchill, *Aileen: Life and Death of*

a Serial Killer (2003), 3 Disc Limited Edition, including Patty Jenkins's *Monster* and Nick Broomfield's documentaries, Metrodome, 2006.

11. Miriam Basilio, "Corporal Evidence: Representations of Aileen Wuornos," "We're Here: Gay and Lesbian Presence in Art and Art History," Special Issue of *Art Journal*, 55, 4, 1996, pp. 56–61, p. 56.

12. See: ibid.

13. David Schmid tells us that "ironically, when Wuornos was first contacted, shortly after her arrest, by a Hollywood producer interested in making a film about her, Wuornos pleaded with the producer to 'please don't make me a Monster.'" Schmid, *Natural Born Celebrities*, p. 241.

14. Patty Jenkins speaking in "*Monster*: The Vision and the Journey," DVD extras, 3 Disc Limited Edition, Metrodome, 2006.

15. Pearson, "The Trouble with Aileen Wuornos," p. 260. Pearson adds: "This public distancing from Wuornos is striking in light of Oscar-night acceptance speeches by Julia Roberts and Hilary Swank for their respective portrayals of legal assistant turned activist Erin Brochovich [*sic*] and transgendered youth Brandon Teena a few years before," p. 260.

16. Broomfield speaking in "The Making of a Monster," DVD extras, 3 Disc Limited Edition, Metrodome, 2006.

17. Aileen Wuornos with Christopher Berry-Dee, *Monster: My True Story* (London: John Blake, 2004), p. 78.

18. Birch, "Introduction," in *Moving Targets*, 1–6, p. 6.

19. See: Vivien Miller, " 'The Last Vestige of Institutionalized Sexism'? Paternalism, Equal Rights and the Death Penalty in Twentieth and Twenty-First Century Sunbelt America: The Case for Florida," *Journal of American Studies*, 38, 3, 2004, 391–424; Kathryn Ann Farr, "Defeminizing and Dehumanizing Female Murderers: Depictions of Lesbians on Death Row," *Women and Criminal Justice*, 11, 1, 2000, 52–53; and Renée Heberle, "Disciplining Gender; Or, Are Women Getting Away with Murder?," *Signs: Journal of Women in Culture and Society*, 24, 4, 1999, 1103–1112.

20. Elizabeth Comack and Salena Brickey, "Constituting the Violence of Criminalized Women," *Canadian Journal of Criminology and Criminal Justice*, 49, 1, January 2007, 1–36, p. 3.

21. Schmid, *Natural Born Criminals*, p. 13.

22. Megan Sweeney, "Living to Read True Crime: Theorizations from Prison," *Discourse*, 25, 1&2, Winter & Spring 2003, 55–80.

23. Ibid., p. 69.

24. Ibid., p. 68.

25. Ibid.

26. Broomfield, *Aileen Wuornos: The Selling of a Serial Killer* (1993), 3 Disc Limited Edition, including Patty Jenkins's *Monster* and Nick Broomfield's documentaries, Metrodome, 2006.

27. Wuornos with Berry-Dee, *Monster*, p. 229. My italics.

28. Ibid., p. 196. My italics.

29. Claudia Card writes: "Evelina Giobbe, president of a support group for ex-prostitutes, confirmed the credibility of Aileen Wuornos's plea for self-defense in an interview with Geraldo Rivera, saying, 'Women in prostitution are commonly sexually assaulted, raped, battered, and robbed by customers. Aileen's fears are not unfounded. Close to 2,000 men a year used her in prostitution. So to say three to six a day, that seven of them may have assaulted her fits with the stats that are in there. Abstracted from that context, seven men may sound like a lot; in context, it sounds like probably a fraction of those who threatened the life of Aileen Wuornos.'" Cited in Card, "Review of Lynda Hart, *Fatal Women: Lesbian Sexuality and the Mark of Aggression* (London and New York: Routledge, 1994)," *Journal of the History of Sexuality*, 6, 1, July 1995, 150–152, p. 151. And David Schmid adds: "The law enforcement perspective on Wuornos exhibits not only a failure to understand the situation that Wuornos claimed she was in, but also an inability or unwillingness to appreciate that a woman's assessment of the degree of danger in a particular situation may be very different from that of a man." Schmid, *Natural Born Celebrities*, p. 235.

30. Wuornos with Berry-Dee, *Monster*, p. 78.

31. Ibid., p. 188. My italics.

32. Ibid., p. 196.

33. Broomfield and Churchill, *Life and Death of a Serial Killer*. Ken Mentor in his review of Broomfield's *Selling of a Serial Killer* makes this point too: "Wuornos, although not necessarily a sympathetic character, has been exploited by nearly everyone associated with her case, and in fact, her entire life." "Review: Nick Broomfield, *Aileen Wuornos: The Selling of a Serial Killer*," *Teaching Sociology*, 26, 1, January 1998, 89–90, p. 90.

34. Hart, *Fatal Women*, p. 137.

35. Morrissey, *When Women Kill*, p. 39.

36. Comack and Brickey, "Constituting the Violence of Criminalized Women," p. 8.

37. Mentor, "Review of Broomfield," p. 90.

38. Morrissey, *When Women Kill*, p. 39.

39. Pearson, "The Trouble with Aileen Wuornos," p. 265.

40. Cameron and Frazer cite the following, from cataloguers of murder Morris and Blom-Cooper, as a typical example of this reprehensible discursive trend: "Some women may *contribute to their own deaths* by running the risks *associated with prostitution*, of which violent death is *an occupational hazard*. . . . The prostitute, whose client is unknown to her, may be murdered *simply* because she represents a readily accessible sexual object to her killer, to whom anonymity in his victim may be important. More commonly, prostitutes are the only women

prepared to cooperate in the sado-masochistic perversions which form, for the killer, an integral part of the homicidal drive." Terence Morris and Louis Blom-Cooper, *A Calendar of Murder* (London: Michael Joseph, 1964), pp. 276, 323. Cited in *Lust to Kill*, p. 31. Cameron and Frazer's italics.

41. Card, "Review of Hart," p. 151.

42. Pearson, "The Trouble with Aileen Wuornos," p. 262.

43. Cited in ibid.

44. Wuornos with Berry-Dee, *Monster*, p. viii.

45. Footage in Broomfield, *Selling of a Serial Killer*.

46. Schmid, *Natural Born Celebrities*, p. 232.

47. Footage in Broomfield, *Selling of a Serial Killer*.

48. Cited in Basilio, "Corporal Evidence," p. 60.

49. See: Flora Rheta Schreiber, *The Shoemaker: The Anatomy of a Psychotic* (New York: Signet, 1984), esp. p. 367, for the distinctions between psychiatric insanity and legal insanity, and between personality disorders and psychoses. Schreiber's book is an attempt to prove that multiple murderer and rapist Joseph Kallinger was suffering from a severe paranoid schizophrenia that directly led to his crimes, and that he required incarceration and treatment in a psychiatric hospital, rather than detention in a prison. (Kallinger was originally adjudged to be suffering from a personality disorder and therefore convicted as sane and sent to prison, where he killed an inmate following a psychotic hallucination in which an imaginary presence allegedly appeared and told him to do so.)

50. Wuornos with Berry-Dee, *Monster*, pp. 201–202.

51. In Broomfield, *Selling of a Serial Killer*.

52. Broomfield, "Introduction to *Life and Death of a Serial Killer*," DVD extras, 3 Disc Limited Edition, Metrodome, 2006.

53. "Florida Serial Killer Wants Death Penalty," *Advocate*, 3 July 2001. Cited in Pearson, "The Trouble with Aileen Wuornos," p. 268.

54. "Woman Serial Killer Wants to Die," *Chicago Sun-Times*, 20 July 2001, 3. Cited in Pearson, "The Trouble with Aileen Wuornos," p. 268.

55. Schmid, *Natural Born Celebrities*, p. 240.

56. Pearson, "The Trouble with Aileen Wuornos," p. 258.

57. Schmid, *Natural Born Celebrities*, p. 234.

58. Seltzer, *Serial Killers*, p. 135.

59. Reynolds, *Dead Ends*, p. 236.

60. The dialogue of *Monster* is heavily based on Wuornos's 12-year prison correspondence with a lifelong friend to which she agreed to allow Jenkins full access hours before her execution.

61. Valerie Solanas, *SCUM Manifesto* (London: Verso, 2004), p. 66.

62. Both cited in Avital Ronell, "Deviant Payback: The Aims of Valerie Solanas," introduction to Solanas, *SCUM Manifesto*, 1–31, p. 10.

63. Richard Greiner, "Feminists Should Gloat over Their Serial Killer," *Human Events*, 25 March 1994, p. 15. Cited in Pearson, "The Trouble with Aileen Wuornos," p. 257. (Pearson takes Greiner's sound bite as the title of her article, but does not expand upon the implications of this idea.)

64. Karena Rahall, "Aileen Wuornos's Last Resort," *Assaults on Convention: Essays on Lesbian Transgressors*, ed. Nicola Godwin, Belinda Hollows, and Sheridan Nye (London: Cassell, 1996), p. 115. Cited in Pearson, "The Trouble with Aileen Wuornos," p. 257.

65. Skrapec, "The Female Serial Killer," p. 263. My italics.

66. Ronell, "Deviant Payback," p. 9.

67. Reynolds, *Dead Ends*, p. 95.

68. Schmid, *Natural Born Celebrities*, pp. 235–236.

69. Jeffner Allen, *Lesbian Philosophy* (Palo Alto, CA: Institute of Lesbian Studies, 1986), p. 38.

70. Caputi, *Age of Sex Crime*, p. 2.

71. Morrissey, *When Women Kill*, p. 9.

72. Basilio, "Corporal Evidence," p. 60.

73. Broomfield, voice-over in *Life and Death of a Serial Killer*.

74. Heberle, "Disciplining Gender," p. 1103.

75. Ibid., p. 1106.

76. Florida Supreme Court, 644 So.2d 1000 (1994), Justice Kogan concurring.

77. Heberle, "Disciplining Gender," p. 1110.

78. Card, "Review of Hart," p. 152. My italics.

Chapter Seven

1. Paul, *When Kids Kill*, p. 28.

2. This case inspired the Boomtown Rats' 1979 number one single "I Don't Like Mondays."

3. Several films have been inspired by Columbine, including the black comedy *Duck! The Carbine High Massacre* (Hellfire and Smack, 2000), *Heart of America* (Boll, 2003), and *Zero Day* (Coccio, 2003). In this chapter, I shall concentrate only on Michael Moore's 2002 documentary *Bowling for Columbine* and Gus Van Sant's acclaimed narrative film *Elephant* (2003). Alongside these, I read a fictional text, Lionel Shriver's *We Need to Talk about Kevin* (2003), which is written from the viewpoint of the mother of a high school mass killer, and which explicitly references the spate of school killings in North America to which Columbine gave a collective name. Shriver's sophisticated narrative addresses the question of the legitimacy of the idea of innate nature on which discourses about both the killer and the child turn. A film adaptation of the book with the same name, directed by Lynne Ramsay, was released in 2011.

4. Blake Morrison, "Life after James," *Guardian*, Thursday, 6 February 2003, http://www.guardian.co.uk/uk/2003/feb/06/bulger.ukcrime.

5. Young, *Imagining Crime*, p. 115.

6. Ibid., p. 113.

7. The image shown in figure 7 was taken from this website: http://www .dailymail.co.uk/news/article-463121/Vile-game-using-image-Bulger-kidnap-withdrawn-sale.html. The article tells of the withdrawal from sale of a video game that included a facsimile of this iconic image of abduction.

8. Ariès, *Centuries of Childhood*.

9. Chris Jenks, *Childhood* (London: Sage, 1996); Gill Valentine, "Angels and Devils: Moral Landscapes of Childhood," *Society and Space*, 14, 5, 1996, 581–599.

10. Foucault, *Will to Knowledge*, pp. 42–43, 104.

11. Anneke Meyer, *The Child at Risk* (Manchester, UK: Manchester University Press, 2007).

12. In 2010 the British government rejected a proposal to raise the age to 12, despite the fact that in most European countries it is higher, between 14 and 16. (The age of criminal responsibility in Scotland has long been 8 years old, but this is being raised to 12.) The lawyers of Thompson and Venables later successfully appealed to the European Court of Human Rights, who decreed that the boys had been denied a fair hearing and should not have been tried in an adult court with a jury. By that time both killers were 17 years old (Davis, *Children Who Kill*, p. 152).

13. Young, *Imagining Crime*, p. 114.

14. Ibid., p. 115.

15. *Independent on Sunday*, 28 November 1993. My italics. Cited in ibid.

16. Young, *Imagining Crime*, p. 118.

17. Sereny, *Case of Mary Bell*, pp. 72–73.

18. Ibid., p. 80.

19. Sereny, *Cries Unheard: The Story of Mary Bell* [1998] (London: Papermac, 1999), p. 11.

20. Morrison, "Life after James."

21. See: ibid.

22. Morrison, *As If* (London: Granta, 1997), p. 21.

23. Ibid., p. 27.

24. Ibid., p. 36. My italics.

25. Sereny, Preface, *Case of Mary Bell*, p. viii.

26. Young, *Imagining Crime*, p. 142.

27. *Sunday Times*, 28 November 1993. My italics.

28. Blake Morrison, "Life after James."

29. Young, *Imagining Crime*, p. 117.

30. Ibid.

31. Ibid., p. 119.

32. Ibid., p. 118.

33. Davis, *Children Who Kill*, pp. 148–149. My italics.

34. Caputi, *Age of Sex Crime*, p. 70.

35. Young, *Imagining Crime*, p. 126.

36. Ibid., p. 127.

37. *Independent on Sunday*, 17 November 1993.

38. Sereny, Appendix, "The Murder of James Bulger," in *Case of Mary Bell*, 275–333, p. 280.

39. Morrison, *As If*, p. 224.

40. Davis, *Children Who Kill*, p. 16.

41. Paul, *When Kids Kill*, p. 11.

42. Cited in Morrison, *As If*, p. 229.

43. Davis, *Children Who Kill*, p. 149.

44. Cited in *Guardian*, 1 April 1994.

45. Cited in ibid., 13 April 1994.

46. Young, *Imagining Crime*, p. 136.

47. The victims killed in the Columbine massacre were: Cassie Bernall, Steve Curnow, Corey de Pooter, Kelly Fleming, Matt Kechter, Daniel Mauser, Daniel Rohrbough, Rachel Scott, Isaiah Shoels, John Tomlin, Lauren Townsend, Kyle Velasquez, and Coach Dave Sanders.

48. Cited in Dave Cullen, *Columbine* (London: Old Street Publishing, 2009), p. 239.

49. Cullen, *Columbine*, p. 179.

50. Cited in ibid., p. 327.

51. Cullen, *Columbine*, p. 277.

52. Cited in ibid.

53. Cullen, *Columbine*, p. 277.

54. Ibid., p. 335.

55. De Quincey, *On Murder*, p. 5.

56. Red Lake Shooting Conspiracy? CBS News, http://www.cbsnews.com/stories/2005/03/30/national/main683990.shtml

57. www.villagevoice.com/2004–08–31/film/film/.

58. Cited in Cullen, *Columbine*, p. 322.

59. Cullen, *Columbine*, p. 258.

60. Cited in ibid., p. 326.

61. See: Cullen, *Columbine*, p. 72.

62. See: ibid., p. 322.

63. Ibid., p. 241.

64. Ibid., p. 323.

65. Ibid., p. 348.

66. Ibid.

67. There is a continuity error. We are told there were "ten days" between the killings on p. 73; but on p. 284, the Columbine killings are said to have taken place "twelve days" after Kevin's *Thursday*. Lionel Shriver, *We Need to Talk about Kevin* [2003] (London: Serpent's Tale, 2005).

68. Ibid., p. 284.

69. Ibid., p. 172.

70. Ibid., p. 103.

71. Ibid., p. 194.

72. Ibid., p. 291.

73. Ibid., p. 464.

74. Morrison, "Life after James."

75. Shulamith Firestone, *The Dialectic of Sex: The Case for Feminist Revolution* (London: Paladin, 1972), p. 73.

76. Ibid., p. 85.

77. Ibid., p. 101.

78. Edelman, *No Future*.

79. Firestone, *Dialectic of Sex*, p. 73.

80. Ibid., p. 88.

Conclusion

1. Emlyn Williams, *Dr Crippen's Diary: An Invention* (London: Robson Books, 1987).

2. John Douglas and Mark Olshaker, *Mindhunter: Inside the FBI's Elite Serial Killer Unit* (New York: Scribner, 1995), p. 32.

3. See especially: Richard Dyer, *Stars* (London: British Film Institute, 1979).

4. Brady, *Gates of Janus*, p. 41.

5. Seltzer, *Serial Killers*, p. 145.

6. Ibid., p. 142.

7. One of the most recent British cases that testifies to a belief in the power of contagion and corruption by explicit material, and its capacity to lead to murder, is that of Graham Coutts, who strangled to death Jane Longhurst in 2003. Coutts was found to have had on his computer hard drive a collection of pornographic images featuring erotic asphyxiation and simulated death. He claimed that Jane's death had occurred as a result of a consensual erotic asphyxiation transaction that had gone wrong, but the court rejected this defense. A campaign by the victim's mother, Liz Longhurst, led to a law being passed in the UK in 2008 that makes the possession of "extreme pornography" a criminal offence, despite the protests of BDSM and social justice activists, including some femi-

nists. For more, see: Julian Petley, "Pornography, Panopticism and the Criminal Justice and Immigration Act 2008," *Sociology Compass*, 3, 2009, 417–432.

8. Brady, *Gates of Janus*, p. 52.

9. Lacan, *The Seminar, Book VII. The Ethics of Psychoanalysis, 1959–60*, trans. Dennis Porter (London: Routledge, 1992), p. 139.

Index